The Good Health Garden

Growing and Using Healing Foods

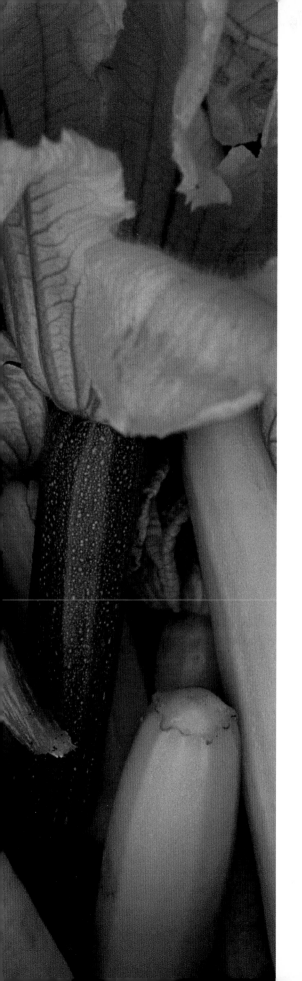

The Good Health Garden

Growing and Using Healing Foods

Anne McIntyre

PUBLISHED BY THE READER'S DIGEST ASSOCIATION LIMITED
LONDON • NEW YORK • SYDNEY • CAPE TOWN • MONTREAL

A READER'S DIGEST BOOK

Published by The Reader's Digest Association Limited
11 Westferry Circus
Canary Wharf
London E14 4HE

Text copyright © 1998 Anne McIntyre
Volume copyright © 1998 Breslich & Foss Limited

ISBN 276 42352 6

The book was designed and produced by
Breslich & Foss Limited
20 Wells Mews
London W1P 3FJ

Project editor: Laura Wilson
Copy editors: Jonathan Hilton, Caroline Taylor
Designer: Margaret Sadler
All photography by Juliette Wade except for p. 105 (top right), The Garden
Picture Library; p. 97 and p. 106 (top right) A-Z Botanical Collection Ltd.
Illustrators: Madeleine David, Amanda Patton,
Polly Raynes

Manufactured in Malaysia
Printed in Belgium

Contents

Introduction

'The love of gardening is a seed that once sown never dies.'

Gertrude Jekyll

Growing fruits, vegetables and herbs in the garden to provide foods and medicines throughout the year is something that our ancestors did for thousands of years. The first gardeners are thought to have lived around ten thousand years ago, in the Middle East, S.E. Asia and Central America, and we know that by Roman times many vegetables which are common today, such as turnips, cabbages, radishes, garlic, lettuce, chicory, gourds and asparagus, were cultivated in European gardens. It is only really over the last century that there has been a shift away from growing food for the kitchen in individual vegetable plots to mass production of food for our increasing urban populations. Now, there is growing disenchantment with the use of pesticides and chemical fertilisers in farming, and the lack of flavour and texture in most shop-bought produce, and a trend is on the move. More and more people are concerned with food as the raw material to maintain their health and that of their families, and are looking towards growing their own as the most economic and reliable means to providing nutrient-rich, toxin-free food.

Naturally it is not only country people but also town and city dwellers who want to make the most of their plots of land, to grow food for their tables and herbs both for their kitchens and their medicine chests. Many people do not possess sufficient space to grow their fruits, vegetables and herbs in neat rows or stylish potagers set apart from their lawns and flower borders, so it has become increasingly necessary to plan the plot of land to maximise productivity. Indeed, garden fashions have changed, and today gardens are expected to be places of both beauty and productivity, the aesthetic value of the garden being equal to that of the food that can be harvested from it. It requires a thoughtful design to provide eye-catching appeal as well as a steady flow of food from the garden for as much of the year as possible.

This book contains a variety of traditional planting designs and layouts which may be useful as springboards for your own creations, and which could be adapted to your particular plot, its size and aspect.

Medieval monastic vegetable gardens were laid out to make the maximum use of limited space in small square or rectangular beds. Vegetables, fruits and herbs were usually planted in neat rows, with room to walk between them to weed and maintain them. In the medieval physic gardens, beds for medicinal herbs would have been of similar design, with an enclosed rectangle or square divided into small rectangular raised beds edged with elm planks. Raised beds aid drainage on heavy, wet soils and enable organic compost to be added at regular intervals to improve soil fertility. This system can be followed today and looks very attractive. It is easy to maintain, and allows you to create a variety of soil conditions in different areas of the garden, making it possible to grow a wide range of produce.

Narrow paths divided the raised beds. These enabled planting and maintenance of the beds and at the same time defined a geometric design which was pleasing to the eye and had symbolic value. Often the monks created a cross in the centre of the garden, the symbol of Christianity, which remains popular to this day.

In vegetable and herb gardens, different produce was grown in each space defined by the paths. This allowed a simple rotation plan, which could easily be adapted for gardens today. The paths were interspersed with pergolas and arbours to support climbers such as roses, hops and vines and as places for tranquillity and contemplation.

Until the 19th century, an English cottager's garden was designed for food production rather than aesthetic value. It was usually small, and cottagers would crowd in as many flowers and herbs as they could. The cottage garden was traditionally laid out with a straight path leading to the front door, and a boundary hedge or wall with a gate – possibly with an arch over the gate or a trellis by the front door supporting climbing roses or honeysuckle. To either side would be neat rows of vegetables and soft fruit edged with flowers and herbs, or there would be a larger plot around the back for such purposes. Almost anything goes in a cottage garden: an area outside the kitchen for herbs, for example, or walls to support espaliered fruit trees. The advantage of a cottage garden design is that it does not require as much maintenance as a more formal garden, and involves a more relaxed approach to gardening. A broad range of vegetables, flowers, herbs and fruits can be grown together, creating a medley of colour shape and produce which is enhanced by a sense of profusion rather than order.

The potager garden is a more decorative, stylised version of a kitchen garden, designed to delight the eye as well as the palate. The potager originated in France where vegetables, fruits, herbs and flowers are often arranged in attractive, symmetrical patterns in a formal layout. Today this is an increasingly popular breakaway from the traditional kitchen garden with its straight rows and allows for greater creativity and individual design using colour, texture shape and form to provide a highly decorative tapestry of food.

The success of potagers depends on their design, and consideration of the size, shape and colour of the plants used. The width and height of each species needs to be taken into consideration, just as much as the colour and texture. Low-growing species should be placed in front of taller ones so that they, too, can have a share of the sun. Flowering annuals – such as marigolds and nasturtiums – can provide vibrant colour not only in the garden but also in the salad bowl. Tall plants for the back could include rhubarb, Swiss chard, spinach, tomatoes, broccoli, Brussels sprouts and peas or broad beans trained onto a trellis or wigwam. For the middle or front, try dwarf beans, beetroot, carrots, celery, chives, basil, cabbage, parsley, onions, radishes and turnips. As the vegetables are harvested, the beautiful pattern will start to disappear, although they can always be harvested in a symmetrical fashion.

Alternatively, for those with a minimal amount of space and/or time available, herbs, vegetables and fruits can all be grown together in a flower border. This looks attractive and it also provides instant companion planting. The border needs to be well located in a sunny position with good rich soil to provide nutrients for such a range of plants to grow so intensively. Vegetables and herbs can be grown in the spaces in between shrubs and flowers; fruit trees will provide beautiful blossom in springtime and fruit in late summer or early autumn, and fruit bushes can be grown as deciduous hedges to provide shelter for the garden. Here again, taller varieties of vegetables should be grown at the back of the bed, along with large architectural herbs such as fennel, borage, angelica or horseradish. Low-growing thyme and Roman chamomile could be placed at the front.

Some like to grow their culinary herbs separately in a herb garden, often just near the kitchen. This needs to be a warm sheltered place with well-drained soil to produce the best results. With all the variety of shapes, textures, colours, not to mention smells, the herb garden can be a place to delight not only the eye and the palate but also the nose – so it is best to place the herb garden where it can be enjoyed for all its virtues. Pots of herbs can be positioned on patios, verandahs, or next to the front door or a window. Many herbs grow quickly into clumps or shrubs and need to planted with plenty of space between them to allow for growth. Any spaces can be filled with annual herbs such as nasturtiums, marigolds, basil and coriander. Small paths through the herb garden will allow for maintenance and easy harvesting.

Even since Roman times, city dwellers have grown herbs and other plants in terracotta pots and containers on balconies and windowsills. For those who have very limited space, herbs can be grown in pots and containers along with a few salad vegetables, such as chicory, rocket, lambs lettuce or winter cress. Basil, coriander, parsley, chives and oregano can be grown alongside these. Pots not only look highly attractive, they also allow some of the more rampant and invasive herbs – such as tarragon, marjoram, chives, mint and lemon balm – to be nicely contained.

Everyone can have some kind of kitchen garden, even if it consists only of a few pots of herbs or salad vegetables on the kitchen windowsill or balcony, peas and beans trailing between the railings, or a hanging basket of tomatoes on the wall. All these can provide fresh, natural food that can be easily grown, and harvested and eaten within minutes, bringing an immense feeling of achievement and satisfaction. Nurturing a seed to its full potential as a food or medicine is a magical experience.

the healing garden

'The lesson I have thoroughly learnt and wish

to pass on to others, is to know the enduring

happiness that the love of

a garden gives.'

Gertrude Jekyll

The pleasures of gardening

There is something about gardens and gardening that is almost compelling. When growing edible and health-giving plants as well as flowers, it is possible to create a place not only of beauty but also of purpose. A garden can be a place in which to sit and relax, and it can also be a place to put your heart and your back into and reap the rewards.

There is immense satisfaction to be gained by tending a garden, and perhaps even more from growing your own food. Not many pursuits in life are able to keep you fit, remove stress, lift your spirits and produce a wealth of nutrient-packed and toxin-free fruits, herbs and vegetables. Organic kitchen gardening can do just that!

It is wonderfully rewarding to spend a few relaxed hours weeding, creating a sense of order and harmony in a previously untidy, overgrown area of the garden. Certainly, some of the challenges when maintaining a multipurpose garden include keeping order amid the range of different kinds of plants, keeping the balance between beauty and productivity, and finding combinations of plants and planting designs that work well for you.

Working in an organic garden provides an opportunity not only to derive food, sustenance, and satisfaction for ourselves, but also to do something positive for the planet on which we live and on which we depend for our existence. We need trees to give us oxygen; grass, and scrub to prevent soil erosion; hedgerows and woodlands to preserve topsoil against wind and rain; and the wild herbs, fruits and vegetables that originally provided us with the cultivated varieties on which we depend for our foods today.

Our ancestors have grown cultivated forms of vegetables for thousands of years and the food we grow in our gardens today allows us to benefit from years of evolution, selection and experiment, yet recent 'progress' has proved far from beneficial. Pesticides and fertilisers may enable us to grow plenty of fruit and vegetables that look perfect and inviting but at what cost to the earth's ecosystem – and to our health? The mass-market

production of many food crops has taken a worrisome direction: genetic engineering can produce food with prolonged shelf life, bright colours and a healthy appearance, but it is at the cost of its flavour and nutritional value. If a food has been transported for a long distance in cold storage, it may look fresh on the supermarket shelf, but its vitamin C and A content will not compare with that of a fruit or vegetable grown at home and eaten fresh from the garden.

Many gardeners are fast coming to realise both the drawbacks of chemical

fertilisers and that insecticides destroy not only pests but also the beneficial organisms that keep other pests at bay. They know that in upsetting the delicate natural balance of their garden, they may well be paving the way for more serious problems ahead. As a result, they are looking for more ecological ways of gardening that use old-fashioned methods of husbandry in conjunction with modern methods of organic gardening – an agreeable blend of the old and the new. The vast inherited pool of garden folklore, from which we have learned methods of gardening such as pruning and propagating, still works well; while modern, disease-resistant plant varieties can eliminate the need for insecticides and chemical fertilisers, and new dwarf forms of vegetables help those of us who have little growing space.

Gardening provides constant stimulation and challenge, for the garden is always changing, and each garden has a life of its own. For our part, we need to work in conjunction with the natural forces in our garden, to our mutual benefit, rather than fighting to control nature with pesticides, insecticides and chemical fertilisers. The give and take in the garden involves working with the end result in mind while taking into consideration what the garden itself needs to enable it to produce to maximum efficiency. Enhancing nature requires treating the garden with care and consideration, and acquiring some knowledge about the needs of the soil and the requirements of the plants you want to grow. Information of this kind is widely available in literature but only experience will help you to store it in your memory. Experience comes from contact with the garden and with the soil through our five senses, and this physical relationship with the natural world will have a beneficial healing effect long before we enjoy the fruits of our labours at the meal table, and learn to appreciate their contribution to health and well-being.

The joy of seeing a beautifully laid out garden, combined with the colours and shapes of the vegetables, fruits, flowers, and herbs, is hard to describe. The sounds in the garden can quieten the mind, and connect us to the world of nature around us: bees humming, birds singing, and the rustle of the leaves in the breeze. The varying textures of plants provide much interest: marigolds are full of resins and gums which make the whole plant sticky to the touch, borage is coarse and hairy, while dill and fennel are light and feathery. The perfumes of plants have the ability to alter mood, awaken the senses and release tension, all within a few minutes. Lemon balm, for example, has an uplifting and calming effect when its scent is inhaled, and has been used for centuries by herbalists for this purpose.

Finally, taste – there is no question that healthy fruits, vegetables and herbs grown organically and picked minutes before eating have a freshness and flavour that can never be equalled by those you buy. This is one of the main reasons why sitting down to a meal containing ingredients which you have grown yourself is so satisfying. Food that is freshly picked from your own garden is packed with vitamins, minerals and trace elements which have had no chance to diminish before they are eaten, and you

were also valued highly by the Greeks and Romans and grown in medieval monasteries by monks who considered them beneficial to the stomach and to 'dry' intestines. Today we know that the fibre in turnips has beneficial effects on the bowel, helping to ensure normal function, preventing constipation, and lowering the risk of bowel disease, including cancer. There are other foods that have not yet been researched but for which several thousand years of human use clearly indicate therapeutic uses. Moreover, the fact that humans have been eating plants and using herbs as medicines for so long means that our bodies have adapted to natural foods in a way that they have not always done to the synthetic components found in many modern medicines.

With such a wonderful array of therapeutic properties – the healing benefits of actually tending a garden and creating a place of beauty, and its productivity – the kitchen garden can be proudly displayed, not hidden from view as it might have been fifty or a hundred years ago. Dreary rows of cabbages and sprouts, interspersed with drab looking potatoes are a thing of the past. Today, a profusion of healthy-looking vegetables in all shades from red to green to yellow, intermingled with the bright flowers of medicinal herbs, and the blossoms of fruit trees in spring followed by an abundance of fruit glowing in autumnal sunlight, conjures up a vision of the Garden of Eden – a place of solace, comfort and joy, a wonderful antidote to our stressful lives, a 'good health garden' indeed.

what is paradise?
but a garden, an
orchard of trees and
herbs full of pleasure
and nothing there
but delights.

William Lawson

can be completely certain that they contain no chemical fertilisers or pesticides.

In addition to all the other considerations, there are several ways in which edible plants can benefit our health directly. First, they are a source of a wide range of nutrients that provide our bodies with the building blocks for making new cells, repairing damage and fighting off disease. Second, their cellulose provides fibre which, because it is not broken down in the bowel, helps to maintain a healthy bowel. Finally, they contain a range of pharmacologically active constituents such as mucilage, essential oils, antioxidants and phytosterols which have specifically therapeutic effects. Peppers, carrots, parsley and dandelion leaves, for example, are rich in the antioxidants beta-carotene and vitamin C, both of which help to delay the ageing process, enhance immunity and are thought to help in the prevention of heart and arter-

ial disease and some cancers. We are becoming increasingly aware from the wealth of modern research and media coverage that diet plays an enormous part in maintaining health and preventing diseases. But this knowledge is nothing new; for thousands of years cultures all over the world have utilised food to prevent as well as to treat illness.

It is reassuring to observe that while fashions in diet change from one decade to another, modern research is bearing out many of the ancient medicinal uses of fruits, vegetables and herbs. Today we know that leeks, valued as remedies for the throat and chest by the ancient Greeks and Romans, contain, like their relatives garlic and onions, antiseptic substances that help ward off respiratory infections, colds, flu, sore throats and chest infections; while the mucilage they contain helps to soothe inflammatory conditions such as laryngitis. Turnips

NUTRIENTS CONTAINED IN FOODS

Carbohydrates provide our main source of energy. Simple carbohydrates come in the form of sugars such as glucose and fructose, which occur in fruit. Complex carbohydrates are made up of several sugars and are found in starchy foods such as potatoes, beans, parsnips, turnips, carrots and pumpkins, as well as pasta and bread. When digested, complex carbohydrates are broken down into simple sugars, and require insulin from the pancreas to utilise them in the cells for energy. Such starchy foods also provide other nutrients – minerals, vitamins, and trace elements – and diets in which starchy foods supply around half the daily calorie intake have been shown to help prevent heart and arterial disease, strokes, obesity, gallstones and bowel problems. Calories eaten as starch are less likely to be stored as body fat than calories eaten in the form of fats, and so help to prevent weight gain.

Soluble fibre is found in many fruits and vegetables and has the effect of slowing the rate of digestion in the stomach and intestine, so providing a steady flow of energy as the food is digested and absorbed. Sugars and low-fibre starchy foods are digested and absorbed more rapidly than those containing soluble fibre, which means that blood sugar levels rise quickly, with the help of insulin from the pancreas, but also fall fast. Soluble fibre helps to produce a lower rate of rise and fall in blood sugar, something that is vital to diabetics and those who suffer from hypoglycaemia. It also helps to stabilise energy levels and mood. Diets rich in soluble fibre such as oat bran have been shown to help reduce low-density lipoprotein (LDL) cholesterol, the 'bad cholesterol' which contributes to heart and arterial disease.

Fats in plants are found in the form of fatty acids, which are essential for the absorption of vitamins A, D, E and K from the diet. Fatty acids are vital to normal function of the nervous, immune and hormonal systems, and help maintain the health of the heart and circulatory system, thereby helping to prevent heart disease and strokes.

Proteins are necessary for the formation and repair of cells and as building blocks for making hormones and enzymes. Proteins are synthesised in the body from amino acids which are derived from food. Complete proteins, containing all the essential amino acids, are found in animal proteins – fish, poultry, meat, eggs and milk. No vegetable proteins except soya bean products such as tofu and tempeh contain all the essential amino acids, and therefore two vegetable proteins should be eaten together at the same meal. Beans and other legumes are good sources of protein but must be combined with one of the other two main sources of vegetable protein: nuts and seeds or grains.

Vitamins and minerals are also vital to health. Fifteen vitamins and fifteen minerals can only be obtained from food to help prevent disease. Many are leached from the body through consumption of excess sugar or alcohol, and by the action of diuretics such as coffee and tea. The complexities of the beneficial interactions between vitamins and minerals, as well as of other vital constituents of food, are achieved in nature through a nutrient-rich diet; the same result cannot be achieved by the daily consumption of artificial and isolated supplements. Vitamins, minerals and trace elements can also be lost through cooking and storing fruits and vegetables. Produce is best eaten straight from the garden, either raw, lightly steamed or stir-fried. Boiling in large quantities of water and throwing the cooking water away will result in considerable loss of nutrients.

Antioxidants are present in many foods, and these have the ability to prevent oxidation in the body, which causes the release of harmful substances known as free radicals. Free radicals contribute to heart disease, cancer, degenerative diseases, lowered immunity, cataracts and the ageing process. Vitamins A, C and E, selenium, and many carotenes and flavonoids from food sources have been shown to exert a beneficial effect in a way that chemical supplements of these substances do not. Zinc, copper and selenium deficiencies reduce antioxidant defences, and excess iron increases oxidation. Red and orange fruits and vegetables (red and yellow peppers, tomatoes, carrots, oranges, strawberries, raspberries) and spinach are good sources of the antioxidants beta-carotene, flavonoids and vitamins C and E.

Carotenes give the colour to orange, red and yellow foods; they number in the hundreds and act as antioxidants. Studies have shown that a carotene-rich diet lowers incidences of heart and arterial disease, cataracts and some cancers.

Popular vegetables such as carrots, onions, potatoes and garlic are rich in essential vitamins, minerals and trace elements, and can help to bolster our resistance to disease. In addition, studies have shown that these vegetables can be medically effective in the treatment of a number of ailments including arthritis, heart disease and digestive problems.

vegetables

Onion *Allium cepa*

The onion has been used in healing since 4000 BC. Its benefits were first appreciated by the ancient Egyptians, who respected it both as a panacea and as a symbol of vitality. For centuries, onion has been used to ward off epidemics of infectious diseases, such as typhoid, cholera and the plague, as well as to increase energy and longevity, and modern medical research has served to justify our ancestors' belief in the medicinal properties of this amazing plant.

ONIONS CAN HELP TO TREAT

- *Anaemia*
- *Arthritis*
- *Bronchitis*
- *Catarrh, coughs and colds*
- *Constipation*
- *Cystitis*
- *Flatulence*
- *Flu*
- *Fluid retention*
- *Gout*
- *High blood pressure*
- *High cholesterol*
- *Pharyngitis*
- *Rhinitis*
- *Sinusitis*
- *Worms*

INTERNAL USE

Raw onions are antiseptic and enhance the body's ability to fight against a long list of bacteria, including salmonella. They are also effective against respiratory infections and can be used in the treatment of gastrointestinal infections and urinary tract infections such as cystitis. The pungent onion has a heating effect, increasing the circulation and causing sweating, which is useful in cold, damp weather to ward off infection. It also helps to lower fevers and sweat out colds and flu. Onions can be used to treat sore throats, catarrh and sinusitis as they have a decongestant action. They act as an expectorant for coughs and bronchitis.

Raw onions act as a stimulant to the digestive system and liver, and thereby make an excellent nutritional energy tonic as they enhance the digestion and absorption of nutrients. Thus, they can also be used as a pick-me-up, and when recovering from illness. Onions have earned a reputation as a blood purifier and detoxifying remedy. They have diuretic properties and can be used for water retention, arthritis and gout. A few tablespoons of onion wine taken first thing each morning for 8–10 days in a row is an excellent remedy for expelling worms.

Traditionally, both onions and garlic have been used to benefit the heart and circulation, and they can help to reduce blood pressure and narrowing of the arteries, and to guard against heart attacks. Modern research has shown that they have a lowering effect on harmful cholesterol, and half a raw onion eaten daily is said to significantly lessen the chance of a heart attack. Both raw and cooked onions can help to lower blood pressure, and prevent clots. Onions have been used in folk medicine to reduce blood sugar levels, which could be useful to diabetics, and research has shown that both raw and cooked onions do, in fact, have this effect. It is also thought that, due to their sulphur compounds, they may be useful as a remedy against cancer.

EXTERNAL USE

Onions have many external applications: for example, for wasp and bee stings, rub a slice of raw onion over the affected area. For warts, chop onions, cover them with salt and leave them overnight. Store the juice that collects in a bottle, and dab the warts with it twice daily. Onion juice can also be applied to burns or as an antiseptic for cuts and grazes. The juice can also be used for toothache – simply place a small piece of cotton wool soaked in onion juice into the cavity. Poultices of cooked onion paste applied to abscesses, whitlows and boils can give speedy relief. Grated onions can be made into a poultice to apply to chilblains.

When the leaf tips turn yellow, bend the leaves over at right angles and slightly loosen the roots with a fork.

HOW TO GROW

Seeds are obtainable but onions are easiest raised from 'sets'. Add well-rotted manure before planting, and lime if your soil is acid. Sow seeds in February or March under glass or in a warm bed in April. Harden off seedlings started indoors and plant out seedlings or sets in April, 10 cm (4 in) apart, with 25 cm (10 in) between rows. Mulch in the summer. Dig up onions in August after loosening the roots (*see left*) and spread them in the sun to dry the foliage.

Onion
recipes & remedies

Any type of onion, including spring onions, can be used to make the following remedies.

Onion wine

A useful remedy to expel worms from the intestines.

1 large onion, finely chopped
4 tablespoons (60 ml) honey
570 ml (1 pint) white wine

Add the onion and honey to the wine, and leave to soak for 48 hours, shaking frequently. Strain, and take 2–4 tablespoons (30–60 ml) daily. The wine will keep for up to 3 days if it is refrigerated.

Infusion of onions

For colds, catarrh, coughs and bronchitis.

4 medium-sized onions, sliced
1 litre (1³/4 pints) hot water

Soak the onion slices for 2–3 hours in hot water. Take one glassful (6 fl oz) twice daily.

Onion decoction

A refreshing drink that is particularly helpful for catarrh.

3 medium-sized onions cut into quarters
250 ml (9 fl oz) water
Honey to taste

Simmer the onions in water for 5–10 minutes. Strain, add honey to taste and drink as a beverage as necessary.

Onion skin tea

Tea made from boiled onion skins can help to improve poor circulation, especially in cases of gout.

10 onion skins
1 litre (1³/4 pints) water

Simmer the onion skins in water for 10 minutes. This quantity may be drunk each day for as long as symptoms persist.

Onion syrup

For colds, catarrh, coughs and bronchitis.

2 medium-sized onions, chopped
2 tablespoons (30 ml) honey

Place the chopped onions into a bowl, drizzle with honey and leave covered at room temperature overnight to produce a juice. Take 1 tablespoon (15 ml) every 2 hours.

Leek *Allium porrum*

The leek has been praised for its medicinal benefits for thousands of years. The ancient Greeks recommended leeks to improve the voice, and for a few days every month, the Roman Emperor Nero apparently ate only leeks and oil, to keep his throat healthy in order to sing well during his competitive appearances at festivals. The leek has been a popular remedy for the respiratory system ever since.

LEEKS CAN HELP TO TREAT

- *Atherosclerosis*
- *Boils and abscesses*
- *Bowel infections*
- *Catarrh, coughs and colds*
- *Chest infections*
- *Colic*
- *Cuts and grazes*
- *Diarrhoea*
- *Flatulence*
- *Insect bites and stings*
- *Minor burns and scalds*
- *Poor circulation*
- *Sore throats*
- *Urinary infections*

INTERNAL USE

Leeks remain an effective medicine for the respiratory tract. They have warming and stimulating properties that help to loosen phlegm, and an expectorant action that helps to clear congestion from the nose and bronchial system. In addition, leeks, like other members of the *Allium* family, have antiseptic properties that help to ward off colds, sore throats and chest infections. These warming and antiseptic properties can also be put to good use in the digestive system. Leek broth, leek soup or braised leeks can be taken to ease diarrhoea. Leeks can help to re-establish the normal bacterial population in the gut after a bowel infection, during and after a course of antibiotics, or when suffering from candidiasis. They also have a relaxing effect in the digestive tract, helping to relieve cramp, colic, wind and distension. They stimulate the appetite and improve the digestion, and by aiding peristalsis, are mildly laxative. The mucilage in leeks has a soothing action, which can help to relieve inflammatory conditions such as colitis.

Leeks have a diuretic action, enhancing the elimination of fluid and wastes via the urinary tract. Their combined diuretic and antiseptic properties can be useful when treating fluid retention or urinary infections, such as urethritis and cystitis.

The leek is a rich source of potassium, magnesium, silica, iron and calcium, as well as in vitamins C and B complex. Its warming properties stimulate the circulation and are generally invigorating, and since leeks are nutritious and easily digested, they make an excellent tonic for convalescence. As a broth, leeks provide a good, nutrient-rich food to replace minerals lost during sickness and diarrhoea. Like onions and garlic, leeks help to protect the heart and arteries, and to prevent atherosclerosis and high blood pressure.

EXTERNAL USE

A leek poultice can be used as an antiseptic for cuts and grazes. A cut leek can be rubbed on to insect bites and stings to relieve pain and swelling. Warm cooked leeks can be mashed to make a paste, which, when applied on gauze, can help to draw poisons out of boils and abscesses. Leeks cooked in milk make a soothing and healing lotion to apply to inflamed skin and minor burns.

HOW TO GROW

Leeks like rich, well-drained soil with plenty of organic matter. The seeds should be germinated indoors in late winter or outdoors in spring. If they are outdoors in a seed bed, sow the seeds 1.5 cm (½ in) apart, in rows 15 cm (6 in) apart in March or April. Plant them out in their cropping positions between June and August when 20 cm (8 in) high. Using a dibber, make holes in firm ground 20 cm (8 in) deep and 15–20 cm (6–8 in) apart in staggered rows. Drop the leeks in gently, roots downwards, then fill with water in order to settle the soil around the roots. The seedlings will soon settle without the soil being replaced. Leeks can be planted out in the space left by early potatoes. They should be 'earthed up' periodically (*see left*), hoed in summer to keep the weeds down, and kept watered during dry weather. They can be harvested from November to March.

To 'earth up', draw in soil around the base of the leek with a hoe in order to prevent light getting to the plant. This will increase the length of the white stem.

Leek
recipes & remedies

Young leeks can be eaten raw as part of a salad. However, they are usually served steamed or braised.

Leek broth

A good mineral-rich food to take when suffering from cystitis, diarrhoea or gastroenteritis.

8–10 leeks, chopped
2–3 litres (3^{1}/$_2$–5^{1}/$_4$ pints) water

Simmer the leeks gently in water for 1^{1}/$_2$–2 hours. Serve the broth with the leeks intact or pass them through a blender first, depending on preference.

Syrup of leeks

Good for sore throats, catarrh, colds and chest infections.

2–3 leeks, chopped
1 litre (1^3/$_4$ pints) water
Honey to taste

Cook the leeks in the water until soft and extract the juice by squeezing through muslin. Add honey to taste and give 1 teaspoon (5 ml) 3–6 times daily for respiratory infections. Store in the refrigerator.

Leek poultice

A useful antiseptic for cuts and grazes.

1 leek, chopped
1–2 litres (1^3/$_4$–3^{1}/$_2$ pints) water

Wash and chop a leek. Cook it gently in the water until soft. When cool enough to handle, place between 2 pieces of gauze and bind it to the affected part with a cotton bandage.

Leek, garlic and ginger soup

A warming soup, helpful for warding off colds, flu, sore throats and chest infections, and for clearing catarrhal congestion.

1 tablespoon olive oil
4 medium-sized leeks trimmed and finely sliced
2 cloves garlic, finely chopped
1 tablespoon chopped fresh ginger
1 litre (1^3/$_4$ pints) water or vegetable stock
Salt and freshly ground pepper

Heat the oil in a large saucepan over a low heat. Add the leeks, cover and cook for 10 minutes, or until just softened. Add the garlic, ginger and water or stock, increase the heat and bring to the boil. Reduce the heat, cover the saucepan and simmer the soup for 20 minutes, or until the leeks are tender. Remove the saucepan from the heat, and allow the soup to cool a little, then purée in a food processor or blender until smooth. Rinse out the saucepan, add the soup and reheat gently. Season to taste with salt and pepper, and serve.

Garlic *Allium sativum*

Garlic is one of the most remarkable food or herb remedies in existence, and has been revered as a rejuvenator and aphrodisiac in many cultures for thousands of years, despite its antisocial effects. The ancient Greeks sang its praises, and the Egyptian pharaoh Cheops was well aware of its energy-giving properties when he ordered the workmen building the Great Pyramid to have a daily ration of garlic; this was designed not only to give them strength but also to protect them against epidemics, as it has long been known for its ability to fight infection.

GARLIC CAN HELP TO TREAT

- *Asthma*
- *Catarrh, coughs and colds*
- *Chest infections*
- *Chilblains*
- *Circulatory disease*
- *High blood pressure*
- *High cholesterol*
- *Low immunity*
- *Poor circulation*
- *Sore throats*
- *Tiredness and lethargy*
- *Worms*

INTERNAL USE

As a result of garlic's invigorating properties, it has been considered the vital ingredient of many an elixir of life. In 5th-century Greece it was apparently sold by street vendors chanting: 'It is truth. Garlic gives man youth.' They were not far wrong, because modern research has verified garlic's rejuvenating properties by revealing the presence of antioxidant substances that help to delay the ageing process by protecting the body against damage from free radicals. It has also been found that garlic's antioxidant substances help to guard against degenerative diseases such as heart disease and cancer. The sulphur compounds in garlic are reported to slow down the growth of tumours.

Garlic has powerful antibacterial, antifungal, antiviral and antiparasitic properties, and when crushed not only is garlic's powerful odour released but also its natural antibacterial substance, allicin, which has been shown to have antibiotic properties. When taken internally, garlic exerts its antibacterial effects throughout the digestive, respiratory, urinary and reproductive tracts. It makes an excellent remedy for sore throats and colds. It helps to re-establish the normal bacterial population of the gut after taking orthodox antibiotics for an infection. It is an effective remedy for worms when taken first thing in the morning on an empty stomach. Its warming and stimulating properties have a decongestant action in the respiratory system, helping to clear catarrh, sinusitis and bronchial congestion. It also acts as an expectorant and can be helpful to clear coughs and chest infections. Because of its diaphoretic properties, garlic helps to bring down fevers. Garlic has a warming and invigorating effect on the digestion, stimulating the secretion of digestive enzymes and of bile from the liver. It promotes appetite and improves digestion and absorption, helping to ensure regular bowel movements and thereby keeping the bowel free of excess toxins.

Garlic has been valued in India as a remedy for the heart and circulation since the first century AD. Ayurvedic physicians have used garlic for preventing heart disease, and in China and Japan it has been taken for centuries to lower blood pressure. Modern research has again confirmed its ancient use, showing that, if taken regularly, garlic can significantly lower the level of harmful cholesterol, thereby helping to prevent and treat atherosclerosis and high blood pressure. By reducing blood pressure and the tendency to clotting, garlic can help to prevent heart attacks and strokes. It has a vasodilatory action, opening the blood vessels and improving blood flow through them, thus helping to relieve and prevent a wide range of circulatory disorders and promoting a feeling of warmth and well-being.

When harvesting, ease the plants out of the ground with a fork to avoid damaging them.

HOW TO GROW

Garlic does best in well-drained, well-manured soil in a sunny position. Propagate by planting cloves in late February or March, pointed end upwards, 15 cm (6 in) apart. Harvest between August and September and dry plants in the sun before tying them in bunches and storing them in a cool, dry place.

Garlic
recipes & remedies

To be beneficial, garlic needs to be eaten raw, since cooking destroys about 95% of its medicinal value.

Garlic syrup

An excellent remedy for coughs, colds and sore throats.

4 garlic cloves, thinly sliced
Honey to cover

Cover the sliced garlic with honey and leave for 2–3 hours. Crush to extract the juice, and take teaspoonfuls throughout the day.

Garlic oil

For rheumatism, arthritis, sprains and strains, and chest infections.

6 garlic cloves, peeled and crushed
250 ml (9 fl oz) olive oil

Place the crushed cloves in a sterilised bottle and cover with olive oil. Seal and leave for 1 or 2 weeks. Press through muslin and store the oil in a sterilised bottle. Massage it regularly into the affected areas of the body.

Celery *Apium graveolens* var. *dulce*

Celery is a tasty vegetable with a distinct pungent flavour, and makes a crisp addition to salads. The celery we grow today is the descendant of wild celery (*A. graveolens*), which was highly valued by the ancient Egyptians, Greeks and Chinese, both as a flavouring and as a medicine. The Romans used to wear a wreath of celery around their heads to ease a hangover. By medieval times, celery was popular for its ability to relieve aches and pains, to calm the nerves and benefit the digestion.

CELERY CAN HELP TO TREAT

- *Arthritis*
- *Constipation*
- *Gout*
- *High blood pressure*
- *High cholesterol*
- *Mild depression*
- *Stress*
- *Urinary infections*
- *Weak digestion*

INTERNAL USE

Celery has been valued as a remedy to lower blood pressure since about 200 BC, and modern research has shown that eating a couple of stalks of fresh celery daily can help to reduce blood pressure and harmful cholesterol levels. The substance responsible for lowering blood pressure has been identified as 3-n-butylphthalide, which acts by blocking the enzyme that makes catecholamines, which are stress-hormones. This substance dilates the arteries and reduces contraction in arterial muscles caused by stress, and is probably most useful for treating stress-related hypertension.

Celery has a mild diuretic effect, especially the seeds, which contain appreciable amounts of apiol in their volatile oil, which has an antiseptic effect on the urinary system. Celery helps to enhance the elimination of excess fluid and toxins via the urinary system and has long been used to treat gout and arthritis as well as urinary infections. While orthodox diuretics can leach potassium from the system unless they are combined with a potassium supplement, celery comes ready packed with a good dose of this substance.

Modern research has shown that celery contains at least eight different compounds that may be effective against cancer, including substances that may have the ability to neutralise the effects of some carcinogens. Eating raw celery on a regular basis may also help to protect against stomach cancer.

Celery has always been popular with dieters because it is low in calories and high in fibre, while its diuretic action reduces excess fluid. The stalks are moderately nutritious, but the top leaves are more so as they contain more calcium, iron, potassium and vitamins A and C than the stalks. The leaves should be included when making soups, casseroles and salads. Celery seeds and stalks both have a stimulating effect on the digestive tract: celery seed tea makes an excellent after-dinner *digestif*. Celery seeds have also been used by herbalists for centuries to raise the spirits and benefit the nervous system. Celery, being high in fibre, will help to ensure regular bowel function and prevent and relieve constipation.

Caution: Celery eaten either before or after vigorous exercise has been known to induce allergic responses in sensitive people.

HOW TO GROW

There are two types of celery: self-blanching and trench celery. Both like rich, moist soil and grow well in alkaline, peaty areas. For both types, sow indoors in mid to late spring in seed boxes, and leave uncovered. Transplant into trays or pots when 2 small celery leaves appear on each seedling, spacing the plants 5 cm (2 in) apart. Harden off as the weather becomes warmer and plant out in cropping positions in May and June.

Plant out self-blanching celery in holes 30 cm (1 ft) apart, with 45 cm (18 in) between rows. Firm the soil around the roots, water and mulch. Harvest from August to September.

For trench celery dig a trench 30 cm (1 ft) deep and 40 cm (16 in) wide. Half fill it with well-rotted manure and cover with 7.5 cm (3 in) topsoil. Plant the young celery with 5 or 6 leaves 30 cm (1 ft) apart. In August, break off odd side shoots, gather the leaves and stems in a bunch and earth up. Wrap the leaves and stems in black polythene. Water, and spade soil into the trench around the plants, covering them up to the leaves. Harvest in September or October, lifting the plants with a fork.

Celery
recipes & remedies

Tender young hearts are delicious raw, and stalks are often eaten with a cheese filling. They make a good alternative to bread or crackers as a base for hors-d'oeuvres or snacks, when they can be stuffed with pâté or cream cheese.

Celery seed tea

An excellent after-dinner drink to aid digestion.

50 g (2 oz) celery seeds
570 ml (1 pint) boiling water

Add the seeds to the water and cover the container. Leave to infuse for 5–10 minutes. Strain and allow the liquid to cool. Drink 1 cupful after meals.

Celery juice

Drink half a glass first thing for 15–20 days as a remedy for rheumatic ailments.

4–6 celery stalks

Remove the leaves and wash the stalks thoroughly, then extract the juice using a juice extractor.

Horseradish *Armoracia rusticana*

Horseradish is probably native to south-east Europe but it is widely cultivated all over northern Europe and North America, and is often found growing wild on banks and roadsides. It is popular for its large tap roots, which make an excellent, intensely pungent condiment. Freshly grated horseradish is traditionally eaten as horseradish sauce with beef and fish, often mixed with grated apple and cream or yoghurt to reduce its biting pungency.

The leaves look like large dock leaves and also have a very pungent taste – when young and tender they can be chopped and mixed (in moderation) in green salads. Both leaf and root are rich in vitamin C.

INTERNAL USE

Horseradish has been respected as a food and medicine since at least the time of the Romans, and it was one of the five bitter herbs eaten by the Jews at the feast of the Passover. In medieval Europe it was taken to improve digestion and in the 17th century Culpeper prescribed it for external use to treat sciatica, gout, joint pain and 'hard swellings of the spleen and liver'. It was not until the mid 17th century that it became popular as a condiment in Britain, served with meat to ease its digestion.

Horseradish is a powerful and stimulating remedy, increasing circulation and promoting warmth throughout the body – excellent for those who feel the cold and suffer from poor circulation in winter. Its pungency has a beneficial effect throughout the digestive tract when used in small amounts. It enhances appetite and stimulates digestive juices and bile, thereby aiding digestion. It helps to ensure regular bowel function and the movement of wastes through the system. By increasing the blood flow to the tissues and removal of waste products from the body, horseradish acts as a good detoxifying remedy. These qualities are augmented by its diuretic action (provided mainly by its constituent asparagin), which hastens the elimination of fluid and toxins from the body. So, horseradish has often been used to cleanse the body, to clear the skin, and to treat problems such as boils and abscesses as well as arthritis and gout.

In the respiratory system, horseradish has a stimulating decongestant and expectorant action, and horseradish syrup has long been used to help relieve coughs, colds, fevers, flu, catarrh, sinusitis and hay fever. The powerful antibiotic effect it has is excellent for urinary and respiratory infections. In addition, horseradish makes a good energy-giving tonic.

EXTERNAL USE

A poultice of grated raw horseradish stimulates the circulation and has long been a folk remedy for easing arthritic pain. When applied, it should not come into direct contact with the skin since it can cause irritation and even blistering.

Caution: Horseradish should not be used for symptoms characterised by heat such as acidity, gastritis and peptic ulcers, nor for people with kidney or thyroid problems.

HORSERADISH CAN HELP TO TREAT

- *Arthritis*
- *Boils and abscesses*
- *Bronchial congestion*
- *Catarrh, coughs and colds*
- *Chilblains*
- *Constipation*
- *Fevers and flu*
- *Fluid retention*
- *Gout*
- *Hay fever*
- *Indigestion*
- *Poor appetite*
- *Poor circulation*
- *Sinusitis*
- *Skin problems*
- *Tiredness and lethargy*

Horseradish should be deadheaded regularly to ensure continued flowering, and the roots dug up from August onwards.

HOW TO GROW

Horseradish likes well-drained soil and prefers full sun, although it will tolerate partial shade. It grows up to 50 cm (20 in) tall. Propagate it either by sowing seeds in early spring, or by planting roots, which can be bought or dug up in the autumn of the previous year and stored. Planting holes should be 60 cm (2 ft) apart, and 25 cm (14 in) deep for roots. Horseradish grown from a root should be left in the ground for 2 years. It self-seeds readily, and once it begins to spread it can be hard to get rid of.

Horseradish
recipes & remedies

Horseradish gives off fumes that are more powerful than onions, which can cause the eyes to smart and run while preparing it. One way to avoid this is to grate or shred it in a food processor, rather than by hand.

Horseradish vinegar

To stimulate the appetite and aid digestion.

1 large horseradish root, washed, peeled and grated
1 onion, chopped
570 ml (1 pint) cider vinegar

When grating the horseradish root, take care not to get any juice in your eyes. Fill a sterilised bottle or jar with the horseradish and onion. Heat the vinegar in a pan until it just starts to simmer and pour it into the bottle or jar. Cover and leave it to cool. Strain and store in a sterilised bottle. Shake well and leave it to stand for 4–6 weeks, shaking a few times a day. Take 1 teaspoonful (5 ml) in hot water 3–6 times daily when the need arises.

Horseradish syrup

A remedy for hayfever, bronchitis and coughs.

1 large horseradish root, washed, peeled and grated
Honey to cover

Place the grated horseradish root in a bowl and pour the honey over it. Cover the bowl and leave for 24 hours.

Press through a sieve or muslin and store juice in a sterilised airtight bottle in the refrigerator. Take 1 teaspoon (5 ml) 3–6 times daily when symptoms arise.

Horseradish sauce

An excellent warming digestive and circulatory stimulant which aids the digestion of rich foods and heavy meats. Serve with cold meat or as a salad dip.

4 tablespoons grated fresh horseradish
1 tablespoon Dijon mustard
1 teaspoon cider vinegar
Pinch of paprika
4 tablespoons natural yoghurt
1 teaspoon fresh lemon juice

Mix the horseradish, mustard, vinegar and paprika together in a small bowl. Add the yoghurt and lemon juice and stir until smooth. Chill before serving.

Asparagus *Asparagus officinalis*

Asparagus is best known as a culinary delicacy, enjoyed particularly in spring when the succulent new shoots, known as 'spears', lightly steamed and drizzled with warmed butter or olive oil, provide a tasty hors-d'oeuvre. What is not so well known is that several varieties of asparagus have been valued as medicines for more than 2,000 years. The ancient Egyptians cultivated it, as did the Greeks, who recommended it for rheumatism and urinary problems. In medieval monasteries it was valued for its detoxifying properties.

ASPARAGUS CAN HELP TO TREAT

- *Arthritis*
- *Cataracts*
- *Constipation*
- *Fluid retention*
- *Low immunity*
- *Skin problems*
- *Tiredness and lethargy*
- *Urinary infections*
- *Vitamin and mineral deficiency*
- *Worms*

INTERNAL USE

Today, *A. officinalis* is used principally for its powerful diuretic effect, brought about mainly by its active constituent, asparagine, a substance that helps to hasten the elimination of toxins and excess fluid from the body. It is helpful for relieving urinary infections and it also has a beneficial cleansing effect on the system.

Asparagus was popular in the past in the treatment of chronic arthritis, rheumatism and gout as well as skin problems. The rhizomes have been used in decoctions for their even stronger diuretic effect.

The cleansing properties of asparagus are augmented by the beneficial effect that this vegetable is thought to have on the functioning of the intestines and the liver, the great detoxifying organ of the body. It also stimulates bowel function and makes an effective remedy for mild constipation. Its aspargusic acid has the ability to expel worms from the body and has been used to treat schistosomiasis, which is an inflammatory condition of the liver.

Asparagus not only tastes delicious but is also a nutritious food. It contains folic acid, vitamins A, B complex and C , manganese, iron, phosphorus and protein. It makes a good slimming food, too, being high in fibre and low in calories (unless covered in olive oil or butter of course). The antioxidant vitamins A and C help to prevent damage to the cells caused by the presence of free radicals, and thereby help to slow the ageing process, which perhaps explains why asparagus has the reputation of being a rejuvenative and restorative.

Another antioxidant substance found in asparagus – glutathione – has recently been shown to help prevent the formation of cataracts and is thought to have anticancer properties, as well as helping to boost the body's ability to combat viruses.

HOW TO GROW

Asparagus plants are perennials and require a permanent bed in a sunny, sheltered site, where they can remain productive for up to 20 years. They grow best in a rich, sandy, well-drained soil with a nutritious top dressing of organic matter. On heavy soils they are best grown in raised beds.

Asparagus may be grown from 1- to 3-year-old crowns or from seed. Dig in plenty of garden compost or well-rotted manure the year before planting and remove perennial weeds. Crowns should be planted in April, in a trench 30 cm (1 ft) wide and 20 cm (8 in) deep, with a ridge in the middle. Plant crowns in holes 10 cm (4 in) deep and cover with 5 cm (2 in) of sifted soil. Rows should be 30–45 cm (12–20 in) apart.

When planting asparagus crowns, spread the roots over the ridge you have made in the centre of the trench before covering with soil.

If planting from seed, soak them in water for at least a day before sowing in warm soil in April. They should be planted about 30–45 cm (12–18 in) apart, in rows 45 cm (18 in) apart. Thin them to about 15 cm (6 in) apart when they reach a height of 15 cm (6 in).

Plants can be harvested in their second or third year, in May or June. Cut the spears 2.5–5 cm (1–2 in) below the level of the soil when they are 13–18 cm (5–7 in) high. In late autumn, the foliage should be cut back to 2.5–5 cm (1–2 in) from the ground.

Asparagus
recipes & remedies

Asparagus spears can be steamed or boiled in water until they are tender, and eaten. The water left over from this can be drunk 2–3 times a day as a cleansing diuretic. Alternatively, it can be prepared as a decoction.

Asparagus decoction

Excellent for urinary problems.

25 g (1 oz) asparagus, chopped
570 ml (1 pint) water

Place the chopped asparagus in the water. Bring it to the boil and then allow it to simmer for 20 minutes. Strain and allow it to cool. Drink 1 cupful 2–3 times a day.

Hand and foot bath

A recommended treatment for stimulating the liver.

55 g (2 oz) asparagus, crushed
55 g (2 oz) asparagus rhizomes, washed
1 litre (2 pints) water

Place the asparagus and rhizomes in the water and bring to the boil. Simmer for 15 minutes. Strain and allow the liquid to cool to body temperature. Soak the feet for 8 minutes in the morning and the hands for 8 minutes in the evening.

Brassicas *Brassica oleracea* varieties

Botanically speaking, the brassicas (members of the Cruciferae family) include cabbage and related green crops, such as kale, broccoli, Brussels sprouts and cauliflower, as well as horseradish, kohlrabi, radishes, rape, sea kale and turnips. Cabbage, kale, broccoli, Brussels sprouts and cauliflower all have very similar properties and they can be used medicinally almost interchangeably. All of these vegetables contain both nitrogen and sulphur compounds, which can create wind in some susceptible people. It is the sulphur content that you can smell when these brassicas are cooked for too long.

BRASSICAS CAN HELP TO TREAT

- *Alcoholism*
- *Anaemia*
- *Arthritis*
- *Boils and abscesses*
- *Chilblains*
- *Colitis*
- *Constipation*
- *Coughs and colds*
- *Cuts and grazes*
- *Gastritis*
- *Gout*
- *Indigestion, heartburn*
- *Liver problems*
- *Low immunity*
- *Minor burns and scalds*
- *Poor lactation*
- *Sinusitis*
- *Skin problems*
- *Varicose veins*
- *Vitamin and mineral deficiency*

CABBAGE *B. oleracea* var. *capitata*

Cabbage is one of the most ancient and treasured remedies in history. In one form or another, it has been cultivated for about 4,000 years, and it has earned the reputation of a panacea for all ills with such names as 'poor man's medicine chest' and 'doctor of the poor'.

INTERNAL USE

Today, eaten raw or lightly steamed, cabbages are a valuable source of vitamins, minerals and trace elements. They contain vitamins A, B, C and E, and minerals calcium, sulphur, silica, magnesium, iodine, iron and phosphorus. Their antioxidant vitamins help to protect the body against degenerative diseases, including cancer, and to slow the effects of ageing. Being rich in iron and chlorophyll, they make a good remedy for anaemia. They have a reputation as a nerve tonic, and can be used to treat anxiety, insomnia, depression and exhaustion. Cabbage was used by sailors to prevent scurvy and it was recommended for pregnant women and breast-feeding mothers to increase milk production.

Cabbage has an ancient reputation as a remedy for purifying the blood, and still today, a decoction of raw cabbage taken daily makes a good spring cleanser to detoxify the system and it can be helpful for clearing such skin problems as acne and boils. It can also act as a diuretic, hastening the elimination of toxins via the urine, and has long been eaten in soups or taken as a decoction to help ease fluid retention, kidney stones, arthritis and gout.

Extensive modern research into the medicinal benefits of the cabbage largely confirms its ancient uses in folk medicine. It has been shown to help stimulate the immune system and the production of antibodies, and it is a useful remedy for fighting off bacterial and viral infection. It contains sulphur compounds, which may be responsible for its antiseptic, antibiotic and disinfectant actions, particularly in the respiratory system. It was used as a folk remedy, in the form of soup or tea, for respiratory infections, colds, sinusitis, coughs and sore throats, and it was also an old remedy for tuberculosis.

Cabbage can be used to help heal ulcers. It contains mucilage that coats the lining of the digestive tract and protects it from irritants and excess acid, and an amino acid, methionine, found only in raw cabbage, which promotes healing. It should be taken raw or juiced for best results: 2–3 glasses (12–18 fl oz) of freshly extracted juice taken between meals can help to relieve peptic ulcers, gastritis, heartburn and ulcerative colitis. Cabbage also benefits the digestion in other ways – it stimulates the appetite and can relieve constipation. An old Russian folk cure for chronic constipation was half a glass (3 fl oz) of salted cabbage juice taken before each meal. As a tonic to the liver, cabbage has long been used to treat cirrhosis of the liver as well as lethargy, irritability and headaches, symptoms all associated with a sluggish liver. It is also an ancient remedy for headaches and hangovers, and was also used to dry out alcoholics. Recent research has confirmed that cabbage can be beneficial to the liver, and that it contains a substance called glutamine, which can help both peptic ulcers and alcoholism. Research has also indicated that eating cabbage regularly may help to reduce blood sugar and so may be of some benefit to diabetics.

Like other types of brassica, such as broccoli, cauliflower and Brussels sprouts, cabbage has been thoroughly researched for its protective

action against cancer. Cabbage, in particular, has been found to help lower the risk of cancer – especially cancer of the colon and the growth of polyps, which are often a prelude to cancer – and, when eaten raw, to help protect against the effects of radiation. The more that is eaten, the better the effect. This is probably due to the many tumour-inhibiting chemical constituents it contains – bioflavonoids, indoles, genistein and monoterpenes. Cabbage also appears to enhance the body's ability to metabolise oestrogen and helps to reduce susceptibility to breast, uterine and ovarian cancers if eaten regularly.

EXTERNAL USE

Cabbage leaves have a soothing antiseptic and healing effect and they have an ability to draw out toxins from the skin. A cabbage-leaf poultice is a traditional remedy for wounds, burns and scalds, boils and carbuncles, bruises and sprains, ulcers, blisters, cold sores and shingles, and bites and stings. Its anti-inflammatory action can benefit swollen and painful joints, arthritis and gout, and it can help to relieve the pain of neuralgia, sciatica, toothache, headaches,

migraine and lumbago. Traditionally, it was applied over the abdomen and left overnight to treat peptic ulcers and bowel problems. Applied to the lower abdomen during the day and night, it may be useful to soothe cystitis and renal colic, and to relieve fluid retention.

A cabbage poultice applied to the chest and cabbage tea or juice taken internally during the day is reputed to relieve the pain and soreness of a harsh cough, and to help to clear a chest infection. If applied to the throat it can help to soothe a sore throat, tonsillitis and laryngitis. The leaves, once steeped in olive oil, can be applied to chapped skin, chilblains, ulcers, varicose veins and phlebitis, abscesses and boils.

Cabbage juice can be used as a gargle for sore throats, a lotion for burns, bites, cold sores, acne, impetigo and squeezed into the ear for earache. Tepid cabbage water is excellent for bathing sore, tired eyes.

Caution: All brassicas should be avoided by people who have overactive thyroid glands. Sauerkraut is high in tyramine and can sometimes trigger migraine headaches.

HOW TO GROW

By growing different types of cabbage, you can enjoy this vegetable all year around:

Spring cabbage: Sow in July or August, harvest in April and May.

Summer cabbage: Sow in April, harvest in August and September.

Winter cabbage: Sow in April or May, harvest between October and February.

Cabbages, as do all brassicas, like sun and rich, alkaline, well-drained soil with plenty of organic matter. Sow seeds about 1.5 cm ($^1/_2$ in) deep in trays or a seed bed, leaving about 3.5 cm (1$^1/_2$ in) between seeds. Time your sowing according to variety (*see above*). When plants are 7.5 cm (3 in) high, replant in their cropping position 30–45 cm (12–18 in) apart, in staggered rows 45–60 cm (18–24 in) apart. Harvest cabbages as required, then dig up and dispose of the roots.

KALE *B. oleracea,* Acephala group

Kale was probably the earliest kind of cultivated cabbage and it is nearest to the original wild cabbage – the colewort. These early cabbages probably had more stalk than anything else, and kale still has tall, thick stems.

INTERNAL USE

Kale, like cabbage, is a good source of minerals and vitamins, notably beta-carotene, vitamins C and E, iron, folic acid and a form of calcium that is easily absorbed by the body. It is similar in therapeutic value to its relatives – broccoli, cabbage, Brussels sprouts and cauliflower – being rich in antioxidants and other powerful cancer-fighting phytochemicals, including a substance called sulphoraphane that blocks the action of several carcinogens. It also contains indoles, which enhance the liver's metabolism of oestrogen, and so helps to speed up its excretion from the system, thereby reducing the risk of breast cancer. Indoles and other substances, such as beta-carotene and bioflavonoids, also stimulate the production of those enzymes that protect against cancer.

Kale makes an excellent and nutritious tonic for anyone who is anaemic or feeling tired, lethargic and run down. Its rich iron content is readily absorbed, due to the presence of vitamin C,

and acts to enhance energy levels, immunity and healing.

It is best to cook kale only lightly, either steamed or stir-fried, to preserve its therapeutic properties. The addition of such spices as coriander and cumin, or herbs such as rosemary or thyme, will help to neutralise some of this vegetable's wind-producing properties.

HOW TO GROW

Kale should be sown in seed beds in April or May about 1.5 cm ($^1/_2$ in) deep, and thinned to 7.5 cm (3 in) apart when the seedlings are large enough to handle. In July, transplant them, 45 cm (18 in) apart, in soil that has been well watered the previous day. Kale needs firm soil with garden compost or well-rotted manure added the previous year. Water in dry weather, earth up (*see page 170*) and stake in the autumn. To harvest, remove individual leaves from the stem with a knife from December to March. For continued cropping, avoid stripping the plant.

CAULIFLOWER *B. oleracea,* Botrytis group

The cauliflower is thought to have been native to Turkey, Syria and Egypt, and was apparently mentioned in texts around 540 BC. It was first recorded in Britain by the herbalist John Gerard, but was not a frequently eaten vegetable until the end of the 18th century. Although it originated in the East, the cauliflower will survive frosts and light freezes, which, many people believe, improve its flavour. Mature cauliflowers are more frost-resistant than seedlings.

INTERNAL USE

Cauliflowers are a good source of minerals and vitamins, particularly vitamin C, folic acid, potassium and bioflavonoids. They are low in calories, which is helpful for slimmers, and high in fibre, ensuring healthy bowel function. They also protect the bowel from damage caused by irritants and toxins, and can protect against cancer. Like other brassicas, such as cabbage, broccoli and Brussels sprouts, cauliflower contains substances that are thought to help to reduce the risk of cancer, particularly of the breast and the colon. As do all crucifers, it contains antioxidants, which capture free radicals that cause damage to cells and predispose to heart disease, degenerative diseases such as arthritis, and to cancer development. They also neutralise chemicals in the body that activate carcinogens. The crucifers may also help to cleanse the body of carcinogens such as pollution from air, pesticides from foodstuffs, and chemicals, by a detoxification process. The indoles and other anticancer substances present in crucifers have the ability to increase the secretion of glutathione, which can destroy carcinogens and help to enhance the secretion of enzymes that speed up detoxification and thereby protect the DNA of the cells from damage caused by carcinogens. It is important to remember not to cook cauliflower for long, since indoles are destroyed by heavy cooking.

HOW TO GROW

There are varieties of cauliflower that can be grown for summer, autumn and winter cropping. Cauliflowers need alkaline soil and are harder to grow than broccoli or sprouts. The soil should be firm, fertile and well-limed. Do not dig before planting. For varieties that crop in late summer and autumn, sow seeds between March and May, 1.5 cm (¹/2 in) deep in a seed bed, transfer to their cropping position at 6–8 weeks when they have 4 leaves, and plant out in staggered rows 45–60 cm (18–24 in) apart. Mulch and keep plants well watered. Early cauliflowers can be sown in October, overwintered indoors and planted out in March. To harvest, cut the heads off and dig up and dispose of the root.

BRUSSELS SPROUTS *B. oleracea,* Gemmifera group

As their name indicates, Brussels sprouts were first recorded, around 600 years ago, as growing in Belgium. They reached England and France by the 19th century, where they have enjoyed mixed popularity ever since.

INTERNAL USE

Brussels sprouts are a good source of beta-carotene, folic acid, antioxidant vitamins A, C and E, bioflavonoids, iron, potassium and fibre. Like their relatives – cabbage, broccoli and

cauliflower – sprouts are also thought to help to protect against cancer and other degenerative diseases, and to regulate the body's oestrogen balance. They contain a substance called sulphoraphane, which helps to stimulate enzymes to cleanse the body of carcinogens. They also contain indoles, which, along with the antioxidants, help to protect against cancer, notably breast cancer, by speeding up the metabolism and removal of oestrogen from the body. The folic acid contained in Brussels sprouts is beneficial, particularly to pregnant women, as it is vital to the development of the baby's brain and spinal cord that occurs during the first few weeks of pregnancy. Brussels sprouts are best steamed or lightly cooked, otherwise their indole and vitamin C content will be destroyed. Vitamin C is vital for the efficient absorption of iron from food, a healthy immune system, skin and cardiovascular system and may help to prevent damage caused by free radicals.

HOW TO GROW
Brussels sprouts like firm, fertile soil and a sunny but sheltered spot. They are usually cultivated in the same way as cabbages (*see page 28*), but they can also be started off in seed trays indoors and planted out, 60 cm (24 in) apart, when the seedlings have 4–5 leaves. As the plants grow, earth them up if necessary to prevent them from falling over. Individual plants can yield up to 900 g (2 lb) of sprouts. Harvest them when they are the size of walnuts and still closed. Snap or cut them off the plant, starting from the bottom. Discard the remaining roots after harvesting.

BROCCOLI *B. oleracea,* Italica group
Broccoli, like cabbage, was apparently grown by the ancient Egyptians, Greeks and Romans and is said to have originated in Crete, Cyprus or the Eastern Mediterranean. It was valued medicinally in early times, and was used to treat headaches, diarrhoea, stomach disorders and gout. There are two types of broccoli: calabrese, which is harvested in summer or autumn; and sprouting broccoli, which can be either purple or green, which is harvested in winter.

INTERNAL USE
Broccoli is rich in nutrients, most notably the antioxidant vitamins A and C, beta-carotene, calcium, potassium, iron and folic acid, and has properties very similar to its relatives. Its abundant antioxidants help to safeguard the body against damage caused by free radicals and so protect against degenerative diseases such as arthritis, heart disease and cancer. There is some evidence to suggest that people who eat more broccoli are less likely to develop cancer of the lungs, breast, cervix, colon, prostate, larynx, oesophagus and bladder. The indoles have been shown to speed up the metabolism and removal of oestrogen from the body, and so help to prevent breast cancer. The folic acid in broccoli can help to prevent the virus that is related to the development of cervical cancer, to protect the lungs against cancer. It is also vital to pregnant women for the normal development of the brain and spinal cord in the baby.

Broccoli is also a good source of chromium, a substance that helps to regulate insulin and blood sugar. It has been shown to increase the efficiency of insulin so that the body requires less of it – a fact that is useful to non-insulin-dependent diabetics. Broccoli is high in soluble fibre, which not only helps to ensure healthy bowel function but also helps to reduce the levels of cholesterol in the blood.

Broccoli is best eaten raw or lightly cooked, steamed or stir-fried. Over-cooking and boiling tends to reduce the vitamin C content and destroys the protein and cancer-protecting substances such as indoles.

HOW TO GROW
Broccoli and calabrese grow best in soil that is firm, not loose, and not too rich in nitrogen. Calabrese is usually sown in its final position. The seedlings should be thinned to 5 cm (2 in) when they are large enough to handle, and kept well watered. Calabrese can be harvested between August and October. Broccoli seeds should be sown outdoors in a seed bed in April or May, 2.5 cm (1 in) apart. When the plants are 10 cm (4 in) high, transplant them 10 cm (4 in) apart in all directions. Keep them well watered and harvest between March and May.

Brassica
recipes & remedies

Spices added to brassicas when cooking – such as coriander seed, cumin or caraway – will help to reduce flatulence. Cabbage is most effective when eaten raw, since some compounds are destroyed by cooking.

Salted cabbage juice

An excellent remedy for constipation and a sluggish liver.

900 g (2 lb) cabbage, finely shredded
Salt to cover

Place the shredded cabbage in a large dish. Pour salt over it and leave for half an hour until the cabbage is moist. Strain the juice and take 1–2 teaspoons (5–10 ml) 3 times daily.

Cabbage syrup

A soothing remedy for colds, coughs, bronchitis and sore throats.

150 g (6 oz) cabbage leaves, finely
shredded
Honey to cover

Cover the shredded leaves with honey. Leave overnight and then press through a sieve to collect the syrup. Take 1 teaspoon (5 ml) every 2 hours for as long as the symptoms persist.

Cabbage leaf poultice

Apply to the appropriate area to ease the pain of arthritis, cystitis, coughs or sore throats.

Use as many green leaves as possible, cutting out the middle ribs. Warm them in a little hot water, iron them (with a tea towel over the leaves), or hang them over a radiator until dry. Crush the dry leaves with a rolling pin and apply several layers, holding them in place with a bandage. Change the leaves every few hours.

Cauliflower with dill vinaigrette

The excellent digestive and warming properties of dill are beneficially combined here with cauliflower, which, like other brassicas, can be hard to digest. Broccoli can be used instead of cauliflower if preferred.

1 medium-sized cauliflower
1 tablespoon Dijon mustard
1 tablespoon cider vinegar
3 tablespoons extra virgin olive oil
Chopped fresh herbs: 2 tablespoons
dill and 1 tablespoon parsley
Salt and freshly ground pepper

Cut the cauliflower into bite-sized pieces. Steam for 2–3 minutes, or until just tender (al dente), then rinse in cold water and drain well. Place in a salad bowl. Put the mustard and cider vinegar into a small bowl and whisk to combine. Slowly whisk in the olive oil. Add the herbs and season to taste with salt and pepper. Pour the dressing over the cauliflower. Toss lightly, then chill before serving.

Turnip *Brassica rapa,* Rapifera group

The turnip, like the swede, is a native of Europe and a member of the Crucifereae, or cabbage, family. The turnip has been cultivated since about 3000 BC, first in Mesopotamia. It was popular with the ancient Greeks, and was introduced into other parts of Europe by the Romans. Turnips were grown in the kitchen gardens of the medieval monasteries and they were eaten fresh or preserved in vinegar or brine. They were considered beneficial to the stomach, to moisten 'dry intestines', and as a diuretic.

TURNIPS CAN HELP TO TREAT

- *Acne*
- *Arthritis*
- *Bladder infections*
- *Boils and abscesses*
- *Bowel disorders*
- *Catarrh, coughs and colds*
- *Chilblains*
- *Constipation*
- *Eczema*
- *Fluid retention*
- *Gout*
- *Low immunity*
- *Vitamin and mineral deficiency*

INTERNAL USE

Turnips are highly nutritious, containing vitamins A and C, and minerals including calcium, phosphorus, magnesium, sulphur, iodine and potassium. Turnip tops are particularly high in vitamins A and C, calcium, iron and copper. As a result, turnips have a reputation as an energy-giving tonic and as a remedy to cleanse the blood, useful for clearing skin problems. Turnip greens, with their high calcium content, are good for building and maintaining healthy bones and teeth, and are good for both children and post-menopausal women. The whole of the turnip plant was traditionally used to combat scurvy and for correcting the nutritional deficiencies responsible for lethargy and low spirits.

Turnips have long been valued for their beneficial effect on the urinary system. They have been used as a remedy for fluid retention, urinary infections, obesity, gout and arthritis, and kidney stones (largely formed of uric acid).

The sulphur compounds found in turnips contribute to their valuable antibacterial properties, which are particularly beneficial to the respiratory system. Turnip juice can be an effective decongestant; 1 teaspoon (5 ml) of the juice taken three times daily makes a useful remedy for children's colds, coughs and catarrh.

The fibre in turnips also benefits the digestive system, ensuring normal bowel function and helping to prevent constipation and other bowel problems, which may help to reduce the risk of disease, including bowel cancer.

Recent research has indicated that turnips may enhance general immunity. Both the root and the green tops are high in substances called glucosinolates, which have been reported to help block the development of cancer. Raw turnips are higher in glucosinolates than cooked ones. The dark green leaves are also rich in chlorophyll and in carotenoids, including beta-carotene, which research has indicated to be anticarcinogenic. They are delicious when cooked, steamed until tender. Turnips have also been shown to accelerate the metabolism of oestrogen, which may help to guard against the development of oestrogen-dependent tumours, such as breast cancer.

EXTERNAL USE

Turnips are reputed to have a soothing and healing effect on the skin and they have been used in hot poultices in order to draw out boils and abscesses and to help to heal chilblains. They can also be applied in poultices to ease the aching muscles and painful joints associated with rheumatism, arthritis and gout.

For a good flavour and texture, turnips should be harvested when young, after about 70 days.

HOW TO GROW

Grow in light shade in alkaline soil, which should be prepared with plenty of garden compost or well-rotted manure dug in the autumn before planting. Sow seeds outside every three weeks from late March to July for a continuous supply, and again in August for winter cropping. Seeds should be sown about 1.5 cm ($^{1}/_{2}$ in) deep, in rows 30 cm (1 ft) apart. Thin to 10 cm (4 in) apart when large enough to handle, and then to 15 cm (6 in) 3 weeks later. Keep turnips watered, especially in dry weather.

Turnip
recipes & remedies

Turnip leaves can be cut to about 1.5 cm (½ in) above the roots within 4 weeks of sowing, and then lightly steamed or boiled.

Turnip syrup

Makes a soothing decongestant.

1 turnip, sliced
Honey to cover

Cover the turnip slices with honey. After 2–3 hours the honey will have drawn out the juice to form a syrup. Take 1–2 teaspoons every 2–3 hours while symptoms persist. Store in a sterilised jar in the refrigerator.

Turnip purée

A traditional remedy for bronchitis.

450 g (1 lb) turnips, sliced
3 teaspoons (15 ml) milk or olive oil

Steam or boil the turnips in a little water. Once soft, purée in a blender, adding the milk or olive oil. Take 2–3 tablespoons 2–3 times a day.

Turnip poultice

Apply hot to draw out boils and abscesses, to heal chilblains and relieve painful joints.

½ quantity turnip purée (see previous recipe)
2 pieces gauze
Light cotton bandage

Place sufficient turnip purée to cover the affected area between 2 pieces of gauze. Bind it to the affected area with the bandage (*see page 161 for further information*).

Turnip and dill soup

A highly nutritious soup, rich in vitamin A, calcium and magnesium, which cleanses and strengthens the immune system and is excellent for a weak digestion.

1 tablespoon olive oil
1 large onion, finely chopped
450 g (1 lb) turnips, peeled and finely chopped
3 tablespoons fresh dill
Salt and freshly ground pepper
850 ml (1½ pints) water or vegetable stock

Heat the oil in a large saucepan over a low heat. Add the onion, cover and cook for 10 minutes, or until translucent but not browned. Add the turnip and three quarters of the dill, stir well and season to taste with salt and pepper. Cover and cook gently for 30 minutes, adding a little water or stock if too dry. Add the remaining water or stock, increase the heat and bring almost to the boil. Remove the saucepan from the heat and allow to cool a little. Purée the soup in a food processor or blender until smooth. Rinse out the saucepan, add the soup and reheat gently. Garnish with the remaining dill and serve.

Peppers *Capsicum annuum* var. *annuum*

There are many varieties of pepper: sweet peppers, bell peppers, chilli peppers, paprika, cayenne, tabasco. Some are sweet and mild, others hot and pungent. They all derive from the same wild species (*C. annuum*) that came originally from Central and South America: in fact, peppers were grown in Mexico as far back as 7000 BC. Pre-Columbian ceramics decorated with peppers confirm that the Aztecs cultivated and used them, and by the time peppers were introduced to Europe by Christopher Columbus in 1493, most of the varieties with which we are now familiar had been developed.

SWEET PEPPERS CAN HELP TO TREAT

- *Allergies*
- *Cardiovascular problems*
- *Respiratory infections*

HOT PEPPERS CAN HELP TO TREAT

- *Catarrh, coughs and colds*
- *Chilblains*
- *Fevers*
- *Gastrointestinal infections*
- *Inflammation*
- *Neuralgia*
- *Period pains*
- *Poor circulation*
- *Sinusitis*

INTERNAL USE

Peppers are rich in beta-carotene and vitamin C, natural antioxidants that help to protect against degenerative diseases, cancer, and cardiovascular diseases such as atherosclerosis and angina. Peppers contain bioflavonoids, which research has indicated have anticancer properties, as well as phenolic acids and plant sterols, both of which may help to inhibit the formation of tumours. Regularly eating fresh, raw peppers enhances immunity and helps the body to fight off infections such as colds, flu and coughs, and may help to protect against eczema and asthma.

Cayenne pepper and other hot, spicy peppers are powerful stimulants, particularly to the heart and circulation, and make an excellent warming remedy for those with poor circulation and associated problems such as chilblains, cold extremities, tiredness and depression. If eaten or taken in a hot drink at the onset of a cold or flu, cayenne increases sweating and so enhances the body's fight against infection. Cayenne has a bactericidal action, it is rich in vitamin C and it makes a wonderful remedy for the respiratory system. The pungency of cayenne acts as an effective decongestant in the chest and upper respiratory tract, easing expectoration and relieving stuffiness, catarrh and sinusitis.

Cayenne also has a revitalising effect on both body and mind, dispelling tiredness, lethargy, nervous debility and depression. The burning sensation experienced on the tongue caused by eating cayenne or chillies sets off messages to the brain to stimulate the secretion of endorphins, which are opiate-like substances that can block pain and induce a feeling of well-being, even euphoria. Research has shown that hot peppers have an analgesic effect and can ease the pain of toothache, shingles and migraine.

Cayenne's pungency has a stimulating effect throughout the digestive tract, improving appetite, digestion and the absorption of food. It can help to relieve symptoms of a weak digestion, such as diarrhoea, wind, nausea and pain.

In the reproductive system, cayenne's warming properties help to relieve the spasm and pain caused by poor circulation to and from the area, and can bring on delayed periods. According to modern research, cayenne can help to ease circulation problems. It helps to prevent blood clots and has the ability to lower harmful cholesterol.

EXTERNAL USE

Hot peppers can be used as local stimulants in ointments and liniments to relieve arthritic and muscular pain, neuralgia, bruises and back pain. Their pungency helps to bring out inflammation and by numbing the skin to relieve pain. Cayenne pepper powder placed in woollen socks makes an excellent remedy for poor circulation and unbroken chilblains.

HOW TO GROW

Peppers like moist, free-draining soil with plenty of organic matter and a warm, sheltered spot. Sow seeds indoors under glass in March, and transplant to a pot or growbag when they have grown 3–4 leaves, and keep warm. Continue to grow in a pot or growbag in the greenhouse or, if they are bound for outdoors, harden them off and plant outside in late May or June, 45 cm (18 in) apart. They should be secured to stakes, and will need humidity in order to set.

Peppers can either be cut when green, in July or August if in a greenhouse, or in August or September if grown outdoors. If yellow or red peppers are preferred, they can be left on the plant to ripen.

Pepper
recipes & remedies

If the pungency of hot peppers proves hard to swallow, it is advisable to start with small amounts and gradually build up a tolerance. It is best avoided by those prone to overheating and acidity of the stomach, since it may aggravate the problem.

Cayenne, elderflower and peppermint tea

To relieve fevers, flu, colds and catarrh.

570 ml (1 pint) boiling water
15 g (¹/2 oz) elderflowers
15 g (¹/2 oz) peppermint leaves
1 pinch cayenne pepper

Pour the water over the herbs and leave them to infuse for 15 minutes. Drink 1 cupful, hot, 3–6 times daily while symptoms persist.

Heating liniment

For muscle pain, rheumatism, arthritis, neuralgia, sprains and strains. The oils below can be bought at health or beauty shops.

¹/4 teaspoon (1.25 ml) capsicum tincture (see page 159)

25 drops rosemary oil
25 drops lavender oil
50 ml (2 fl oz) almond oil

Combine the ingredients together and massage daily into the affected area.

Gargle or mouthwash

For throat and mouth infections.

40 g (1¹/2 oz) sage leaves
40 g (1¹/2 oz) thyme
2 teaspoons (10 ml) cayenne pepper
500 ml (18 fl oz) cider vinegar

Combine the ingredients together in a large jar and leave them covered to macerate for 2 weeks. Strain and store in a sterilised airtight bottle. Use 1 teaspoon (5 ml) in a little warm water 2–3 times daily while symptoms persist.

Chicory *Cichorium intybus*

Chicory can often be seen growing wild on embankments and roadsides, with leaves like its relative, the dandelion, and exquisite bright blue, daisy-like flowers. The many cultivated varieties such as radicchio (*see photo right*) or blanched chicory (*see below*) maintain the medicinal benefits of the wild plant, and the roots, leaves, and flowers can all be used (although roots have the strongest effect). The leaves of the different varieties add a pleasantly bitter taste to salads, while the flowers add interest and colour.

CHICORY CAN HELP TO TREAT

- *Arthritis*
- *Constipation*
- *Fluid retention*
- *Gout*
- *Headaches*
- *Indigestion and heartburn*
- *Liver and gall bladder problems*
- *Tiredness and lethargy*
- *Urinary infections*

INTERNAL USE

Chicory has been well known as a vegetable and as a medicine since the time of the ancient Egyptians; it is mentioned on a papyrus dating back about 4,000 years. The Greeks and Romans enjoyed it as a vegetable and the Roman physician Galen referred to chicory coffee as 'the friend of the liver', recognising its benefit to the liver and gall bladder (for which it is still valued today). In the Bible, it was one of the bitter herbs that God commanded the Israelites to eat with lamb at Passover.

As with the dandelion, chicory stimulates the flow of saliva and other digestive juices. It enhances the appetite, promotes digestion and absorption, and can be used to improve a sluggish digestion and to relieve indigestion and heartburn. Chicory can help to stimulate the function of the bowels, the liver and gall bladder. It makes an effective remedy for mild constipation and for conditions that are often associated with a sluggish liver, such as headaches, lethargy, irritability and skin problems. It may be helpful in treating gallstones.

Chicory also has a diuretic effect, enhancing the elimination of fluid and toxins from the system. This helps to cleanse the blood and can be helpful to people suffering from arthritis and gout. Its antibacterial properties combined with the diuretic action may help to relieve urinary infections such as cystitis and urethritis.

HOW TO GROW

Chicory likes a rich soil, with plenty of garden compost or well-rotted manure. The seeds should be sown outdoors in drills in May or June, and thinned to about 20 cm (9 in) apart when seedlings are large enough to handle. They should be kept well watered, especially in dry weather. To harvest chicory, cut the leaves about 2.5 cm (1 in) from the base and lift the root out of the soil using a fork. The roots can then be stored until required for making remedies or coffee (*see opposite*), or forced for blanching (*see below*). Chicory root can also be dried by chopping it and placing it on a tray in a low oven and roasting until it is dry and brittle.

To blanch chicory
Roots should be cut down to about 20 cm (9 in) before being stored in a cool place until required for forcing (November to February).

Plant 3 or 4 roots in a 25 cm (10 in) diameter pot and water thoroughly. After planting, cover with an upended pot to block out the light, and keep it in a warm place.

The blanched leaves should be ready for cutting about a month from planting. Once the leaves have been cut, the roots can be composted or used for remedies (see opposite).

Chicory
recipes & remedies

Varieties of chicory with a long taproot are dried, roasted and ground to blend with coffee.

Chicory root decoction

A remedy to improve digestion.

55 g (2 oz) fresh chicory root or
    25 g (1 oz) dried root, washed and
    chopped
700 ml (1¼ pints) water

Add the washed and chopped chicory root to the water in a saucepan and bring it to the boil. Simmer for 20 minutes. Strain and drink 1 cupful 3 times daily.

Chicory coffee

Chicory helps to counteract the stimulating effects of caffeine, and acts as an excellent digestive.

55 g (2 oz) fresh chicory root or
    25 g (1 oz) dried root

Place root on baking tray in oven at 180°C (350°F or gas mark 4) for around one hour, or until brittle. Grind the chicory root in a coffee grinder and use 1–2 teaspoons (5–10 ml) of the powder per cup of hot water.

Cucumber *Cucumis sativus*

The cucumber is a member of the Cucubitaceae, or gourd, family, which includes melons, pumpkins, courgettes and other squashes. It comes originally from the East, where it has been grown for thousands of years and where its cooling, refreshing and thirst-quenching properties were appreciated in the heat. Those people from the more temperate climates, however, viewed the cucumber very differently: the herbalist John Gerard claimed that it 'filleth the veines with naughty cold humours'.

CUCUMBERS CAN HELP TO TREAT

- *Arthritis*
- *Bladder infections*
- *Eczema*
- *Fevers*
- *Fluid retention*
- *Gastritis*
- *Gout*
- *Heat rash*
- *Inflammatory eye problems*
- *Insect bites and stings*
- *Overheating*
- *Sunburn*
- *Urticaria*

INTERNAL USE

Cucumber seeds are mentioned in 18th-century medical pharmacopoeias as being one of the four coldest seeds, useful for cooling hot, inflammatory problems, and cucumbers are still popular as a refreshing summer food today. In spite of consisting of 96.4% water, they are, when left with the peel on, nourishing. They contain vitamins A and C, and minerals including sulphur, manganese, phosphorus, silicon, sodium, calcium and potassium. This mineral content helps to prevent nails from splitting, and to maintain healthy hair; the potassium helps to regulate blood pressure.

The low calorific value of cucumbers makes them popular with dieters. Their mild diuretic action may help weight loss where there is fluid retention, and is helpful for relieving bladder infections. Cucumbers have earned a reputation as a cleansing remedy for increasing the elimination of wastes, including excess uric acid – thus helping those suffering from arthritis and gout – in fact they have long been used as a remedy for inflammatory joint problems.

The cooling properties of the cucumber have been used in many different ways. Cucumber was used as a folk remedy for fevers – it was given as a juice or as cucumber water, or even placed alongside a sick infant, when the heat of the fever was said to be absorbed by the cucumber. It has also been used to remedy excessive heat and inflammation in the body. Today it is still valued for its cooling properties, and in France, cooked cucumber is a popular remedy to aid liver function and for treating intestinal disorders and infections.

EXTERNAL USE

Cucumbers have long been famous as a cooling and soothing remedy for problems of the skin. The juice can be used to soothe urticaria and eczema, as well as prickly heat and sunburn, and makes a noticeable improvement fairly quickly. Cucumber juice mixed with equal parts of rosewater can be applied to skin problems, as well as to chapped lips, and helps to reduce pain and inflammation of insect bites and stings. Many have applied cucumber slices to their eyelids to cool sore or inflamed eyes and to tone up the skin around them. Cucumber is often used to cleanse and tone the skin, particularly when it is oily, and prone to spots or blemishes, and to soften hard skin.

HOW TO GROW

There are two sorts of cucumber: outdoor, or ridge, cucumbers and indoor cucumbers.

Outdoor varieties should be grown on ridges of soil in a sunny, sheltered position and their shoots allowed to trail on the ground. Dig holes to one spade's depth, 60 cm (2 ft) apart, and fill them with a mixture of manure and soil. Sow seeds in May or June (earlier if under cloches) and water well. Cucumbers do not transplant well and are best planted in their cropping position. After 5–6 leaves appear, pinch out the growing points. Cucumbers should be harvested when fully ripe (August or September).

Indoor varieties need warmth, humidity and plenty of watering and feeding. Sow 2 seeds about 1.5 cm (1/2 in) deep in a 7.5 cm (3 in) pot in March or April. When 2–3 leaves have developed, thin to one plant per pot. Support the growing plants with canes or horizontal wires. Pinch out the tips of the leading shoots, feed every 2 weeks with potash fertiliser once the fruits have started to grow and mist regularly with warm water. Indoor cucumbers can be harvested between June and September.

Cucumber
recipes & remedies

As part of a meal, especially one that contains hot and spicy dishes, cucumber-based dishes, such as Indian raita, can help to cool the stomach and prevent irritation.

Cucumber juice

Can be used to help bring down a fever, especially in children.

1 cucumber, peeled and thinly sliced

Place the cucumber slices in a bowl for 2 hours and then collect the juice by filtering it through fine muslin, pressing the slices thoroughly to squeeze out all the liquid. Take 1–2 teaspoonfuls every 2 hours.

Grated cucumber

A useful remedy to soothe sunburn, stings and other inflammatory skin problems.

1 cucumber, peeled

Grate the cucumber so that it is semi-liquid, and massage it into the affected area.

Cucumber raita

A cooling accompaniment to a hot spicy meal. The mint aids digestion and the natural yoghurt benefits the bacterial population in the intestines.

½ cucumber, peeled and diced
150 ml (¼ pint) Greek yoghurt
2 tablespoons chopped fresh mint leaves
Fine sea salt
A squeeze of lemon juice
A sprig of fresh mint, to garnish

Combine the diced cucumber, yoghurt and chopped mint in a bowl. Add sea salt and a squeeze of lemon juice to taste. Transfer to a serving dish. Chill, garnish with a sprig of fresh mint and serve.

Cucumber and coriander salad

A cooling salad which cleanses the system of harmful toxins – excellent for hot summer days.

¼ head lettuce, shredded
1 bunch watercress, de-stalked
½ cucumber, peeled and thinly sliced
A few sprigs of fresh coriander, chopped
Extra virgin olive oil
Fresh lemon juice
Fine sea salt

Arrange the lettuce on a plate or in a salad bowl. Add the watercress and cucumber, and sprinkle with the coriander. Drizzle a little olive oil over the salad, add a squeeze of lemon juice and a little sea salt to taste, toss lightly, and serve at once.

Marrow, squash, pumpkin and courgette *Cucurbita* spp.

Marrows, squashes, pumpkins and gourds (collectively known as cucurbits) are all members of the Cucurbitaceae family, and are some of the oldest vegetables in existence. The cucurbits also include some of the most curious-looking vegetables, and many are named according to their shapes: turban gourds, crookneck squash, banana squash. They also include some of the biggest vegetables – the largest pumpkins, for example, have weighed in at more than 500 kg (1000 lb).

CUCURBITS CAN HELP TO TREAT

- *Bowel disorders*
- *Colitis*
- *Gastritis*
- *Headaches*
- *Indigestion*
- *Overheating*
- *Peptic ulcers*
- *Prostate problems*
- *Worms*

INTERNAL USE

Cucurbits have been used medicinally for centuries, but it was not until the beginning of the 19th century that one of their most valuable therapeutic properties was discovered – the ability of pumpkin seeds to help expel worms from the body. This is due to the presence of a substance known as cucurbitive, which very effectively treats roundworms, threadworms and tapeworms without irritating the bowel.

All cucurbits are a rich source of nutrients, notably the natural antioxidants beta-carotene, folic acid, vitamins C and E, which have been shown to help prevent cancer, and minerals including potassium, iron, calcium, magnesium, phosphate, copper and zinc. Research has discovered traces of other cancer-preventing substances in squash seeds, known as protease trypsin inhibitors, which can prevent activation of viruses and carcinogens in the digestive tract. It is thought that the deep orange squashes in particular, those highest in beta-carotene, can help to lower the risk of lung, oesophageal, stomach, bladder, prostate and laryngeal cancers when eaten regularly. By deactivating carcinogens, squashes appear to protect against lung cancer in smokers as well as passive smokers.

Eaten as a vegetable, the fibre in squashes has a beneficial effect in the bowel, ensuring regular bowel movements and protecting against diseases of the bowel such as diverticulitis and cancer. The fibre binds to toxins and carcinogens and then helps to carry them out of the body via the bowel.

Pumpkin seeds are rich in fibre, protein and essential fatty acids, vitamins B and E, as well as zinc, iron and calcium. Not only do they enhance immunity but they also have particular significance for the male reproductive tract, where they may help to reduce benign enlargement of the prostate gland. Research has now shown that the amino acids alamine, glycine and glutamic acid in the seeds can reduce the symptoms of prostate enlargement, such as the frequency of urination that leads to disturbed sleep. The high zinc content of pumpkin seeds also helps to balance male hormone levels, and so may help to prevent prostate problems.

EXTERNAL USE

The pulp of raw pumpkin can be applied as a poultice to soothe burns and headaches, and the seeds can also be pounded with oatmeal and applied to the skin to remove blemishes.

HOW TO GROW

Cucurbits like warm, moist conditions and need rich soil with plenty of organic matter dug into it. They prefer partial shade and should be grown well away from other crops so that they do not smother them. Seeds should be sown under cloches in April or May, or in the open in late May or June. Plant seeds edgeways 2.5 cm (1 in) deep, in 7.5 cm (3 in) diameter pots. Seedlings can be planted out once they have grown 4–6 leaves. Put in firm supports if these are required, and plant in compost-filled holes. Water the roots, not the leaves, especially in dry weather. Marrows should be planted 1–1.2 m (3–4ft) apart each way, pumpkins 1.2 m (4 ft) apart, and courgettes 1 m (3 ft) apart with 1m (3 ft) between rows. Harvest cucurbits, with their stalks on, from July to October.

Cucurbit
recipes & remedies

As well as being eaten as a main course or side dish, cucurbits, such as marrows and pumpkins, can be made into jams and pickles.

Pumpkin seed and honey paste

An effective remedy for expelling worms from the body.

35–40 g (1 1/4–1 1/2 oz) pumpkin seeds
35–40 g (1 1/4–1 1/2 oz) honey

Strip the pumpkin seeds of their outer covering and pound them with a pestle and mortar to make a paste. Mix them with equal parts of honey and take first thing in the morning before breakfast in 3 doses, about 20 minutes apart. Continue for 2 more days.

Pumpkin and oatmeal paste

An excellent remedy for skin blemishes.

50 g (2 oz) pumpkin seeds
50 g (2 oz) oatmeal

Strip the pumpkin seeds of their outer covering and pound them to make a paste. Combine them with the oatmeal and apply to the skin for 10–15 minutes. Rinse off with warm water or rosewater.

Pumpkin seed tea

Helpful for prostate disorders.

100 g (3 1/2 oz) unshelled pumpkin seeds
1 litre (2 pints) water

Simmer the pumpkin seeds in water for 20 minutes, strain and take a glassful (6 fl oz) 3 times a day.

Steamed courgettes

A nutritious remedy to help regulate the bowels.

450 g (1 lb) courgettes, chopped

Chop the courgettes into 2.5 cm (1 in) lengths. Place them in a steamer and steam for 5–10 minutes, or until tender.

Artichoke *Cynara scolymus*

The artichoke is a magnificent architectural plant for the back of an ornamental border or herb garden. It is perennial in temperate climates and has large silvery leaves and grey-blue, thistle-like flowers. It is one of the oldest cultivated vegetables, and was grown by the ancient Egyptians, Greeks and Romans alike. It was introduced to Europe by the Arabs in the 15th century and to Britain in the 16th century. The Arabs recommended the leaves as a medicine, particularly to treat the liver and sluggish digestion.

ARTICHOKES CAN HELP TO TREAT

- *Acne*
- *Arteriosclerosis*
- *Arthritis*
- *Atherosclerosis*
- *Eczema*
- *Fluid retention*
- *Gout*
- *Heartburn*
- *Indigestion*
- *Nausea*
- *Poor appetite*
- *Urticaria*

INTERNAL USE

Europeans have long respected the artichoke as a 'friend of the liver'. The bitters in artichoke leaves act to stimulate the flow of digestive juices and aid bile secretion from the liver and gall bladder. This explains why extracts of artichoke have traditionally been included in bitter alcoholic apéritifs and digestifs, to whet the appetite before a meal and to ease the digestion of food afterwards, as well as to support a liver that has been overworked by the excesses of a rich and heavy meal with alcohol.

Modern practice and research support the ancient use of artichoke as a medicine. In Europe particularly, the artichoke is popular as a medicine to lower cholesterol and triglycerides, and to treat atherosclerosis and arteriosclerosis. Cynarin, a substance found in the leaves, has been shown to help improve liver and gall bladder function as well as to lower cholesterol levels. Artichoke leaves in teas and tinctures are used by modern herbalists to help to remedy weak digestion, poor appetite, heartburn, nausea, liver insufficiency and skin problems such as acne, eczema and urticaria. Artichokes also have diuretic properties, enhancing the elimination of fluid and toxins from the system. So, with

their beneficial action on the liver as well as on the kidneys, artichokes make a good cleansing remedy, helping to clear the skin and to relieve arthritis and gout.

HOW TO GROW

Artichokes grow 1–1.75 m (3–5 ft) tall and like rich, light, well-drained soil. They will not grow well in heavy clay. They prefer a warm climate, and may not survive the winter unless they are grown in the milder parts of Europe and North America. In any event, they should be protected from frost.

Artichokes are usually grown from offsets collected from healthy, productive plants (*see below*). Although they tend to be more productive in their second and third years than in their first, artichokes do not normally continue to grow after 5 years, and the heads tend to be smaller with a tougher texture. Artichoke shoots should be planted in shallow holes in late March or April, 1.2 m (4 ft) apart, and mulched and watered well. The heads should be harvested when the leaves are tightly wrapped and still green from the second year onwards, in June and July. If they are left on the plant, they will turn into huge, beautiful thistle flowers.

The stems should be cut back in October or November, and they should be protected from winter frost by earthing up.

To propagate, select healthy shoots from existing plants that are over 3 years old and remove, using a spade or large, sharp knife, making sure that each shoot retains some of its roots.

Remove the buds as soon as they appear in the first year. This will encourage further growth. The heads can be harvested from the second year onwards.

Artichoke
recipes & remedies

Artichokes can be steamed or cooked in boiling water for 15–30 minutes, drained and left to cool. The tender parts of the leaves can be eaten. One by one, tear each leaf away from the base and dip it in vinaigrette, butter or mustard sauce.

Artichoke leaf infusion

To aid liver and gall bladder function and to help lower blood cholesterol.

25 g (1 oz) dried artichoke leaves or
    50 g (2 oz) fresh leaves,
    chopped
570ml (1 pint) boiling water

Place the chopped leaves in a large teapot. Pour on the water. Cover and leave to infuse for 10–15 minutes. Drink 1 cupful 3 times daily.

Carrot *Daucus carota*

The humble carrot, a native of Afghanistan, was well known to the ancients. It was discussed by the Greeks in writings dating back to 500 BC and was used by Hippocrates in 430 BC. The familiar garden carrot, now grown all over the world, is the cultivated variety of the wild carrot, an umbelliferous plant, also called Queen Anne's Lace. The name *Daucus* comes from the Greek *daio* meaning to burn, on account of the pungent and stimulating qualities of carrots, particularly the seeds.

CARROTS CAN HELP TO TREAT

- *Anaemia*
- *Arthritis*
- *Boils and abscesses*
- *Bronchial congestion*
- *Constipation*
- *Cuts and grazes*
- *Cystitis*
- *Diarrhoea*
- *Flatulence*
- *Fluid retention*
- *Gout*
- *Heart and arterial disease*
- *Intestinal infections*
- *Liver problems*
- *Minor burns and scalds*
- *Poor night vision*
- *Respiratory infections*
- *Vitamin and mineral deficiency*

INTERNAL USE

Carrots are highly nutritious, being rich in vitamins A, B complex and C, in minerals including iron, calcium, potassium and sodium, and in beta-carotene, asparagin and daucarine. They have long been praised as a restorative remedy, promoting growth and vitality, helping to build healthy tissue and skin, for use in debility, convalescence, mineral deficiency, rickets, dental caries and anaemia. Recently, carrots have been shown to increase haemoglobin and red blood cell counts. Their high vitamin A content has meant that carrots have long been considered excellent for promoting good night vision and for the general care of the eyes.

Carrots are renowned for their digestive properties. They regulate intestinal activity, promoting bowel function, and can be useful both in easing constipation and preventing diarrhoea. They have the ability to soothe the mucous membranes throughout the digestive tract, which helps to reduce irritation and inflammation. Puréed carrot can be given even to small infants to treat digestive problems. Carrots can be used to relieve flatulence, irritable bowel syndrome and intestinal infections. A carrot-juice fast for 1 to 2 days is a well-known cleansing therapy for the liver, and can also help to clear up skin problems. An infusion of carrot tops has been used to treat eczema and acne.

In 1960, Russian scientists identified a chemical ingredient in carrots called daucarine, which has been shown to dilate blood vessels, particularly those in the head, helping to protect against arterial and heart disease. Since then, the carotenoids in carrots have been found to have antioxidant properties, which confirms their folk use as a circulatory remedy, since antioxidants help to reduce damage caused by free radicals and thereby to reduce degenerative diseases, notably in the heart and arteries.

Beta-carotene is now thought to inhibit the development and growth of tumours, particularly in smoking-related cancers, in the lungs and pancreas. Studies have shown that eating at least one raw or lightly cooked carrot daily may be enough to have this effect.

Caution: Although carrots are very nutritious, eating too many can give the skin a yellow tinge known as carotenemia, which will disappear when consumption is reduced.

EXTERNAL USE

Grated raw carrot can be used in the form of a poultice as an antiseptic and to speed up the healing of wounds, burns, boils, abscesses and styes. Carrot broth can be applied to chilblains and chapped skin, to soothe itching in eczema and to treat impetigo and cold sores. It can also be used as an antiseptic mouthwash and as a gargle for sore throats.

HOW TO GROW

Early carrots, for summer eating, are usually short and fat, and main or late crop carrots are longer and more suitable for storing. Both prefer a light, well-drained, sandy soil with plenty of organic matter dug into it. Warm the soil for early sowings by using cloches, and rake the soil to a fine tilth before sowing. Sow seed about 1.5 cm (½ in) deep in drills spaced at 20 cm (8 in) intervals, in March or April for early varieties and mid April to July for later ones. Both should be thinned to 2.5 cm (1 in) apart with 7.5–10 cm (3–4 in) between rows when large enough to handle. Early varieties can be harvested as required from June to July, and later ones from July to October.

Carrot
recipes & remedies

For maximum nutritional benefit drink carrot juice or eat carrots raw or lightly steamed or stir-fried. Once cooked, their soothing and anti-inflammatory properties come into their own.

Carrot juice

A remedy for expelling threadworms in children. Taken with honey and a little water, it is also useful for treating colds and coughs.

3–4 carrots, washed and cleaned

Juice the carrots in an extractor. Adults can take 1 glassful (6 fl oz) daily before breakfast. For children under 12 years, dilute the carrot juice with an equal amount of water.

Carrot broth

Soothes chilblains, cold sores and impetigo, and can also be used as a gargle for sore throats.

450 g (1 lb) carrots, washed and cleaned
850 ml (1 1/2 pints) water

Place the carrots in the water, boil until they are soft and then blend.

Cooked carrot purée

A remedy for diarrhoea in infants. If symptoms persist, consult your doctor.

450 g (1 lb) carrots, washed and cleaned
1.2 litres (2 pints) water
1 teaspoon (5 ml) olive oil
Salt and pepper to taste

Place the carrots in the water and boil until soft. Blend, strain and add a little olive oil and salt and pepper to taste, with sufficient of the cooking water to make up 1.2 litres (2 pints) again.

Rocket *Eruca vesicaria* subsp. *sativa*

Rocket, with its pungent, spicy leaves that resemble dandelion leaves, is becoming increasingly popular as a salad vegetable. Rocket has been grown at least since the time of the ancient Greeks and Romans and was known for its medicinal values in those times: the Greek physician Dioscorides knew rocket as 'a digestive and good for the belly'. It is a native of the Mediterranean and of eastern Asia, and derives its Latin name from the ancients' observation of the plant: *Eruca* means 'downy stemmed' and *vesicaria* means 'like a bladder' – a reference to the seed pods. It now grows wild in many parts of Europe and Asia.

ROCKET CAN HELP TO TREAT

- *Anaemia*
- *Bronchial congestion*
- *Bruises*
- *Catarrh, coughs and colds*
- *Constipation*
- *Inflammation*
- *Low immunity*
- *Poor circulation*
- *Tiredness and lethargy*
- *Weak digestion*

INTERNAL USE

One of the early names for this plant is rocket cress and other names include arugula and roquette. The strong mustardlike flavour of rocket leaves was popular in Elizabethan times both as a food and as a medicine. Its stimulating effect on the circulation increases energy and produces a sense of well-being. Its pungency stimulates the appetite and may improve the digestion and absorption of food. It also helps to cleanse the digestive system, removing stagnant food by its mild laxative action, and its cleansing effect also enhances general health and vitality.

The stimulating properties of rocket leaves can also be felt in the respiratory tract, where they aid in clearing congestion by helping to loosen phlegm and easing expectoration from the chest area. The seed pods are also edible and, like the leaves, were long considered to have certain aphrodisiac properties. Dioscorides was well aware of this, writing in the 1st century AD: 'this being eaten raw in any great quantitie doth provoke venery and the seed of it also doth work ye like effect'.

The leaves are rich in vitamins A and C and minerals, notably iron, calcium and potassium. They were once eaten to prevent scurvy, and in large amounts were given as an emetic to induce vomiting to clear toxins from the stomach. The natural antioxidants contained in the leaves enhance immunity and help prevent damage to the body caused by free radicals. Thus rocket, like other members of the crucifer family, helps to protect against cardiovascular disease, degenerative diseases and cancer. Rocket leaves are best picked when they are young to add to salads, and they go better with blander salad vegetables such as lettuce and cucumber. They can also be boiled or steamed, stir-fried or added to pasta dishes. When used medicinally, they are usually picked later, just as they are going into flower, when their pungency is more obvious.

EXTERNAL USE

The oils contained in rocket leaves are similar to mustard oils, which have a stimulating effect when used locally, speeding the healing process and reducing inflammation. Traditionally, the oil of rocket was applied as a poultice to bruises.

HOW TO GROW

Rocket is an annual that grows fast in most soils, but it does especially well in cool climates, when planted in rich, moisture-retentive soil in partial shade. If it is planted in full sun it tends to bolt. Sow seeds in mid spring to early summer, about 1.5 cm (½ in) deep, with 30 cm (1 ft) between rows, every 2–3 weeks from mid spring to summer. Keep the seedlings well watered, and thin them to 15 cm (6 in) apart when they are large enough to handle. Leaves can be harvested regularly after 6–8 weeks, to encourage fresh growth.

Do not discard the early thinnings, since they are delicious when used in salads, and mature plants can either be harvested whole or individual leaves can be clipped off as required for 'cut-and-come-again' growth.

Do not allow the soil to dry out in hot weather.

Rocket
recipes & remedies

Rocket leaves have been known for thousands of years for their cleansing and stimulating effect on the system. They are best eaten raw in salads, especially as a starter before other foods are eaten.

Rocket and garlic vinaigrette

An excellent dish to enhance immunity and clear congestion.

110 g (4 oz) rocket leaves, washed
2 cloves garlic, crushed
3 tablespoons (45 ml) olive oil
1 tablespoon (15 ml) white wine
      vinegar
Salt and pepper to taste

Mix together thoroughly the olive oil, vinegar, garlic and salt and pepper to taste. Drizzle over the rocket leaves and eat as an hors-d'oeuvre.

Fennel *Foeniculum vulgare*

Fennel is an attractive, statuesque perennial with blue-green feathery leaves and large umbels of flowers and then seeds. It is a native of the Mediterranean and is a familiar sight in wild open spaces, by roadsides and on waste ground all over Europe. The whole plant has a lovely, sweet liquorice smell and taste, which has long been valued in the kitchen, and for making liqueurs, perfumes and medicines. The soft green leaves make a delicious garnish, traditionally used for fish dishes, as fennel is said to counteract the oiliness in fish. The seeds are often used in making bread, cakes and biscuits.

FENNEL CAN
HELP TO TREAT

- *Arthritis*
- *Bronchial congestion*
- *Colic*
- *Coughs*
- *Flatulence*
- *Fluid retention*
- *Heartburn*
- *Indigestion*
- *Menopausal problems*
- *Nausea*
- *Period pains*
- *Poor appetite*
- *Poor lactation*

Fennel was valued as a food and medicine by the ancient Egyptians, Greeks, Romans and Chinese. The Egyptians used fennel to treat eye problems, and it was said that fennel enabled the eyes to see clearly the beauty of nature. A decoction of fennel seed is still recommended as a remedy to bathe inflamed eyes, and until about fifty years ago it was customary to wash the eyes of a newborn baby with fennel water. According to Greek mythology, Prometheus hid the fire of the sun in a hollow fennel stalk and brought it to earth to benefit the human race. Fennel was said by the Greeks to give men strength; it was given to athletes to improve their performance, and they adopted it as their symbol of victory.

The Greeks also used fennel as a detoxifying remedy and diuretic, and prescribed it as a slimming aid. Hippocrates recommended it for stimulating milk flow in nursing mothers, as herbalists still do today. In the Middle Ages the seeds were chewed to relieve the pangs of hunger, especially while fasting during Lent.

The swollen stem-base of the Italian Florence fennel (*F. vulgare* var. *dulce*) has a crisp and crunchy texture, a mild aniseed taste, and makes an excellent side dish.

Earth up fennel regularly from the time when the bulb is the size of a golf ball until harvesting.

INTERNAL USE

It is as a digestive remedy that fennel is best known today. It has a warming and relaxing effect throughout the digestive tract, stimulating the appetite and promoting the digestion and absorption of food, particularly of carbohydrates and fats. It helps to relieve tension and spasm in the gut, and fennel seeds are included in gripe water for babies, helping to relieve colic or soothe an uncomfortable or restless baby. Fennel tea can help to settle the stomach and relieve wind, nausea, indigestion and heartburn.

As a diuretic, fennel enhances the elimination of fluid and toxins from the system via the urinary tract and it can be used to help treat fluid retention and as a cleansing remedy for arthritis. Its relaxing or antispasmodic effects extend to the uterus as well, where it can help to reduce period pains, while its hormone-like action is used to regulate the menstrual cycle and is helpful during the menopause. For the respiratory system, fennel can loosen bronchial congestion and aid expectoration.

HOW TO GROW

Herb fennel (*Foeniculum vulgare*) likes well-drained, medium-rich soil and full sun. It can be propagated by sowing seeds from February to May in cropping position, and thinning to 30 cm (1 ft) when the seedlings are large enough to handle. The leaves can be harvested throughout the summer months, and the seeds collected from September to October.

Florence fennel (*F. vulgare* var. *dulce*) prefers well-drained, sandy soil with plenty of well-rotted manure or garden compost. It should be sown about 1.5 cm (1/2 in) deep in drills 45 cm (18 in) apart in late April and thinned to 30 cm (1 ft) apart when seedlings are large enough to handle. Keep plants watered in dry weather and earth them up (*see left*). Harvest in August or September.

Fennel
recipes & remedies

Fennel is often eaten with beans and vegetables such as cabbage and broccoli, to aid their digestion and help to prevent wind.

Fennel soup

A soup to stimulate the appetite and aid digestion by priming the digestive tract for the food to follow. As a mild diuretic, fennel can also help to relieve fluid retention.

2 fennel bulbs
2 tablespoons olive oil
2 medium-sized potatoes, peeled
    and diced
1 litre (1 3/4 pints) water or vegetable
    stock
Salt and freshly ground pepper

Cut the feathery leaves from the fennel and set aside. Trim the bulb and cut into chunks. Heat the olive oil in a large saucepan over a moderate heat. Add the potatoes and fennel and sauté, stirring, for 5–10 minutes, until slightly softened. Pour in the water or stock and bring to the boil, then reduce the heat, cover and simmer the soup for 20–25 minutes, until the vegetables are tender – test a large piece with the point of a knife. Remove the saucepan from the heat, and allow to cool a little, then purée the soup in a food processor or blender until smooth. Rinse out the saucepan, add the soup and reheat. Season to taste with salt and pepper, garnish with the reserved fennel leaves and serve.

Lettuce *Lactuca sativa*

The garden lettuce is a cultivated variety of the wild lettuce (*L. serriola* or *L. virosa*), which can still be found growing on chalky soil throughout the British Isles, as well as uncultivated land from Asia to northern Europe. Lettuce derives its Latin name from the milky juice (*lactis* in Latin) that exudes from the stem. This juice used to be collected once it had oxidised and turned brown. It was then used for its opiate content as a substitute for opium or laudanum to kill pain, and as a sedative. The juice of the garden lettuce, which is less powerful than that of the wild lettuce, was often used in the past to soothe restless infants to sleep.

LETTUCES CAN HELP TO TREAT

- *Anxiety and tension*
- *Catarrh, coughs and colds*
- *Constipation*
- *Gastritis*
- *Insomnia*
- *Irritable bowel syndrome*
- *Nervous indigestion*
- *Peptic ulcer*
- *Poor appetite*

It is probable that the garden lettuce first originated in Turkey or Iran, though suggestions concerning its origins range from Siberia to North Africa. It is thought to have been cultivated first by the ancient Egyptians around 4500 BC and was probably introduced as a food to Britain by the Romans, and by the 16th century there were apparently eight varieties. Lettuce seeds accompanied the early settlers to North America.

INTERNAL USE

The wild lettuce was used to stimulate the appetite, to enhance digestion and liver function and to remedy constipation. John Parkinson, the 17th-century herbalist, said that 'lettuce eaten raw or boyled, helpeth to loosen the belly, and the boyled more than the raw', while the 16th-century herbalist John Gerard wrote that the cultivated lettuce 'is very proper for hot bilious dispositions'. Lettuce is still used for its calming and relaxing properties to help relieve nervous tension and insomnia. Throughout history it has been valued for its anaphrodisiac properties, and it used to be combined with marjoram for this purpose.

Lettuce is still used therapeutically for its cooling and anti-inflammatory properties when there is heat and inflammation. It can be used for ulceration or spasm in the digestive tract, as in gastritis, peptic ulcers, colitis and irritable bowel syndrome. Its antispasmodic properties can help to relax tension and spasm throughout the body. Lettuce has a cooling and moistening action in the respiratory system, helping to loosen and soothe dry, harsh and irritating coughs and easing production of phlegm; it is particularly helpful in this respect when taken with garlic or thyme.

Lettuces contain many beneficial vitamins and minerals – including antioxidants beta-carotene and vitamin C, folic acid, calcium, potassium and iron. The antioxidants help to prevent damage caused by free radicals and so protect against degenerative diseases, heart disease, cataracts and cancer. Lettuces are useful to dieters, when eaten without an oily dressing, as they are low in calories yet high in fibre, so they are quite filling. The darker the leaf, the more beta-carotene and vitamin C it contains – dark-leafed varieties also contain bioflavonoids, which work in conjunction with vitamin C and antioxidants to help to prevent cancer.

HOW TO GROW

The four main types of lettuce are butterhead, Cos, loosehead and crispheart, and they thrive in the same conditions: rich, well-drained soil with plenty of organic matter. They can be used as an intercrop between larger vegetables such as cabbages and Brussels sprouts. Seeds for summer varieties should be sown every few weeks from April to July to ensure a continuous supply for summer and autumn, and seeds can also be sown under cloches from October to January for harvesting between March and May. They should be sown about 1.5 cm (½ in) deep in well-prepared ground, in rows 30 cm (1 ft) apart. When the seedlings are large enough to handle, they should be thinned to 10–25 cm (4–10 in) between plants, depending on the variety being grown. Thinnings can be transplanted fairly easily. Seedlings grown under glass should have a second thinning in late February or early March, if needed, to 15 cm (6 in) apart. Harvest lettuces as required. For all but the 'cut-and-come-again' varieties, pull the whole plant out of the ground and cut off the root for composting.

Lettuce
recipes & remedies

Lettuce can be used to make infusions and soups. Soup is a good way of using up leaves of lettuces which have matured and gone to seed.

Lettuce tea

A traditional remedy for sleeplessness or constipation. Especially good for those who cannot digest raw lettuce.

3–4 lettuce leaves, washed
300 ml (^{1}/2 pint) water

Simmer leaves in water for 15 minutes. Strain and drink a hot cupful before going to bed.

Lettuce soup

570 ml (1 pint) vegetable stock
400 g (14 oz) lettuce, chopped
30 ml (2 tablespoons) olive oil
1 onion, finely chopped
1 clove garlic, crushed
225 g (8 oz) potatoes, peeled and
     diced
Salt and pepper to taste
150 ml (5 fl oz) natural yoghurt

Bring the stock to the boil. Place the lettuce in a heatproof dish, and add the stock. Heat the oil in a saucepan, and add the onion, garlic and potatoes. Fry over a gentle heat for 10 minutes. Add the lettuce and stock, and season. Bring to the boil then simmer for 2–3 minutes. Allow to cool, transfer to a blender and blend to smooth consistency. Re-heat and add yoghurt before serving.

Tomato *Lycopersicon esculentum*

Tomatoes were brought to Europe from South America in the 16th century by the Spanish conquistadors. As a member of the poisonous nightshade family (Solanaceae), the tomato was considered to be as potentially dangerous as deadly nightshade. The earliest record of the tomato in Europe is by the Italian botanist Mattiolus, in 1544, who described the yellow-fruited variety that the Italians called *pomodoro*. The red tomato gained a reputation as an aphrodisiac, and it was known as 'love apple', perhaps because its deep, rich colour represented love and passion.

TOMATOES CAN HELP TO TREAT

- *Anaemia*
- *Constipation*
- *Fluid retention*
- *Heart and circulatory problems*
- *Insect bites and stings*
- *Vitamin and mineral deficiency*

INTERNAL USE

Tomatoes are highly nutritious, rich in vitamins A, C and E, as well as folic acid, iron and phosphorus. They have long been used to aid the digestion and assimilation of starchy and fatty foods, and as a laxative, helping to cleanse the bowel of stagnant wastes and toxins. They have also been used for their diuretic properties, aiding the elimination of fluids and wastes via the urinary system, so they make a good cleansing food. Tomato juice has long been used to help boost energy and vitality and to detoxify the system. The vitamins A and C are particularly helpful when it comes to the prevention and treatment of infections, and to speed healing.

The natural antioxidants contained in tomatoes, including beta-carotene and vitamins C and E, help to protect the body against damage caused by free radicals and thereby help to prevent degenerative diseases, heart and circulatory problems and cancer, and to slow the ageing process. Recent research has also associated tomatoes with a reduced risk of cancer and heart disease, which is related probably to one of the carotenoids named lycopene, also present in grapefruit and watermelon. They are thought to help protect particularly against cancer of the stomach, lung and prostate. Other research has indicated that eating tomatoes regularly may help to prevent appendicitis. Unusually, the cancer-preventing properties of tomatoes appear to be enhanced by cooking, which releases the fat-soluble lycopene, and cooking them in a little olive oil is even better. Fresh tomatoes are obviously the most nutritious form to use, but canned tomatoes and tomato paste contain only a little less vitamin C than fresh.

EXTERNAL USE

Acne sufferers may find relief by rubbing slices of tomato on their spots, and some people rub tomato leaves on their skin to relieve the irritation of insect bites.

Caution: Tomatoes can cause allergic reactions in some susceptible people, including headaches, urticaria and joint inflammation. They can also cause indigestion and heartburn. People who suffer from arthritis and kidney stones should avoid tomatoes because of their oxalic acid content. The leaves can produce an allergic reaction, usually in the form of a rash, in some individuals.

HOW TO GROW

Tomatoes can be grown in the greenhouse in pots or growbags, or in sunny garden beds, depending on the variety and prevailing weather conditions. Either buy young plants or sow seeds indoors from January to March in 13 cm (5 in) diameter pots. Prick out to 1 plant per 7.5 cm (3 in) pot when the seedlings have developed leaves and are safe to handle. When planting, place plants 60 cm (2 ft) apart. Stake before planting and continue to tie the plant to the stake as it grows. Keep the plant regularly watered – if it is left to dry out and is then flooded, the fruit will split. From June to October, pick the fruit as it ripens.

Pinch out side shoots as they grow and pull off the small shoots that grow between the branches.

Tomato
recipes & remedies

Unripe, or green, tomatoes may be used for some recipes, but they vary nutritionally in that red ones contain four times as much vitamin A as green ones.

Spicy tomato juice

A healthy, warming drink on a cold day.

450 g (1 lb) tomatoes, skinned
$^1/_2$ lemon, juiced
1 teaspoon (5 ml) white wine vinegar
Worcestershire sauce to taste
Salt and pepper to taste
$^1/_4$ teaspoon (1.5 ml) chilli or coriander, chopped

Blend the tomatoes until liquid and sieve. Add the lemon juice, white wine vinegar, Worcestershire sauce and salt and pepper. Dilute with mineral water and chill. Sprinkle with the chopped chilli or coriander before serving.

Tomato and yoghurt juice

A nutritious start to the day. The yoghurt helps to offset the heating qualities of the tomatoes.

3 medium tomatoes, skinned, liquidised and sieved – enough to make 150 ml (5 fl oz) juice
150 ml (5 fl oz) still mineral water
1 tablespoon(15 ml) plain live yoghurt
1 sprig mint, bruised
Salt and pepper to taste

Combine tomato juice and mineral water. Stir in the yoghurt. Add the mint and season with salt and pepper as required.

Parsnip *Pastinacea sativa* subsp. *sativa*

This sweet and starchy vegetable is a cultivated variety of the wild parsnip (*P. s.* subsp. *sylvestris*), which is still found growing wild in hedgerows and grassy fields throughout central and southern Europe as well as in the British Isles. It is thought that parsnips were first cultivated as a vegetable by the ancient Greeks and Romans and they were introduced to northern Europe by the Romans. Parsnips were known to have been grown by monks in medieval monastery gardens and they were vital for providing sustenance for the days when eating meat was forbidden.

PARSNIPS CAN HELP TO TREAT

- *Constipation*
- *Low energy*
- *Vitamin and mineral deficiency*

Parsnips were traditionally eaten during Lent with salt fish and became popular in beer, wine, jam and cake-making because of their high sugar content. The 16th-century herbalist John Gerard mentioned that his friend, a Mr Plat, had made bread from parsnips, but Gerard said, 'which I have made no tryall of, nor mean to do'. Parsnip roots, being sweet and starchy, were valued as nutritious foods for warming and fattening but there was a superstition that if they were left long in the ground they could cause insanity and were known as 'madnips'.

The seeds of the wild parsnip were made into medicines by apothecaries for their aromatic properties. They were used for intermittent fevers. A decoction of wild parsnip root was a valued remedy for a sluggish liver and jaundice. In Gerard's day, parsnips were called 'mypes' and were turned into a marmalade used medicinally to improve appetite and as a restorative for invalids.

John Wesley wrote in his *Primitive Physic*: 'wild parsnip both leaves and stalks bruised seem to have been a favourite application; and a very popular internal remedy for cancer, asthma, consumption and similar diseases.'

In traditional folk medicine, parsnips have been considered to be energy-boosting due to their sugar and starch content, and parsnip soup can be given to the elderly and to those convalescing as a nourishing and digestible restorative.

Parsnips are thought to be good for the stomach and to support the kidneys, and they are valued for their diuretic and cleansing properties.

INTERNAL USES

Today, the sweet, pungent taste and starchy texture of parsnips makes them a popular vegetable and ingredient of soups and casseroles. Although starchy, parsnips are low in calories and high in fibre and so make a good food for people watching their weight. They are rich in vitamins C and E and potassium and contain some folic acid. Being high in fibre, parsnips help to keep the bowels regular and to prevent diseases of the bowel. As a member of the parsley family (Umbellifereae) – which includes carrots, celery and parsley – parsnips contain substances called terpenes, which research has shown may help to reduce the spread of cancer cells and to deactivate carcinogenic substances that cause tumours.

HOW TO GROW

Parsnips do best in well-drained, friable soil, which needs to be deep because they have long roots. Parsnips, which should be planted in March or April, are not lifted until November at the earliest, so they stay in the ground for a long time, but do not require much attention. Seeds take up to 4 weeks to germinate, so it is a good idea to plant them with radishes. These can be sown between the rows and used as markers for hoeing. Lettuces can also be sown between the rows. Seeds should be sown in the cropping positions in clusters of three at about 20 cm (9 in) intervals, and thinned to one plant per cluster when seedlings are large enough to handle.

Parsnips can either be lifted in November and stored in sand, or left in the open and harvested as required during the early winter months.

Parsnip
recipes & remedies

The parsnip's taste improves considerably after being subjected to a few frosts, which convert some of the stored starch into sugar. This makes the vegetable sweeter and more flavoursome.

Parsnip purée

Useful for regulating the bowels.

450 g (1 lb) parsnips, washed and
    chopped
1.2 litres (2 pints) water
1 teaspoon (5 ml) olive oil
Salt and pepper to taste

Cook the parsnips in a little water until they are soft. Strain, blend and add a little olive oil and salt and pepper to taste, with sufficient of the cooking water to make up 1.2 litres (2 pints) again.

Roast parsnips

An easily digested and nourishing food for the elderly and convalescent.

1 medium-sized parsnip per person,
    peeled and chopped into 4 pieces
A pan of boiling water
1 teaspoon (5 ml) olive or corn oil per
    parsnip

Blanch the parsnips in the water for 5 minutes. Heat the oven to 180°C (350°F or gas mark 4), pour the oil into a baking pan and put the pan in the oven for 5 minutes to heat the oil. Remove from the oven, add the parsnips and cook for around 40 minutes, turning them several times, until they are brown and crispy.

Beans *Phaseolus vulgaris*

The French bean, broad bean and haricot bean are just some of the cultivars of *P. vulgaris,* which originated in Central and South America and where it can still be found in mountain regions growing wild. The bean was cultivated in ancient times – seeds were found in deposits at Cuitarrero cave in Peru dating back to 6000 BC, and in cave deposits in the Tehuacan Valley in Central Mexico dating to 4000 BC. They were taken to North America, and seeds found in New Mexico date to around 300 BC. In the 16th century, the Spanish conquistadors brought beans to Europe.

There are many different varieties of bean, which vary in the way they grow, and in the colour and texture of their pod and seed. Those with rather papery pods, such as lima beans (*P. lunatus*), tend to be grown simply for their beans; those such as runner beans (*P. coccineus*) with tough pods can be eaten in their entirety when young and as shelled beans when more mature; and those such as French beans (*P. vulgaris*) with tender, fleshy and stringless pods are grown mainly to be eaten as whole green beans.

INTERNAL USE

Fresh green beans are an excellent source of nutrition, containing vitamins A, B and C, protein and folic acid, as well as calcium, copper, phosphorus, iron, magnesium and zinc. Being high in fibre they promote healthy bowel function. By speeding food through the intestines they help prevent the bowel wall from coming into contact with toxins, irritants and potential carcinogens for any length of time. Beans also help to stimulate liver and pancreatic function and thus help to control blood sugar levels.

The vitamins and minerals contained in green beans are vital to the normal function of the nervous and immune systems, and so they can help those feeling tired and run down, and aid the body to combat infection. Beans' diuretic action aids excretion of fluid and toxins, and thereby may help those prone to arthritis and gout as well as to fluid retention.

Dried beans are high in soluble fibre, which helps to regulate the bowels, and can be used to help relieve constipation, haemorrhoids and other bowel problems related to constipation.

Beans can also help to reduce low-density lipoprotein cholesterol. Eating a cup of beans a day has been shown to reduce cholesterol levels. Other studies have shown that eating dried beans regularly lowers blood pressure, making them excellent for preventing and treating cardiovascular problems.

In addition, beans contain substances known as protease inhibitors, enzymes that reduce the activation of carcinogens in the bowel. Protease inhibitors have been shown to deactivate oncogenes – genetic carriers in normal cells that can lead to cancer. Beans also contain lignans, which are thought to have anticancer properties, and when acted on by bacteria in the bowel they are converted to hormonelike compounds that may reduce the incidence of breast and colon cancer.

HOW TO GROW

Broad beans prefer a slightly sandy soil. For an early crop, sow seeds in November 20 cm (8 in) apart in drills about 20 cm (9 in) apart. Germination time is 1–2 weeks. The top of the stem should be pinched out as the first pods form. Tall-growing varieties need support: place stakes at 30 cm (1 ft) intervals on each side of the row and string twine between them. Early crops can be harvested from May onwards, and later crops, sown in March or April, from June onwards.

French beans like light, sandy soil. Sow them indoors in April, harden the plants off, and plant out when 5–7.5 cm (2–3 in) high, 15 cm (6 in) apart, and 30 cm (1 ft) between rows. Or sow seeds outdoors in May or June, 5 cm (2 in) deep and spaced as above. Harvest from June to October when the pods are 10 cm (4 in) long. Continuous picking encourages cropping.

Haricot beans are French beans that have been left to mature and dry on the plant. When the pods have turned a pale brown, pull the plant up, pick the pods and dry them, shelling them when they split.

Bean
recipes & remedies

Dried beans tend to produce wind in those who lack the enzymes to break down complex bean sugars. These sugars are attacked by bacteria in the bowel, producing wind. If dried beans are soaked in water before cooking, they are less likely to have this effect.

Cooked dried beans

Eating a cupful a day, mixed in with other foods if preferred, may reduce harmful cholesterol levels.

450 g (1 lb) pinto beans
1.2 litres (2 pints) water
Salt to taste

Cover the beans with water and soak them for several hours or overnight. Drain and simmer the beans in fresh water until soft. Flavour with salt. Eat with other vegetables, in a casserole, or cold in a salad with vinaigrette dressing.

Pea *Pisum sativum*

Peas have been cultivated in southern Europe and in Asia for thousands of years, and eaten either as succulent fresh peas when immature, or in soups and stews when ripe and dried. They are said to be native to the eastern Mediterranean, from Turkey eastwards to Syria, Iraq and Iran, and were probably first grown in Turkey. The ancient Greeks and Romans were fond of peas, although they did not use them medicinally – apparently they were provided for eating in the pits of theatres (as we might use popcorn). They were introduced to the rest of Europe by the Romans.

PEAS CAN HELP TO TREAT

- *Constipation*
- *High cholesterol*
- *Tiredness and lethargy*

INTERNAL USE

Peas are rich in vitamins A, B complex and C, as well as the minerals phosphorus, iron and potassium. They are high in pectin and other kinds of fibre, which not only help to ensure good bowel function but also to control harmful cholesterol levels. It is said that there is more fibre in peas than in almost any other food. The edible pods of mangetouts are also high in fibre – an excellent food to relieve constipation.

Peas are members of the legume family (Leguminoseae) and, like their relatives, are particularly nutritious when combined with grains, whether used fresh or dried. Being high in complex carbohydrates, they make an excellent energy-giving food and are particularly good for diabetics, since they help to control blood sugar levels.

Peas contain substances known as protease inhibitors, which research has indicated have the ability to deactivate certain viruses and carcinogens in the intestines. So peas are potentially a good remedy for preventing infections and helping to prevent cancer formation. Studies have linked the regular intake of peas with a lowered incidence of appendicitis.

Peas were the first food to be canned and then frozen, and are one of the few foods that actually

Peas are best picked when young and tender. Feel the pods first to check whether the peas inside have developed. Regular picking will encourage cropping.

benefit from being frozen. Sugars in fresh peas are rapidly converted to starch as soon as they are picked and this process is halted by refrigeration or freezing.

In folk medicine, peas have long been used as an aid to digestion, to settle the stomach and reduce heat and inflammation from acidity or gastritis. They have a mild diuretic action, helping to clear toxins from the system.

Caution: Studies indicate the possibility that phyto-oestrogens contained in peas may reduce fertility. And the purines in peas could precipitate an attack of gout in susceptible people if eaten in large amounts.

EXTERNAL USE

In Germany, children with measles used to be sponged with the water in which peas had been boiled, and a poultice made with cooked peas was applied to boils and abscesses.

HOW TO GROW

Both podded garden peas and mangetouts like rich, light, well-drained soil. Dig in garden compost or well-rotted manure the winter before planting, and dig the plot again before sowing the seeds. Depending on the variety, these are sown as an early crop, in March, as a main crop in April or May, or as a main crop in June or July.

Either make a V-shaped drill 5 cm (2 in) deep, and sow the seeds 5 cm (2 in) apart, or make a flat-bottomed drill approximately 10 cm (4 in) wide and sow two staggered rows with seeds 12 cm (4 1/2 in) apart in each direction. After sowing, cover the drills with soil and tread down. Erect support posts and wires or plastic mesh to the correct height for the particular variety being grown. Initially, place sticks on either side of the drill when the plants are about 7.5 cm (3 in) high, since this will encourage them to climb.

Pea
recipes & remedies

Peas and mangetouts can be eaten raw and are most nutritious eaten in this way. Alternatively, they can be steamed, boiled or stir-fried and eaten in soups or risottos.

Pea and pea pod purée

Used to settle the stomach and as an aid to digestion.

450 g (1 lb) peas (including pods)
1 small onion, chopped
300 ml (½ pint) water
Fresh herbs to flavour

Wash the pea pods and place them in a saucepan with the onion. Add water and simmer with the lid on for 15 minutes, or until tender. Blend in a food processor with some of the cooking water to a rough purée texture. Sieve and add fresh herbs of your choice to flavour.

Pea poultice

An effective remedy when applied to boils and abscesses.

225 g (8 oz) peas, cooked and
        puréed
2 pieces gauze
Light cotton bandage

Place sufficient puréed peas to cover the affected part of the body between 2 pieces of gauze. Bind it to the affected area with the cotton bandage (see *page 161*).

Radish *Raphanus sativus*

The pungent radish has a long history – it probably originated in China and is recorded as growing there as early as the 7th century BC. The ancient Egyptians valued it highly for its energy-giving properties, and the slaves who built the giant pyramids were fed by the Pharaohs on a diet of garlic, onions and radishes. The radish was revered by the ancient Greeks: 'such is the frivolity of the Greeks that in the temple of Apollo at Delphi, it is said, the radish is so greatly preferred to all other articles of diet as to be represented there in gold, the beet in silver and the turnip rape in lead'.

RADISHES CAN
HELP TO TREAT

- *Bronchial congestion*
- *Catarrh, coughs and colds*
- *Eczema*
- *Fluid retention*
- *Gout*
- *Liver and gall bladder problems*
- *Poor appetite*
- *Respiratory infections*
- *Rheumatism*
- *Sinusitis*
- *Urticaria*
- *Weak digestion*

INTERNAL USE

There are several different kinds of radish which all have the same medicinal properties, although they vary in degree in relation to their pungency. The long black radish, which has a stronger taste and a more pronounced action than the pink radish, is popular in France and southern Europe, where its ability to help cleanse the liver and invigorate the system is well known. An extract of black radish or freshly expressed juice has often been used to help treat gall bladder and liver disorders such as cholecystitis, gall stones and hepatic pain. Mooli, a long white type of radish, is popular in India and is similarly valued for its reputed liver-regenerative properties and as a remedy for constipation. In France, the pink radish was recommended as a folk remedy, to be taken first thing in the morning for liver problems and allergic skin conditions such as urticaria. Radish syrup was prescribed for bronchial catarrh, coughs and whooping cough.

As soon as they are chewed, fresh radishes stimulate the flow of digestive juices and saliva in the mouth, whetting the appetite and generally enhancing digestion. Radishes can therefore benefit people with weak digestion and those who suffer from constipation. Their pungent, stimulating effect is also felt in the respiratory system, where its decongestant action helps to clear bronchial congestion and blocked sinuses and acts as an expectorant. Being rich in vitamin C, they enhance the efforts of the immune system to fight off infection.

Radishes have a mild diuretic action, helping to hasten the excretion of toxins, including uric acid, from the system. This explains their long history of use for aiding the relief of arthritis, rheumatism and gout, as well as urinary problems such as gravel, stones and fluid retention.

All types of radish are rich in vitamin C and folic acid, and also contain calcium, copper, iron, potassium, sulphur and phosphorus. Their pungency helps to stimulate the circulation and acts as a tonic to the system by helping to boost the efficiency of each cell through the increased blood flow to and from the tissues. As a member of the mustard family (Cruciferae), radishes contain phytochemicals, such as antioxidants and bioflavonoids, which research indicates may be helpful in the prevention of cancer. The leaves of the radish can be added to salads and can be taken in teas for their diuretic effect.

EXTERNAL USE

Fresh radish pulp can be rubbed on corns and carbuncles to make them disappear.

Caution: Radishes may not suit people who suffer from inflammatory digestive problems, gastritis or ulcers. They can cause allergies in sensitive people as they contain salicylate, a compound similar to the active ingredient in aspirin.

HOW TO GROW

Radishes are an easy-to-grow, trouble-free salad crop that can be sown every 2 weeks and does best if grown in light, moisture-retentive soil. Shade them by putting them near taller plants such as parsnips and keep them well watered in dry weather.

Summer radishes should be sown between March and September, and winter varieties between June and August, in drills about 1.5 cm (^{1}/$_2$ in) deep and 15 cm (6 in) apart. They should be thinned to 2.5 cm (1 in) apart, and harvested from 4–6 weeks after sowing.

Radish
recipes & remedies

Radishes help to whet the appetite, which is why they are often included in hors-d'oeuvres. They must be chewed well, however, since some people find them hard to digest.

Radish syrup

This can be used to relieve chesty coughs.

3–4 black or pink radishes, thinly
    sliced
Honey to cover

Sprinkle honey over the slices of radish and strain off the juice after 24 hours. This quantity can be taken at night to relieve symptoms and so encourage a good night's sleep. Larger quantities can be stored in a sterilised airtight jar.

Radish leaf tea

A traditional diuretic remedy for water retention to help clear toxins from the system.

50 g (2 oz) radish leaves, washed
570 ml (1 pint) boiling water

Add the radish leaves to the water. Cover the container and leave to infuse for 10 minutes. Strain and allow to cool. Drink 1 cupful after meals.

Potato *Solanum tuberosum*

The potato was first domesticated and grown by Peruvian Indians in the Andes in about 3000 BC. In the 15th century, the Spanish conquistadors, seeing how highly the potato was valued in South America, took it back to Europe, where other root vegetables, such as carrots and turnips, had long been popular. Legend has it that the potato was first introduced to England in the second half of the 16th century by Sir Francis Drake, who bought a consignment of potatoes in the Colombian port of Cartagena. Others maintain that the potato was sent back to England in 1506, from Virginia in eastern North America, by colonists sent out by Sir Walter Raleigh.

POTATOES CAN HELP TO TREAT

- *Acid indigestion*
- *Arteriosclerosis*
- *Arthritis*
- *Chilblains*
- *Colitis*
- *Constipation*
- *Cuts and grazes*
- *Diverticulitis*
- *Gastritis*
- *High blood pressure*
- *Minor burns and scalds*
- *Stomach ulcers*
- *Sunburn*
- *Ulcers*

INTERNAL USE

Potatoes are high in fibre and carbohydrate and contain proteins, vitamin C (especially when fresh) and minerals – notably potassium – and trace elements. The minerals and vitamins are concentrated in and around the peel, which also has antioxidant properties that help to prevent damage caused to cells by free radicals, thereby helping to protect the body against degenerative diseases, cancer and the ravages of the ageing process. The fibre in potatoes is useful to the health of the bowel, ensuring regular movements and helping to prevent bowel disease, including cancer.

Potato juice has long been popular as a folk remedy. Dr Vogel, the Swiss naturopathic doctor, maintained that raw potato juice had proved its worth in the treatment of arthritis and was a good remedy for stomach ulcers, relaxing spasm and colic in the stomach and bowel, and helping to reduce excess acid in the stomach. It was traditionally used for indigestion, gastritis, peptic ulcers, liver disorders, gall stones, constipation and haemorrhoids.

Potatoes may help to soothe the urinary system, and they have a mild diuretic action. Being rich in potassium, they help to replace any potassium lost through diuresis. This potassium content is also good for the circulation, and for the regulation of blood pressure, and in fact potatoes are a popular traditional remedy for the heart circulation.

EXTERNAL USE

Raw potato juice has a soothing and an anti-inflammatory action, and encourages healing. It can be applied to relieve skin problems, to treat cuts and grazes, minor burns and wounds, sores and ulcers, chilblains and sunburn.

Caution: The potato is a member of the nightshade family. The stalks, leaves and green berries of the plant share some of the narcotic and poisonous properties of nightshades, as do tubers that have turned green.

HOW TO GROW

Potatoes are divided into first early, second early and maincrop. Earlies cannot be stored, but maincrops are intended for storing over winter. Potatoes do best in sandy soil with a high humus content. Tubers are planted in late March or early April for first earlies, mid-April for second earlies, and late April for maincrops.

Method 1: Dig a trench 20 cm (8 in) wide and 30 cm (1 ft) deep and stand the sprouted seed potatoes with their tops 15 cm (6 in) below the ground.

Method 2: Make 10–12 cm (4–5 in) holes, 30 cm (1 ft) apart, and push the potatoes into them, sprout upwards.

Potatoes need to be earthed up when the shoots are around 15 cm (6 in) high, and this should be repeated every 3 weeks. Water the trenches in between the rows. First early potatoes should be harvested in June and July, second earlies in August and September, and maincrop potatoes in September and October.

Buy healthy seed tubers for all varieties in January or February and lay them in trays, eye-up, in a light, frost-free place to sprout.

Potato
recipes & remedies

Grated raw potato and raw potato skins can help to prevent degenerative diseases, including heart disease. When baked or steamed in their skins, potatoes retain much of their nutritional value and are easily digested. Use a juicer to extract the potato juice.

Decoction of potato peelings

This may help to reduce high blood pressure.

Skins of 4–5 potatoes, washed
570 ml (1 pint) boiling water

Boil the potato skins for 15 minutes, then strain and cool. Drink 1–2 cupfuls of the liquid daily.

Raw potato juice

This is a helpful remedy for both stomach ulcers and arthritis.

Juice of 3–4 potatoes
Honey, carrot or lemon juice to taste

Add the flavouring to the potato juice and drink half a glass (3 fl oz) 4 times a day for 1 month.

Potato lotion

Apply externally for cuts, grazes, minor burns, sores and ulcers, chilblains and sunburn.

Juice of 3–4 potatoes
Olive oil or milk

Mix the potato juice with equal amounts of either olive oil or milk and apply to the affected area.

Spinach *Spinacia oleracea*

The origins of spinach are lost in the mists of time, but it is one of the oldest known vegetables and is thought to have come from the Middle East, around Persia. The ancient Greeks and Romans grew it, and the Arabs were fond of it and took it to Spain with them in the 10th century, from where it was taken to the rest of Europe. It was grown by the monks in many medieval monasteries in Europe, and was part of many a peasant's diet at that time.

SPINACH CAN HELP TO TREAT

- *Anaemia*
- *Constipation*
- *Fluid retention*
- *High cholesterol*
- *Low immunity*
- *Poor appetite*
- *Skin problems*
- *Tiredness and lethargy*
- *Vitamin and mineral deficiency*
- *Weak digestion*

INTERNAL USE

Spinach is considered a strengthening and energising vegetable, perhaps due to its iron content, which enhances oxygenation of the blood. The absorption of oxygen is enhanced by spinach's vitamin C content, although this is hindered to some degree by its oxalic acid content.

It makes a good food for those feeling tired, run down, recovering from illness, and for the anaemic and elderly. It is easily digested by most, and has properties that help in enhancing appetite and stimulating the digestion and absorption of food by increasing secretion of digestive enzymes and bile. It is rich in minerals and vitamins, including vitamin C, beta-carotene, iron, folic acid, potassium, magnesium, protein and chlorophyll. Spinach has a mild laxative action, helping to clear wastes from the bowel, and also has diuretic properties, aiding the elimination of fluid as well as toxins from the system. This explains its overall cooling and cleansing action, useful for helping to clear skin problems. The potassium in spinach makes up for any losses caused by increased urination.

Spinach makes a good food to enhance immunity and to help fight off infection. The antioxidants beta-carotene and vitamin C contained in spinach help to protect the body from damage caused by free radicals and so help to pre-vent degenerative diseases, heart disease and cancer. Spinach may help to lower harmful cholesterol levels. The bioflavonoids abundant in spinach, which impart the dark green colour to the leaves, are thought to help deactivate carcinogens and, therefore, inhibit tumour formation. Among these bioflavonoids are the carotenoids, beta-carotene and lutein, which have both been shown in recent research to help prevent cancer of the colon, stomach, lungs and the prostate. Chlorophyll has also been shown to inhibit the action of carcinogens. Folic acid, contained in spinach, not only helps prevent anaemia but is also vital for pregnant women for normal development of the brain and spinal cord of the baby.

Spinach is a good source of protein for vegetarians, but is best when eaten with a grain as it lacks the amino acid methionine, which prevents it from being a complete first-class protein.

Caution: Due to the high oxalic acid content of spinach, it is contra-indicated in gout and arthritis and should be avoided by anyone suffering from kidney or bladder stones.

HOW TO GROW

Spinach needs a rich, fertile and well-drained soil with a high nitrogen content. There are three varieties: summer spinach, which is sown

When harvesting, do not strip plants entirely. Do not cut the leaves, but pick them by bending them downwards.

between March and July and harvested between June and October; perpetual spinach, which is sown between April and July and can be harvested throughout the year; and New Zealand spinach, which is sown during April and harvested between June and September. Seeds for all varieties should be sown every few weeks to ensure a continual crop. Sow spinach seeds 2 cm (1 in) deep, leaving 45 cm (18 in) between rows. Seedlings should be thinned to about 30 cm (1 ft) apart when they become large enough to handle.

Spinach
recipes & remedies

Spinach can be enjoyed as a cooked vegetable or when eaten raw in salads. It should be used as soon after picking as possible, as it deteriorates quickly.

Spinach and carrot juice

A nutritious and revitalising tonic for those feeling tired or run down.

225 g (8 oz) spinach, washed
3 carrots, washed

Using a juicer, extract the liquid from the spinach and carrots. Drink ½ glassful (3 fl oz) daily while symptoms persist. Store excess juice in a sterilised airtight container in the refrigerator.

Steamed spinach

A good iron tonic for the anaemic.

225 g (8 oz) spinach, washed
2 teaspoons (10 ml) olive oil
Salt to taste

Steam the spinach lightly for 5–10 minutes. Add the olive oil and salt to taste.

Spanakorizo

Greek-style spinach with rice is delicious, nourishing and excellent for those with weak digestions, elderly people and convalescents.

3 tablespoons olive oil
1–2 large onions (or 1 bunch spring onions), chopped
1.3kg (3 lb) spinach, de-stalked
600 ml (1 pint) water or vegetable stock
Salt and freshly ground pepper
175 g (6 oz) basmati rice
2 tablespoons chopped fresh dill

Heat the oil in a large saucepan over a low heat. Add the onions, cover and cook for about 10 minutes, or until the onions are translucent but not browned. Wash the spinach and shake off any water left. Add to the onions. Cover and cook for 5 minutes, or until wilted. Pour in the water or stock, add salt and pepper to taste, increase the heat and bring to the boil. Add the rice, stir well and cover the saucepan. Reduce the heat to low once more and leave to simmer for 15–20 minutes, until the water is absorbed and the rice is cooked. Stir in the chopped dill. Cover and allow to stand for 5 minutes before serving.

fruit

Whether raw or cooked, fruit is the most delicious form of natural medicine available. The taste and smell of organic fruit is wonderful, and the simple pleasure of picking an apple or pear from your own tree is hard to beat. Refreshing to the taste buds and cleansing to the system, an excellent source of vitamins, minerals and natural antibiotics, fruit is the ideal food for eating your way to good health.

Strawberry *Fragaria* x *ananassa*

The sweet and succulent taste of strawberries has been appreciated for thousands of years. The ancient Greeks called the strawberry *komaros*, which means 'a mouthful', in reference to its convenient size, while the Romans called it *fragaria* because of its delicate fragrance. Izaak Walton in his *The Compleat Angler* records the quote of Dr Butler, a 16th-century physician: 'Doubtless God could have made a better berry, but doubtless God never did.' Its fragrance alone was said to be refreshing to the spirits.

STRAWBERRIES CAN HELP TO TREAT

- *Acne*
- *Cold sores*
- *Constipation*
- *Fevers*
- *Fluid retention*
- *Heat rash*
- *Infections*
- *Inflammatory eye problems*
- *Skin problems*
- *Sunburn*
- *Vitamin and mineral deficiency*

Throughout history the strawberry has been valued not only as a food but also as a medicine. It has long been considered to have cleansing properties, due to a combination of its laxative and diuretic actions, and has been used to purify the blood and as a cooling remedy for hot inflammatory problems. It has also been used for liver problems, inflammatory eye conditions and to relieve fevers.

INTERNAL USE

Strawberries are highly nutritious. They are rich in vitamins A and C, and in the minerals iron, magnesium, potassium, sulphur, calcium and silicon. This explains their historical use as a tonic for convalescents. The calcium and magnesium aid normal function of the nervous system, which might help to lift the spirits and calm the nerves. The seeds are rich in pectin and other soluble fibres, providing a mild laxative effect and possibly helping to reduce harmful cholesterol levels. However, the seeds may cause irritation to some sensitive people with inflammatory digestive problems such as colitis and diverticulitis.

Recent research has shown that strawberries may help to prevent cancer and degenerative diseases. The antioxidant vitamins A and C help to stop damage caused by free radicals, while the polyphenols contained in strawberries help to combat cancer. The bioflavonoids, including anthocyanin and ellagic acid, have even been shown to help prevent some cancers. Strawberries also have the ability to inhibit the formation of nitro-samines, which are potent carcinogens formed in the intestines under certain chemical conditions.

Strawberries can aid the immune system and they have been shown to have antibacterial and antiviral actions, helping to inhibit the polio virus and Coxsackie virus.

EXTERNAL USE

Rubbing a strawberry on a cold sore may well prove an effective remedy, and strawberries can also be used externally for skin problems such as acne, heat rash and sunburn.

Caution: Strawberries can cause serious allergies in susceptible people as they contain salicylates, a compound similar to the active ingredient in aspirin. Their oxalic acid may cause irritation to the bladder and kidneys in some people and inhibit absorption of nutrients, such as iron and calcium.

HOW TO GROW

Strawberries like a sunny position, slightly acid, well-drained soil and plenty of organic matter. They can be grown in beds or containers.

When the berries form, spread straw around the base of each plant to keep the fruit off the soil. Polythene sheets may be used instead of straw.

Plant in the late summer to harvest the following year, not more than about 45 cm (18 in) apart, in rows 90 cm (3 ft) apart. Dig a hole about 5 cm (2 in) deeper than the root system for each plant. Water the plants in and keep them watered in dry weather. Pinch off the runners as they form (do not layer them; it is better to buy new ones). Pick the fruit by the stalks to avoid bruising when ripe (June to July). Remove the straw (*see left*) and cut off the leaves after cropping. Plants will need to be renewed every five years.

Strawberry
recipes & remedies

The best way to use strawberry fruits medicinally is simply to eat them, or apply them to the body, fresh. Strawberry leaves, however, like the fruit, have cooling and astringent properties, and they are also used medicinally, especially for diarrhoea, kidney and bladder infections, fluid retention, and as a gargle and mouthwash for ulcers and sore throats.

Strawberry leaf tea

This can either be drunk or used as a gargle.

570 ml (1 pint) boiling water
25 g (1 oz) fresh strawberry leaves, rinsed

Pour the water over the leaves in a teapot and leave to infuse for 10 minutes. Strain, and drink 1 cupful, 2–3 times daily.

Apricot *Prunus armenaica*

This richly coloured, velvet-textured fruit is a native of Central Asia and can be found growing wild in China. Apothecaries in the 16th century were familiar with its therapeutic uses. The herbalist John Gerard wrote: 'being first eaten before the meat they easily descend and cause other meats to pass down the sooner.' He was referring to the laxative properties of apricots, which are particularly apparent in apricots from the Hunza area of the Himalayas, where some people apparently live for more than 120 years.

APRICOTS CAN HELP TO TREAT

- *Anaemia*
- *Anxiety and tension*
- *Bowel disorders*
- *Constipation*
- *Loss of appetite*
- *Nervous indigestion*
- *Tiredness and lethargy*
- *Vitamin and mineral deficiency*
- *Weak digestion*

INTERNAL USE

All apricots are high in fibre and low in calories, and they are an excellent food for those suffering from constipation and those watching their weight. Dried apricots make a good alternative for sweet or fatty snacks, being naturally sweet, and have the added bonus of being highly nutritious. They are rich in vitamins A, B and C, and contain protein, magnesium, phosphorus, iron, calcium, potassium, sulphur and manganese; they are particularly rich in iron when dried, and contain plenty of vitamin C to ease its absorption. So apricots make a good, easily digested and nutrient-rich food for those feeling weak and run down, anaemic, or recovering from illness or stress, for pregnant women, children and the elderly.

The vitamins and minerals boost the immune system and thereby enhance immunity and the body's fight against disease. The calcium, magnesium and potassium are all essential for normal function of the nervous system and for the muscular system, and help to support the body through times of stress. They have long been used for anxiety, tension, physical and emotional weakness, depression and insomnia.

Apricots have a beneficial effect on the digestive tract. As well as their laxative action they stimulate appetite, promote digestion and absorption and soothe irritation throughout the digestive system. Apricot marmalade is an old English remedy for relieving nausea and nervous indigestion. By relieving constipation they help to protect against bowel disease such as diverticulitis and cancer. They also help to protect against cancer in other ways: their antioxidant vitamins A and C prevent damage caused by free radicals, helping to protect against heart and arterial disease and cancer, and to slow the ageing process – as demonstrated by the people of Hunza in the Himalayas. The beta-carotene in apricots has been shown to offer some protection against cancer of the lung and possibly the pancreas, the skin and the larynx, or any cancer linked to cigarette smoking.

Apricot kernels contain a substance known as laetrile or amygdalin, sometimes called vitamin B_{17}, which has been said to help the body to fight cancer. It is a controversial remedy as apricot kernels also contain cyanide, which is of course poisonous.

Caution: Apricots can cause allergies in some sensitive people as they contain salicylate, a compound similar to the active ingredient in aspirin.

HOW TO GROW

Apricots like a warm, sunny wall or a greenhouse and can be planted either freestanding, if they are in a well-sheltered place, or fan-trained against a sheltered, south-facing wall (*see pages 139 and 142*). Apricots can grow to 2.5 m (8 ft) with a 3.6m (12 ft) spread for fan-trained plants and 4.5 m (15 ft) for a bush. Apricots can be planted between November and March. Bushes should be planted at least 4.5 m (15 ft) apart and staked. The soil should be slightly alkaline, well-drained and not too rich. Water well after planting, then mulch to keep the soil moist.

Apricots need protection from frost when flowering, and should be thinned when fruits are the size of walnuts (April to May). Harvest in July or August when fruit is ripe. Prune to open up the centre of the plant and remove overcrowded branches in summer. For fan-trained trees, rub out the buds in spring (*see page 76*) and pinch out the tips of side-shoots in early summer.

Apricot
recipes & remedies

Apricots can be eaten fresh, dried, or made into preserves. It is worth noting, however, that the sulphur used to preserve commercially produced dried apricots can also cause allergic reactions, so it is always best to buy unsulphured dried apricots which do not look so invitingly orange.

Apricot iron tonic

An excellent remedy for anaemia.

570 ml (1 pint) boiling water
250 g (9 oz) fresh or dried apricots
Honey or sugar to taste

Pour the water over the apricots and leave to infuse for 10 minutes. Strain, and drink 1 cupful twice a day.

Stewed apricots

A tasty and gentle dish to help regulate the bowels.

450 g (1 lb) fresh apricots
300 ml (10 fl oz) fresh apple juice
Water sufficient to cover apricots

Cover the apricots in a pan with water and let them soak for several hours. Bring the water to the boil, add the apple juice and simmer gently for about 30 minutes, or until the apricots are tender and the liquid has reduced to a syrupy consistency. Eat 1 small bowlful, hot or cold, in the evening.

Cherry *Prunus avium & P. cerasus*

Sour cherries such as the morello derive from the wild cherry *P. cerasus*, and the sweet varieties from its near relative the gean, *P. avium*. The gean, with its popular shiny red fruits, seems to have come originally from Asia Minor. In China, the delicate spring cherry blossom symbolises youth, rebirth, hope, fertility and feminine beauty; in Japan, it is the national flower and represents perfection. In Christian symbolism, cherries were a fruit of paradise, an emblem of sweetness and goodness. The fruit as well as the stalk has been respected for its medicinal uses for centuries.

CHERRIES CAN HELP TO TREAT

- *Anaemia*
- *Arthritis*
- *Catarrh, coughs and colds*
- *Constipation (fruit)*
- *Diarrhoea (stalks)*
- *Fluid retention*
- *Gout*
- *Tiredness and lethargy*
- *Urinary infections*
- *Vitamin and mineral deficiency*

According to Culpeper, sour cherries 'are more pleasing to a hot stomach, procure appetite to meat, to help and cut tough phlegm and gross humours; but when these are dried, they are more binding to the belly than when they are fresh, being cooling in hot diseases and welcome to the stomach, and provokes urine'. The stalks certainly have an astringent action, and help to protect the lining of the digestive tract from irritation, inflammation and infection. Their astringency has a binding effect that can be useful for treating diarrhoea when taken as cherry stalk tea. The fruits are more laxative and make a good remedy for constipation.

INTERNAL USE

Both the fruits and the stalks are valued today for their cleansing properties. Their diuretic action helps the elimination of toxins and excess fluid from the body and can thereby help to clear congestion and phlegm, as Culpeper stated, but can also be particularly effective in the treatment of gout and arthritis. They soothe inflammation of the urinary tract and, taken as a cool tea, can help relieve cystitis and other urinary infections.

Cherries, particularly when eaten fresh, are nutritious, rich in vitamins A and C, the antioxidant vitamins, and are a good source of betacarotene, calcium, magnesium, iron, phosphorus, potassium and zinc. It is not difficult to see why cherries have long had a reputation for rejuvenating body and mind, for supporting the nervous system and for reducing stress. Vitamin C, calcium and magnesium are vital to normal function of the nervous system, the sugars help to provide instant energy, while the wealth of nutrients enhance energy and immunity. Cherries help the body to combat infections and make a good food for those feeling tired and run down or recovering from illness. Ripe black cherries have long been used as a folk remedy for coughs and sore throats, and are particularly useful for treating children as they taste so good.

The sour or morello cherry, *P. cerasus*, has smaller and more bitter fruit and comes from Persia and Kurdistan. The bark of the tree was used as a remedy to reduce fevers and for clearing coughs and catarrh. The stalks are considered more powerfully diuretic than those of the sweet cherries, but both are used for urinary problems, fluid retention, arthritis and gout.

The bark of the black cherry (*P. serotina*) is frequently used today in modern herbal practice. It has a sedative effect on the nervous system and particularly on the cough reflex, soothing harsh, irritating or paroxysmal coughs as in whooping cough and croup. Since it contains prussic acid it is best used only on the advice of a qualified medical herbalist.

HOW TO GROW

Cherry trees need rich soil with lots of organic matter. Both sweet cherries and morellos can be grown freestanding or trained against a wall (*see page 139*). A freestanding tree can grow to a height of 8 m (27 ft) and both freestanding and fan-trained trees can grow to a span of 4.5–6 m (15–20 ft). They need to be kept well watered, especially in dry weather.

Sweet cherries fruit on old and young wood. Prune to remove dead wood and crossing branches in summer. When pruning fan-trained sweet cherries, rub out new shoots as necessary in spring (*see page 76*) and pinch out the growing tips of other new shoots in June or July. Morello cherries are self-pollinating and fruit on new wood. They need to be pruned after fruiting.

Cherry
recipes & remedies

Sweet cherries are best eaten fresh on their own or added to fresh fruit salads. Morello cherries are suitable for cooking, especially for making jams and jellies.

Cherry cough syrup for children

Children will happily drink this delicious-tasting cough syrup.

450 g (1 lb) morello cherries
450 g (1 lb) honey
Juice of 1/2 lemon
Water sufficient to cover cherries

Simmer the cherries in water until cooked and strain through coarse muslin, to extract the juice. Add the lemon juice and honey and stir into the consistency of cream. Pour into bottles and seal. Take 1 teaspoon 3 times daily or as required. It will keep for 3 days if refrigerated.

Cherry stalk tea

Useful for treating diarrhoea and for gout, arthritis and urinary problems.

1 litre (1¾ pints) water
25–50 g (1–2 oz) cherry stalks
225 g (8 oz) fresh cherries

Soak the stalks in cold water for 12 hours. Boil for a few minutes and pour on to the fresh cherries. Soak for another hour and strain through a sieve. Take 3–4 cupfuls daily.

Plum *Prunus domestica*

Plum trees in the orchard, laden with fruit, are one of the delights of late summer and early autumn days. There are many different varieties of plum – more than of any other genus of stone fruit – and they can be used interchangeably for compotes, sauces, puddings, jams, jellies and fruit salads. The plum is a close relative of the wild sloe (*P. spinosa*) that comes from Europe and North Africa and of the Eurasian bullace, both of which are sour and astringent, the damson (*P. insititia*), which comes from Damascus, and the greengage (*P. domestica italica*), which was brought to Britain by Sir Thomas Gage.

PLUMS CAN HELP TO TREAT

- *Anaemia*
- *Arthritis*
- *Bowel disorders*
- *Constipation*
- *Flatulence*
- *Fluid retention*
- *Gout*
- *Skin problems*
- *Tiredness and lethargy*
- *Vitamin and mineral deficiency*

Plums and their dried form, prunes, have been valued at least since Roman times for their energy-giving and laxative properties. In the 17th century, Culpeper recommended prunes 'to loosen the belly . . . to procure appetite . . . and cool the stomach'; a decoction of the leaves has long been a folk remedy for constipation, fevers and fluid retention. Decoctions of prunes were vital ingredients of laxative medicines, and were the favoured laxative for children as their action is not preceded by any griping or discomfort. As a household remedy, prunes used to be cooked in water with wine, cinnamon and lemon peel; however, they are perfectly tasty cooked on their own with just a little water, and even the juice alone will be effective enough for small children. Through their very efficient laxative action, plums and prunes help to keep the bowels healthy and to prevent problems such as diverticulitis and bowel cancer from developing.

INTERNAL USE

Plums and prunes are highly nutritious, rich in vitamins B, C and E, and in minerals iron, calcium, phosphorus, magnesium, sodium and manganese. Vitamins C and E have an antioxidant action, helping to protect the body against free radicals and thereby helping to prevent degenerative diseases and slowing the ageing process. When dried, prunes not only stimulate the muscles of the large intestine to produce an effective laxative action but they also provide a concentrated source of energy – useful for athletes, walkers, cyclists, mountain climbers or anyone who wants a high-energy but low-weight food to carry about with them.

Plums or prunes have a diuretic effect, helping to reduce fluid retention and so aiding the elimination of toxins via the urinary system. Accordingly, they make a good detoxifying remedy and can help relieve arthritis and gout. They have a gently stimulating effect on the liver, which augments their cleansing action – making plums useful for clearing the skin, and for symptoms associated with a sluggish liver, such as lethargy, heat, irritability, headaches and poor digestion. Although plums and prunes can initially provoke wind in some people, they can relieve wind and bloating, particularly when this is caused by constipation.

Caution: Plums can cause allergies in sensitive people as they contain salicylate, a compound similar to the active ingredient in aspirin. The kernels of the stones contain amygdalin, which breaks down to hydrogen cyanide in the stomach, so should be avoided.

If your tree is fan-trained, make sure that you 'rub out' with your thumb all those buds that are growing towards or away from the wall, when new growth appears in the spring.

HOW TO GROW

Plums need rich soil with lots of organic matter. They can be free-standing or grown up a wall with supports (*see page 139*). Free-standing trees should be planted 3.6–4.5 m (12–15 ft) apart, and wall-trained trees about 4.5–5.5 m (15–18 ft) apart. Some varieties are cross-pollinating, so check when buying young trees. Trees should be pruned in spring and fruits thinned out when branches are laden in June, and harvested when ripe (August or September).

Plum
recipes & remedies

Both fresh and dried plums can be taken in many forms. Fresh plums can be eaten raw or made into jams and jellies.

Greengage or plum jam

This jam, rich in iron, calcium, magnesium and manganese, is a good concentrated source of energy, and also helps to keep the bowels regular. This recipe makes approx. 2.7 kg (6 lb) jam.

1.8 kg (4 lb) greengages or plums, halved
  and de-stoned
450 ml (³/4 pint) water
1.8 kg (4 lb) preserving sugar

Place the greengages or plums in a preserving pan or large saucepan and pour in the water. Bring to the boil, reduce the heat, cover and simmer until the fruit has softened to a purée. Remove from the heat and stir in the sugar until it is completely dissolved. Return to a high heat and boil for 20 minutes or so, until the setting point is reached. (To test, drop a teaspoonful of the jam on to a cold saucer and refrigerate for 2 minutes, then see if it wrinkles when pushed with a spoon.) Skim off any froth that forms. Spoon into hot sterilised jars and seal with airtight lids.

Peach *Prunus persica*

The peach, a relative of the plum and the apricot, has been grown for centuries not only for its delicious and refreshing fruit but also for its beautiful spring blossom and its medicinal properties, particularly those contained in the leaves and flowers. Its name in Roman times, *persica*, indicates that when the peach first arrived in Europe it was believed to come from Persia; in fact, it originates in China, where the first records of its use date back to 551 BC. It is thought to have come to Europe before the 1st century AD; by the 16th century, the Spanish had taken peaches to South America, from where they spread to North America.

PEACHES CAN HELP TO TREAT

- *Anxiety and tension*
- *Bowel problems*
- *Coughs*
- *Cystitis*
- *Fluid retention*
- *Gastritis*
- *Heartburn*
- *Indigestion*
- *Skin problems*
- *Stress-related digestive problems*
- *Tiredness and lethargy*
- *Urethritis*
- *Vitamin and mineral deficiency*

INTERNAL USE

Fresh, raw, unpeeled, washed peaches are a good source of the antioxidant vitamins A and C, helping to prevent damage to the tissues caused by free radicals, and the effects of the ageing process. Peaches, particularly when dried, provide a rich supply of iron and potassium as well as some calcium, magnesium and phosphorous. Peaches are easily digested. Being rich in easily assimilable sugars, they provide energy, and being high in fibre and with a moistening quality, they make a good laxative. They are therefore an excellent food for sufferers of constipation, and because they have the ability to regulate stomach acidity, for those prone to excess stomach acid, heartburn, indigestion and gastritis. They are cooling and soothing to an irritated gut lining, and with their calming effect on the nervous system, can be helpful for all sorts of stress-related digestive disorders – indigestion, wind, gastritis, colitis, irritable bowel and spastic colon.

Peaches also aid kidney function and have a gentle diuretic action, aiding the elimination of toxins and relieving fluid retention. The juice of peaches will help to soothe an irritated urinary tract, and to relieve cystitis and urethritis. Their cleansing action on the system can clear skin problems, improve energy and give a sense of well-being. They help prevent atherosclerosis and protect against heart and arterial disease by lowering cholesterol. One of the trace elements that peaches contain is boron, which is said to affect the electrical energy in the brain. Having sufficient boron in the diet helps to maintain mental alertness and enhance mental energy and concentration.

An infusion of dried peach flowers was used until recently, particularly in European countries, as a calming remedy for anxiety and nervousness and to calm tantrums in children. The infusion was also recommended to relieve coughs and asthma in children.

EXTERNAL USE

Crushed fresh peaches are said to be an effective beauty aid when applied to the face for a few minutes daily, keeping the skin cool, fresh and youthful.

Caution: Dried peaches may have a preservative containing sulphites, which can cause allergic reactions in some people. Peaches may also cause allergic reactions in those susceptible to salicylate, a compound similar to the active ingredient in aspirin.

Established peach trees should be pruned twice a year; in spring, and in summer, after the fruit has been harvested.

HOW TO GROW

Peach trees can be grown against a wall in temperate regions or as bushes in containers in a greenhouse. They like well-drained, loamy soil. Buy 3-year-old trees and plant from October to January. Prune in February. Fan-trained trees should be spaced 3.6–4.5 m (12–15 ft) apart, and bushes at least 4.5m (15 ft) apart. Mulch outdoor plants after planting, and again every winter. Fruit should be thinned in June and harvested in July and August.

Peach
recipes & remedies

Peaches, like other stone fruits, can be eaten raw, bottled, made into chutneys, compotes and jams, or juice.

Syrup of peach flowers

A traditional recipe recommended for constipation, and suitable for adults and children alike.

1.7 litres (3 pints) boiling water
450 g (1 lb) fresh peach flowers
450 g (1 lb) sugar

Pour the water over the flowers. Cover and leave to soak for 12 hours or more. Bring to the boil again, cover and simmer for 5–10 minutes; strain and add the sugar. Heat gently until it acquires the consistency of a syrup. Store in a tightly sealed, sterilised jar.

Peach compote

A useful remedy for soothing the stomach.

150 ml (5 fl oz) water
250 g (9 oz) sugar
900 g (2 lb) ripe peaches

Peel the peaches, remove the stones and cut the fruit in half. Heat the water and add the sugar, stirring until it is dissolved. Add the peaches and cook over a low heat for about 15 minutes, or until peaches are tender.

Pear *Pyrus communis*

The pear tree has one of the loveliest blossoms in spring, and its enticing fruit is sweet and refreshing; the juice is like pure nectar. There are over 3,000 different varieties of pear today, some of which were probably known to the ancient Greeks and Romans. Pears are mentioned in Homer's *Odyssey*, and Pliny describes 39 varieties; by Elizabethan times, 232 varieties were available. They have long been popular, both raw and cooked, particularly in medieval monasteries, and pears baked in syrup were evidently considered food fit for a king, for they were served at Henry IV's wedding feast.

PEARS CAN HELP TO TREAT

- *Acid indigestion*
- *Arthritis*
- *Colitis*
- *Constipation*
- *Coughs*
- *Cystitis*
- *Diarrhoea*
- *Fluid retention*
- *Gastritis*
- *Gout*
- *Heartburn*
- *High cholesterol*
- *Irritable bowel syndrome*
- *Stress-related digestive problems*
- *Tiredness and lethargy*
- *Vitamin and mineral deficiency*

Perry, an alcoholic drink much like apple cider but made from pears, had become as popular as cider in 17th-century England. The 16th-century herbalist, John Gerard, considered it a good digestive. He wrote: 'it comforteth and warmeth the stomach.' Culpeper recommended pears to cool the blood, and, when sour, to stop bleeding and diarrhoea through their astringent properties.

INTERNAL USE

Today, we can still use pears to benefit the digestion. They are a good source of pectin and fibre, are easy to digest, and make a good food for regulating the bowels, helpful for remedying both diarrhoea and constipation. Their cooling and astringent properties (they contain tannins) are useful in inflammatory conditions of the digestive tract, such as gastritis and colitis, and their low acidity and calming properties help relieve nervous and acidic stomach problems. Pears, therefore, make a good food for people suffering from nervous dyspepsia, acid indigestion, heartburn, irritable bowel syndrome and diverticulitis. They are excellent for those prone to allergies, as they are one of the least allergenic foods (when unsprayed and not treated with preservatives). For this reason, they make a good first food when weaning young babies.

When unpeeled, pears are a delicious source of vitamins A, B and C, and of minerals and trace elements including potassium, calcium, magnesium, iron and manganese. Being high in natural sugars, they make a good source of quick energy, particularly when dried. They contain pectin, a soluble fibre that helps to control cholesterol, so pears can contribute to the maintenance of a healthy heart and arteries.

Pears have long been used as a remedy for gout and arthritis. They have a mild diuretic action, helping to clear toxins from the system and aiding the excretion of excess fluid, as well as of uric acid. Taken as juice or poached in water, their cooling and cleansing effect is helpful when treating hot arthritic joints, as well as for cystitis and other urinary tract conditions. In the respiratory system, pear has a soothing action, relieving harsh, irritating coughs, particularly if cooked with a little fennel or aniseed.

HOW TO GROW

Most pear trees are not self-fertile so you will need to buy two varieties for cross-pollination to occur. Or you could buy a grafted tree which has three varieties of pear growing from a single stem. Pears can be grown freestanding or up a wall (*see page 139*), and they like a sunny, sheltered position, with rich, well-drained, soil. They can be planted from November to March. Bush trees should be planted 3.6–4.5 m (12–15 ft) apart, and half-standards 6–7.5 m (20–25 ft) apart. Mulch them well every spring and keep them watered in dry weather. Summer pruning is best for trained trees, but standards need no pruning except where there is old, dead wood and overlapping branches. Pears should be picked when ripe, from August to October.

Thin out pears as the young fruits become large enough to turn downwards. Each group of fruits should be thinned to 2 pears only.

Pear
recipes & remedies

Pears should be harvested when the fruit is mature but still hard. Leave the pears to ripen at room temperature before eating them.

Pear compote

Benefits digestion and regulates the bowels.

900 g (2 lb) pears
150 ml (5 fl oz) water
250 g (9 oz) sugar

Peel the pears. Leave whole if small or halve them if large, and remove the seeds. Heat the water and add the sugar, stirring until it is dissolved. Simmer the pears quickly in the resulting syrup for 15–20 minutes. Leave to cool before serving.

Pears with fennel

Useful as a cough remedy.

1 pear, cored, sliced and de-seeded
1/2 teaspoon fennel seeds
1 teaspoon honey
Water sufficient to cover pears

Put all the ingredients in a pan with water. Bring to the boil and simmer for 45 minutes, or until the fruit is tender.

Apple *Malus pumila*

The medicinal benefits of the apple have been well documented since the days of the ancient Greeks and Romans, who considered it to be a universal cure. For years, apples have been used in folk medicine for the treatment of colds, catarrh, flu, fevers, bronchial complaints and heart problems. Cooked apples were considered to be a sedative and an aid to restful sleep. An apple a day really did help to keep the doctor away.

APPLES CAN HELP TO TREAT

- *Arthritis*
- *Catarrh, coughs and colds*
- *Constipation*
- *Cuts and wounds*
- *Diarrhoea*
- *Fevers*
- *Fluid retention*
- *Gastritis*
- *Headaches*
- *Hyperacidity*
- *Indigestion*
- *Irritable bowel syndrome*
- *Liver and gall bladder complaints*
- *Peptic ulcers*
- *Rheumatism*
- *Skin problems*

INTERNAL USE

The apple contains a wealth of vitamins, minerals and other vital nutrients that are easily digested – in fact, the apple itself aids digestion, because its malic and tartaric acids regulate stomach acidity and aid the digestion of protein and fat. It is for this reason that it is traditionally served with fatty meats such as pork and goose. It is said that eating apples helps to dampen the appetite, which is a great bonus for dieters. The apple also has a gentle cleansing action, promoting liver and bowel function, and through its diuretic action it aids the elimination of toxins from the body. The pectin in apples helps to bulk out the stool, making it an effective laxative. Interestingly, apples have been used as a remedy for diarrhoea for the same reason. Pectin has also been shown to protect against the adverse effects of pollution by binding to toxic metals, such as mercury and lead, and carrying them out of the body.

Recent research has indicated that the apple has even more beneficial properties: fresh apples and homemade apple juice both have an antiviral action, and those who eat apples regularly have been shown to have fewer colds and upper respiratory infections. The tannic acid found in apples is very effective against the herpes simplex (cold sore) virus. Other active constituents in apples, which are known as polyphenols, have anti-cancer properties, and apples can also help to lower cholesterol and blood pressure.

EXTERNAL USE

The pulp left over from juicing apples can be applied to soothe skin rashes. Baked apples, with their skins removed and mixed with a few drops of olive oil, can also be used for this purpose, and can be applied to minor cuts and wounds to facilitate healing.

HOW TO GROW

There are some dual-purpose varieties of apple, although most are either dessert (eating) or culinary (cooking) varieties. Each variety may be bought in a number of growth forms (*see page 139*), from dwarf, which is approximately 1.8 m (6 ft) high at maturity, to standard, which can grow to 6–7.5 m (20–25 ft). There are also several supported types available. Some apples are self-fertile and others require another variety to pollinate, so check this when buying. It is also possible to buy grafted trees which have three or four varieties on one plant.

Apples need deep, well-drained, slightly acid soil with lots of organic matter. Buy bare-rooted plants and plant them in a sunny place where they will be sheltered from strong, cold winds and frost. Bush trees should be planted at least 3.6 m (12 ft) apart, or 1.8 m (6 ft) apart in the case of dwarf pyramids. Cordons should be planted at least 1 m (3 ft) apart, with 1.8 m (6 ft) between rows, and espaliers and fan-trained trees about 4.5 m (15 ft) apart. After planting, check the soil regularly around the roots, and firm them down if they have been lifted by frost. Mulch when the soil is warm in early spring. Ideally, keep a 1.2 m (4 ft) circle free of grass and weeds around the base of the tree. Thin the crop around June and harvest, according to variety, early to late autumn.

When picking, lift the apple in the palm of your hand and give it a gentle twist. If it is ripe, it will come away with the stalk attached.

Apple
recipes & remedies

Both eating and cooking apples are excellent for making purées and jams, but eating apples are better for making apple tea as they are sweeter. However, they may lose their flavour and texture when baked, so it is better to use cooking apples.

Baked apples

Good for clearing colds and catarrh.

4 large cooking apples
1 tablespoon butter
25 g (1 oz) raw brown sugar
50 g (2 oz) sultanas
8 cloves
4 teaspoons ground cinnamon
2 tablespoons honey
2 tablespoons water

Core the apples, score a ring around them to prevent bursting and fill the centres with a mixture of butter, sugar, sultanas, cloves and cinnamon. Place the apples in an ovenproof dish and spoon honey and water over them. Bake at 200°C (400°F or gas mark 6) for 30–45 minutes, or until soft.

Apple and mint juice

This makes a refreshing drink that is especially good for treating colds.

Simply juice 5–6 apples and float fresh mint leaves in the glass.

Sage and apple tea

Useful for digestive problems, especially if stress-related.

570 ml (1 pint) boiling water
5–6 fresh sage leaves
2–3 teaspoons fresh apple juice

Make a cup of strong sage tea by infusing the leaves in the water. Leave for 10 minutes and then add the fresh apple juice and serve.

Rhubarb *Rheum* x *hybridum* & *R. palmatum*

Rhubarb is a magnificent architectural plant, related to the dock, and is a native of China and Tibet, where its root has been valued as a medicine since around 3000 BC. The dried root of the medicinal *R. palmatum* was first brought to Europe by Marco Polo. *R.* x *hybridum*, the edible garden rhubarb, was brought to Britain from the Volga region of Russia in 1573, also for the therapeutic properties of its root, but was not enjoyed as a fruit or preserve until the 1800s. Its name may be derived from the Greek *rheo*, to flow, because of the plant's purgative properties.

RHUBARB CAN HELP TO TREAT

- *Constipation*
- *Diarrhoea*
- *Headaches*
- *Infections of the digestive tract*

The medicinal rhubarb *R. palmatum* is used today by medical herbalists and it has been used in China for at least 5000 years as an excellent laxative. It has a bitter taste and a cold quality and is prescribed in Chinese medicine for constipation due to heat, to clear stagnation of undigested food from the system, and to clear excess heat from the body, such as fevers. It is also commonly used in prescriptions for headaches, appendicitis, infectious hepatitis, conjuctivitis, gingivitis, nosebleeds, oedema, bacterial infections and a variety of skin problems. It is a powerful medicine, which should only be used for short periods and on the advice of a qualified herbal practitioner.

INTERNAL USE

The root of both types of rhubarb contains tannins with astringent properties, so that it can be used in small doses to treat diarrhoea. It also contains purgative substances called anthraquinones, and larger doses are excellent for constipation. Lord Nelson is said to have taken powdered rhubarb root on his voyages so that he would have medicine for every eventuality: for diarrhoea, constipation, irritation of the colon and for infections of the digestive tract. An interesting excerpt from an article in *The Lancet*, dated 3 September 1925, written by a Dr R.W. Duckett, reads: 'acute bacilliary dysentery has been treated in that colony [Nairobi, East Africa] almost exclusively with powdered rhubarb for the past 3 years . . . I know of no remedy in medicine which has such a magical effect.'

In small doses, rhubarb root acts as a tonic to the digestion, stimulating appetite and promoting digestion and liver function. The root of the garden rhubarb is similar in action in its fourth or fifth year to that of the medicinal rhubarb, though it is milder.

The stalks of garden rhubarb may have a mild laxative action and have been popular in Europe for improving the appetite and stimulating the liver. They contain plentiful amounts of vitamin C and potassium, as well as some calcium, but this is not absorbed well due to the oxalic acid contained in rhubarb, which blocks calcium absorption. The presence of oxalic acid has meant that rhubarb has long been contraindicated to people who suffer from arthritis and gout and those prone to kidney or bladder stones. The tartness of rhubarb means that most people are tempted to add a lot of sugar or honey to make it palatable, so it can end up being a rather high-calorie food. Adding sweet cecily leaves to the cooking pot will reduce the amount of sugar needed.

For an early crop, rhubarb can be forced in its second year, by placing a pot or bucket over the crown in February.

Caution: Rhubarb leaves are poisonous to eat.

HOW TO GROW

Rhubarb plants have a life of about 15 years. They like rich soil with plenty of nitrogen. Before planting, prepare the site with organic matter. Plant rhubarb as crowns in March, 60 cm (2 ft) apart. Do not harvest in the first year. From the second year onwards, harvest from April by pulling, rather than cutting, the stems. After harvesting, cover the crowns with straw or dead leaves.

Rhubarb
recipes & remedies

Rhubarb can be very acidic, so it is a good idea to combine it with warming spices such as cinnamon or ginger.

Baked spiced rhubarb

Useful for keeping the bowels regular.

900 g (2 lb) rhubarb
175–225 g (6–8 oz) sugar
2 teaspoons ground cinnamon
4 cloves

Pre-heat the oven to 200°C (400°F or gas mark 6). Cut off the rhubarb leaves and trim the root ends. Wash the rhubarb stalks and chop them into 2.5 cm (1 in) pieces. Place them in an ovenproof dish and sprinkle with the sugar and spices. Cover and bake in the oven for approximaately 30 minutes, until they are tender – but not mushy. Leave to cool, still covered, before serving.

Rhubarb and ginger decoction

An excellent remedy for constipation.

13 g (¹/2 oz) rhubarb
13 g (¹/2 oz) fresh ginger root
570 ml (1 pint) water

Place all the ingredients in a pan, cover and simmer gently for 15–20 minutes. Strain and drink 1 cupful 1–3 times daily, depending on need.

Blackcurrant; redcurrant; white currant *Ribes nigrum; R. rubrum;*

R. rubrum White Currant Group

The original currants were small grapes which came from the vicinity of Corinth. They were known as corinthians or corinth raisins, then corantes, and eventually currants. The fruit now known as dried currants is still a variety of grape. The name currant was transferred to these members of the *Grossulariaceae* family – familiar to us as black, red and white currants – due to the similarity in appearance between them and the small grapes from Corinth.

CURRANTS CAN HELP TO TREAT

- *Arthritis*
- *Atherosclerosis*
- *Catarrh, coughs and colds*
- *Constipation*
- *Diarrhoea*
- *Fevers and flu*
- *Fluid retention*
- *Gout*
- *Infections*
- *Insect bites and stings*
- *Mouth ulcers*
- *Poor appetite*
- *Sinusitis*
- *Skin problems*
- *Sore throats*
- *Swollen joints*

INTERNAL USE

Red and white currants have antiseptic properties, and being rich in vitamin C they help to fight off infection. They can be made into a cooling, refreshing drink to bring down fevers and to speed recovery from infections such as colds, flu and chest infections. Their digestive properties help to stimulate appetite and enhance digestion. Red and white currants have diuretic properties, aiding the elimination of excess fluid and toxins via the urinary system. They make a good cleansing remedy for inflammation and infection of the urinary tract, as well as for arthritis, gout and skin problems.

Blackcurrants have similar properties but have more nutritional value with their abundance of vitamin C: 225 g (9 oz) of blackcurrants has 260 mg of vitamin C, while the same amount of red or white currants has only 55 mg. Blackcurrants have long been used as a folk remedy for colds and flu, coughs and chest infections, as the vitamin C enhances immunity and aids the body's fight against infection. It also helps to expel toxins and phlegm from the bronchial tubes. In addition, the tannins in blackcurrants have astringent properties, helping to dry up secretions throughout the body. They therefore make an excellent decongestant and help to dry up catarrh and clear up bronchial congestion. They have a cooling action, reducing heat and inflammation in the body, helping to bring down fevers. Blackcurrant berries and leaves have a diuretic effect, enhancing the elimination of fluid and toxins and were once popular as a remedy for kidney stones. The resulting cleansing action can be used to good effect for easing the effects of arthritis and gout and for clearing skin problems.

Due to their astringent nature, blackcurrants have been used since medieval times as a remedy for diarrhoea. They contain bioflavonoids, notably some called anthocyanosides, which have an antibacterial action, active against the types of bacteria that often cause diarrhoea and gastrointestinal infection. The crushed skins of dried blackcurrants are powdered and marketed in Sweden as an anti-diarrhoeal drug named *Pecarin*. Also some research has shown that anthocyanosides protect the arteries against atherosclerosis, and thus help to protect against heart attacks and strokes.

EXTERNAL USE

A poultice of blackcurrant leaves used to be applied to swollen or inflamed joints, and a fresh leaf rubbed on to insect bites and stings helps to provide swift pain relief. Blackcurrant rob (*see opposite*) is an old country remedy used to relieve sore throats and reduce fevers.

HOW TO GROW

Currants like a heavy, slightly acid soil and a sunny, sheltered position, protected from birds; they will, however, tolerate shade. They should be planted from November to March, pruned in late summer from their second year onwards, and harvested from June to August. The fruit grows on old wood and can be harvested more easily by cutting the whole branch and picking from it.

Currant
recipes & remedies

Hot blackcurrant juice sweetened with a little honey is a delicious drink for adults and children alike, and a good remedy for fevers and respiratory infections. A tablespoon of blackcurrant jam or jelly in a cup of hot water, taken several times a day, used to be popular as a soothing antiseptic remedy for sore throats and colds.

Blackcurrant vinegar

A good remedy for feverish colds.

450 g (1 lb) blackcurrants
Cider vinegar (see method below)
Sugar (see method below)

Rinse the blackcurrants, place them in a bowl and cover with cider vinegar. Leave to stand for 3 days then press through a sieve. Measure the juice, and for every 570 ml (1 pint) of fluid add 500 g (1 lb) of sugar. Heat gently in a pan, bring to the boil and simmer for 5 minutes, removing any foam that appears. Leave to cool and then pour into a sterilised bottle. Add 1 teaspoon to a cup of water and drink as required when suffering from colds and fevers. Store in a cool, dark place for up to 6 months.

Blackcurrant rob

A good remedy for sore throats.
50 g (2 oz) blackcurrants
450 ml (16 fl oz) water
Honey to taste

Simmer the blackcurrants in the water for 10 minutes, then strain and serve with honey to taste.

Redcurrant and raspberry ice cream

A delicious and nutritious pudding, rich in folic acid and so particularly recommended for pregnant women.

300 ml (1/2 pint) water
350 g (12 oz) caster sugar
1 kg (2 1/4 lb) redcurrants
250 g (9 oz) raspberries
juice of 1/2 lemon
900 ml (1 1/2 pints) double cream

Pour the water into a saucepan, add the sugar and stir with a wooden spoon over a low heat until the sugar is completely dissolved. Turn up the heat, bring to the boil and boil for 5 minutes. Remove from the heat and allow to cool. Remove the stalks from the fruit and place the fruit in a large freezerproof container. Stir in the cooled syrup and the lemon juice. Whip the cream until stiff, fold it into the fruit mixture and transfer to the freezer. Once the mixture starts to harden around the edges, remove from the freezer and whisk well to break up the crystals. Return and freeze until firm. Transfer to the refrigerator about 30 minutes before serving.

Gooseberry *Ribes uva-crispa*

The gooseberry is a relative of the currant. Although it is a dessert friut, it appears on tables less often than the sweeter strawberries and raspberries; not only does it taste quite sour (new, sweeter varieties have been developed) but it is unfriendly to harvest because of its prickles. Some say that its name derives from this fruit's long history of use as an ingredient of a tart sauce to accompany goose – its sourness and acidity compensating for the fattiness of the meat. Others say that the name comes from the Old English name for gooseberry, *grozer* or *grosier*.

GOOSEBERRIES CAN HELP TO TREAT

- *Atherosclerosis*
- *Bowel disorders*
- *Constipation*
- *Heart disease*
- *High blood pressure*
- *Low immunity*

The gooseberry has long been reputed to have cooling properties and used to be prepared in vinegar and used internally and externally to cool inflammatory problems. Gooseberries were given as wine, in a fool or in other extracts to bring down fevers; hence its country name 'fever-berry'. Gooseberry jelly is an old remedy for stimulating a sluggish liver and easing digestion of rich and fatty foods. It was considered a good cleansing remedy because of its effect on the liver and its diuretic action, enhancing elimination of toxins via the bowels and the urinary system. The young leaves of gooseberry bushes can be eaten raw in salads. They, too, are valued for their medicinal properties and their ability to dissolve urinary stones.

INTERNAL USE

Gooseberries are still eaten today for their beneficial effect on the digestive tract. They are high in fibre, which acts as a laxative and helps to remedy constipation and prevent bowel disease such as diverticulitis and cancer. The soluble fibre (pectin) helps to lower cholesterol levels, so if eaten regularly, gooseberries will help to prevent atherosclerosis, high blood pressure and heart disease.

Gooseberries are a good source of nutrition, being rich in vitamins A and C, and containing potassium, calcium, phosphorus and iron. Although the vitamins A and C will help to speed recovery from illness, a lot of added sugar will deplete vitamins and minerals in the body and depress immunity. The vitamins have antioxidant properties, helping to protect against damage caused by free radicals and to slow the onset of the ageing process and degenerative diseases including cancer.

Caution: In some people, gooseberries may aggravate arthritic pain.

HOW TO GROW

Gooseberries can be grown as bushes, cordons or fans and, like blackcurrants and raspberries, they need to be protected from bird damage and should be grown under netting or in fruit cages. They do best in moist, well-drained soil, and will bear the heaviest crop if they are grown with plenty of organic matter in the soil, but no lime, in a sheltered position, with either full sun or partial shade.

Buy 2- or 3-year-old specimens and plant them October to March. Bushes and fans should be planted 1.5 m (5 ft) apart and cordons 38 cm (15 in) apart. Fruit should be thinned from May onwards, and it can be harvested between July and August as it ripens.

In winter, prune young gooseberry bushes to achieve an open centre, as this makes the fruit far easier to pick.

Established trees will also need to be pruned in summer. Lateral shoots should be shortened to 5 or 6 leaves (see page 143).

Gooseberry
recipes & remedies

Sweet gooseberries can be eaten raw, but the acidic ones are more suitable for cooking and for making into jam. Gooseberry leaf tea (follow the method on p. 71) is a diuretic which can help to prevent the formation of kidney stones.

Gooseberry and elderflower jelly

An old remedy for easing the digestion of rich and fatty foods.

2.7 kg (6 lb) gooseberries
20 elderflower heads
1 litre (1¾ pints) water
2.7 kg (6 lb) sugar

Top and tail and wash the gooseberries. Rinse the elderflowers and place them and then the gooseberries in a large pan with the water. Simmer gently for half an hour, or until the fruit is soft. Remove the pan from the heat and stir in the sugar. Bring back to the boil and allow to boil rapidly for about 10 minutes until it reaches setting point. Remove any foam and strain through a sieve or a coarse muslin cloth. Pour into sterilised jars and seal.

Gooseberry fool

An English summer pudding which will help to ease digestion of rich and fatty foods. This recipe can also be made with fruits such as rhubarb, raspberries and blackberries.

450 g (1 lb) fresh gooseberries, topped and tailed
caster sugar to taste
300 ml (½ pint) double cream, fromage frais or egg custard

Put the gooseberries into a pan with a little water and cook over a low heat until softened to a purée. Remove from the heat, stir in sugar to taste and allow to cool. Whip the cream until stiff peaks form and combine it (or the fromage frais or custard) with the fruit. Chill before serving.

Blackberry *Rubus fruticosus*

All parts of the blackberry have medicinal virtues which have been known since at least the time of the ancient Greeks. The physician Dioscorides recommended the whole plant – bark, leaves, root and fruit – as a remedy for wounds and ulcers, tender gums and an acid stomach. The plant is rich in astringent tannins which help to dry up secretions and protect mucous membranes throughout the body from irritation, inflammation and infection. This explains why the fruit, the bark and the leaves have long been used to curb diarrhoea and dysentery, gastritis and colitis, stomach and bowel infections, and bleeding of all kinds.

BLACKBERRIES CAN HELP TO TREAT

- *Anaemia*
- *Arthritis*
- *Atherosclerosis*
- *Bleeding gums*
- *Constipation*
- *Coughs and colds*
- *Diarrhoea*
- *Fevers and flu*
- *Gastritis*
- *Haemorrhoids*
- *Heavy periods*
- *High cholesterol*
- *Minor burns and scalds*
- *Mouth ulcers*
- *Poor appetite*
- *Skin problems*
- *Sore throats*
- *Stomach and bowel infections*
- *Urinary infections*

INTERNAL USE

Blackberries are rich in vitamin C, which helps the body's fight against infection and stimulates the action of the 'mucociliary escalator', the tiny hairs in the bronchial tubes that help to clear foreign bodies and infection from the chest. Combined with the astringent properties of the blackberry, this means that the fruit is excellent for the prevention and treatment of colds and flu, coughs and chest infections, sore throats and tonsilitis, catarrh and sinusitis.

A decoction or tincture of blackberry leaves helps to astringe the lining of the uterus and is used by modern herbalists to reduce congestion in the reproductive tract which contributes to heavy bleeding.

Blackberry preparations of all kinds taste delicious and have the added benefit of enhancing the appetite and improving the digestion and absorption of food. Blackberries are nutritious, rich in vitamins A, B, C and E, folic acid, iron and calcium, most of which (except vitamin C) are not lost during cooking. The pectin (a soluble fibre) helps to ensure regular bowel function and to lower harmful cholesterol levels.

The blackberry can provide a good nutritive tonic for children as well as the elderly since it is easy to digest and assimilate. The iron and folic acid are both excellent for pregnant women, the laxative properties help prevent constipation and the pectin helps to protect the heart and arteries from atherosclerosis.

Blackberries and blackberry leaves have a mild diuretic action, which helps to clear excess fluid and toxins from the body via the urinary system. They can be used to treat urinary infections and also as a cleansing remedy for skin problems, arthritis and gout.

Recent research has discovered more therapeutic applications of the blackberry. It has shown that the bioflavonoids which colour the fruit help the body to fight infection and, like the vitamins A, C and E, have a powerful antioxidant action, protecting the body against damage caused by free radicals and helping to prevent degenerative diseases such as cancer.

EXTERNAL USE

A decoction of blackcurrant leaves is useful as a lotion for treating piles and varicose veins, skin problems such as ulcers, abscesses and boils, for cuts and grazes, minor burns and scalds, as a gargle for sore throats and as a mouthwash for ulcers and bleeding gums. If they are used as a lotion or douche, blackberries can help to treat vaginal discharge and infection.

Caution: Blackberries can cause allergic reactions in some sensitive people as they contain salicylate, a compound similar to the active ingredient in aspirin.

HOW TO GROW

Blackberries do best in partial shade and slightly acid soil. Plant November to March, the earlier the better, 30 cm (1 ft) apart for thorned blackberries, 20 cm (8 in) apart for thornless ones. After planting, cut back all stems to 25 cm (10 in). To increase your existing stock of blackberries, layer the tips of the shoots (*see page 143*). This should be done July to September. Tips will be rooted by November, when they should be cut from the parent plant. Pick fruit from August to October as it ripens. Cut canes to soil level as soon as they have fruited. Blackberries fruit on growth that is at least one year old.

Blackberry
recipes & remedies

Wild blackberries should always be picked well away from traffic as they take up heavy metals and pollution from car exhaust fumes.

Blackberry cordial

A wonderfully warming drink for bedtime; relaxing and helpful in warding off winter ills. Delicious diluted with hot or cold water, or poured neat over stewed apples, apple pie, ice cream, yoghurt or fromage frais.

900 g (2 lb) blackberries, or enough to yield 570 ml (1 pint) blackberry juice

450 g (1 lb) sugar or 6 tablespoons honey
10 cloves
5 slices fresh ginger
1 teaspoon ground cinnamon
7 tablespoons brandy

Press ripe raw blackberries through a sieve to obtain the juice. Place in a pan and add the sugar or honey and spices. Bring to the boil over a low heat, stirring until the sugar or honey has dissolved. Simmer for 5 minutes. Leave to cool. When cold, add the brandy and pour into a sterilised bottle and seal.

Blackberry leaf decoction

Useful for helping to reduce congestion in the reproductive tract, especially that associated with heavy periods.

50 g (2 oz) blackberry leaves
650 ml (22 fl oz) water

Place the leaves and the water in a pan. Bring to the boil and simmer gently for 10–15 minutes. Strain. Take 1 cupful 2–3 times daily.

Blackberry syrup

Good for sore throats, irritating coughs or hoarseness – if you don't have time to make the syrup, try a spoonful of blackberry jam instead.

570 ml (1 pint) double-strength infusion of blackberry leaves (see *page 158*)
650 g (1 lb 10 oz) 1:1 mixture of thin honey and refined sugar

Heat the infusion and honey/sugar mixture in a pan. Stir the mixture as it starts to thicken and remove any foam that forms on the surface. Leave to cool before pouring it into a sterilised bottle and seal. Take 1 cupful 2–3 times daily.

Raspberry *Rubus idaeus*

The raspberry is said to have originated in southern Europe and East Asia but can be found growing wild in many parts of Europe and North America. It is not only the raspberry's exquisite taste but also its medicinal properties that have been valued for hundreds of years on both continents. In the past, raspberries were made into wines, cordials and vinegars for medicinal purposes. Raspberry wine and vinegar were considered good remedies for fevers. The vinegar was used as a gargle for sore throats and was often mixed with water and given to children to speed febrile diseases such as chicken pox and measles on their way.

RASPBERRIES CAN HELP TO TREAT

- *Anaemia*
- *Anxiety and tension*
- *Bleeding gums*
- *Catarrh, coughs and colds*
- *Constipation*
- *Diarrhoea*
- *Fevers and flu*
- *Fluid retention*
- *High cholesterol*
- *Indigestion*
- *Mouth ulcers*
- *Nausea*
- *Pain in childbirth*
- *Sore throats*
- *Urinary infections*

INTERNAL USE

Both the fruit and the leaves have astringent properties and can be used to treat diarrhoea and catarrh. They tone the mucous membranes of both the digestive tract and respiratory system, helping to protect them from irritation and infection. This astringency makes them effective when made into a mouthwash for ulcers and bleeding gums.

For many centuries, midwives encouraged women to drink raspberry leaf tea regularly for the last few weeks of their pregnancy to ease childbirth. Research that began during the Second World War has confirmed that the action on the uterus of raspberry leaves and, to some extent, the fruit as well, is not simply an 'old wives' tale', but is very efficient at easing contractions and helping to ensure a safe and speedy delivery. This is a remedy that is still highly valued by women all over the world today, not only to ease the pain of childbirth but also to speed recovery afterwards.

Raspberry leaves also tone the mucous membranes throughout the kidneys and urinary tract and are useful for preventing infections and fluid retention during pregnancy. They have digestive properties that can be effective in quelling nausea in pregnancy, and their sedative properties provide support to the nervous system, helping to reduce anxiety.

Raspberries are rich in vitamins A and C, and contain calcium, phosphorus, iron, potassium and folic acid. The leaves contain potassium, phosphorus, calcium, magnesium, manganese, copper and zinc. These nutrients are excellent for pregnant women, and because raspberries are easily digestible they are a good food for children, the elderly and those convalescing.

The fruit is rich in fibre, which helps to prevent constipation, and in pectin, a soluble fibre that helps to reduce harmful cholesterol levels. The vitamins A and C, as well as other substances, notably the bioflavonoids, have antioxidant actions helping to prevent degenerative diseases and cancer. One of these bioflavonoids, ellagic acid, is particularly useful since it is not destroyed by cooking.

Caution: Raspberries can cause allergic reactions in some susceptible people as they contain salicylate, a compound similar to the active ingredient in aspirin. The oxalic acid in the fruit can cause kidney and bladder stones in some if taken in large amounts, and it inhibits the absorption of iron and calcium.

HOW TO GROW

Raspberries like well-drained, relatively acid soil, and they prefer a sunny, sheltered position. They will need supporting with stakes and wire (*see page 140*). Raspberry roots go down as much as 45 cm (18 in), so the lower soil should be loosened with a fork before planting. Plant the canes between November and March, 38–60 cm (15–24 in) apart, with 1.2–1.8 m (4–6 ft) between rows. After planting, cut them down to about 25 cm (10 in) to a strong, upward-growing bud. Mulch in early spring, and tie the canes into the wire as they grow. Summer-fruiting raspberries will need protection from birds. Pick the fruit when it is ripe.

Cut the old canes out after fruiting. Thin out the new canes, leaving 5 or 6 of the best on each plant, and tie them in. In late winter or early spring cut the tip of each cane off to just above the top wire – about 1.2 m (4 ft).

Raspberry
recipes & remedies

Raspberries are most delicious and beneficial when eaten raw, although they need to be rinsed carefully first. The leaves can be made into tea.

Raspberry vinegar

A useful remedy for sore throats.

1.5 litres (2 pints) cider vinegar
450 g (1 lb) fresh raspberries
900 g (2 lb) sugar

Pour the cider vinegar over the raspberries and leave to stand for 24 hours. Strain through a sieve or muslin bag. Add 450 g (1 lb) sugar to each 570 ml (1 pint) of juice. Heat slowly and stir until the sugar has dissolved. Skim off any foam and pour into a sterilised bottle and seal. Gargle with half a glassful as necessary.

Raspberry leaf tea

To be taken in the last trimester of pregnancy to prepare for childbirth.

25 g (1 oz) raspberry leaves, rinsed
570 ml (1 pint) boiling water
Honey or sugar to taste
Mint or lemon balm if desired

Place the raspberry leaves in a teapot. Pour over the water, cover and leave to infuse for 10–15 minutes. Sweeten with honey or sugar if required and add a few leaves of mint or lemon balm if desired. Drink 2–3 times daily.

Blueberry; bilberry

Vaccinium corymbosum; V. myrtillus

The bilberry, huckleberry or myrtleberry
(*V. myrtillus*) grows wild on moors and heaths in Scotland, the
north and east of England, and in northern Europe. It is the
cousin of the American blueberry (*V. corymbosum*) – famous
for the delicious blueberry pie that has permeated American
folk culture. Many different species of blueberry grow widely
all over the United States. Bilberries and blueberries are
related to cranberries and grow on bushy deciduous shrubs
that bear their purplish-black fruits with their characteristic
blue bloom in autumn.

BLUEBERRIES AND BILBERRIES HELP TO TREAT

- *Bedwetting*
- *Bleeding gums*
- *Bowel infections*
- *Catarrh, coughs and colds*
- *Cuts and grazes*
- *Diarrhoea*
- *Fevers and flu*
- *Haemorrhoids*
- *Inflammatory eye problems*
- *Mouth ulcers*
- *Skin problems*
- *Sore throats*
- *Thrush*
- *Urinary infections*
- *Varicose veins*

INTERNAL USE

Both the leaves and the fruits of the blueberry
and bilberry bush are rich in tannins which have
an astringent action, helping to dry up secretions throughout the body. They can be used to
heal mouth ulcers, bleeding gums and sore
throats. The fresh juice used to be popular as a
remedy for typhoid and other bacterial infections of the gut, and in Scandinavia dried blueberries or bilberries have long been used to treat
childhood bowel infections. Modern research
has confirmed the value of this, finding high
concentrations of both antiviral and antibacterial compounds in blueberries. It appears that
the tannins are responsible for these actions.
Blueberries and bilberries also contain antidiar-
rhoeal compounds called anthocyanosides,
which are particularly effective at aiding the
body's fight against infections.

The astringency of the fruits and leaves,
together with their diuretic effects, make them
useful for treating urinary problems. Blueberries
contain a natural antibiotic substance that prevents bacteria from adhering to, and multiplying
on, the walls of the urinary tract, and instead
helps to flush them out of the system. They also
help to make the urine more acidic and inhospitable to infecting bacteria.

Blueberries and bilberries also have cooling
properties. Taken as a tea or an infusion of the

jelly or jam in hot water, they help to bring down
fevers and relieve inflammation. By astringing
the mucous membranes throughout the body
they help to protect them from inflammation
and infection, so helping to guard against digestive, urinary and respiratory infections.

Blueberries and bilberries are rich in vitamins
A and C, bioflavonoids and iron. They have long
been used to strengthen the eyes and improve
vision, especially at night, as well as an eyewash
for infections and inflammation of the eyes such
as conjunctivitis and blepharitis. The vitamins
and bioflavonoids in these berries have antioxidant properties, helping to protect the body
against damage caused by free radicals and
delaying the onset of the ageing process.

EXTERNAL USE

A decoction of blueberry leaves can be used as a
mouthwash or gargle for infections in the mouth
and throat, and in a lotion for infected skin conditions and vaginal infections. Their astringent
effect is helpful in lotions for varicose veins and
haemorrhoids, for speeding the healing of cuts
and grazes, sores and ulcers, and for skin conditions such as eczema and acne.

**Caution: These berries can cause allergies in
some people, resulting in swollen lips and
eyelids, and in hives.**

HOW TO GROW

Blueberries and bilberries do best in a very acid,
well-drained sandy soil and a sunny position that
is protected from wind and frost. They are slow
to fruit but should be established after 6 years.
Mature bushes may reach 1.8 m (6 ft) high with
a spread of 1.2 m (4 ft). They should be planted
1.5 m (5 ft) apart, November to March. They do
not transplant well, so it is best to buy container-
grown plants. Do not let them dry out, and water
them with rainwater. Tap water may contain
lime in some areas. Harvest the berries as soon
as they are ripe, from July to September.

Blueberry
recipes & remedies

Blueberries and bilberries can be eaten fresh, but they are more usually made into jams, jellies and compotes.

Compote of blueberries or bilberries

Useful for the treatment of bowel and urinary infections.

900 g (2 lb) berries
10 tablespoons water
3 tablespoons honey

Wash the fruit and remove the stems and leaves. Heat the water and honey together in a pan, boil rapidly for 3 minutes and add the fruit. Cook gently over a low heat for 10–15 minutes or until the fruit is soft. Pour into a dish and serve cold.

Blueberry or bilberry leaf decoction

A good remedy for sore throats and mouth ulcers.

25 g (1 oz) berry leaves
570 ml (1 pint) water

Place the leaves and water in a pan and bring to the boil. Simmer for 10–15 minutes, strain and allow to cool before drinking.

Cranberry *Vaccinium macrocarpon*

The cranberry, a creeping plant with wiry stems that crawl over the soil, bearing attractive red berries, is a relative of the blueberry and bilberry. It is a native of North America and likes to grow in damp ground and peaty soil near acidic bogs. It can be found growing wild but is now widely cultivated in North America and Europe, the cultivated varieties bearing larger, juicier fruit than the wild. The cranberry, like the gooseberry, is sour and tart and is not eaten raw, but has traditionally been valued as an ingredient of tart sauces, eaten to complement fatty meats. It often accompanies the Christmas turkey in Europe and North America.

CRANBERRIES CAN HELP TO TREAT

- *Colour and night vision problems*
- *Constipation*
- *Cystitis*
- *Kidney stones*
- *Low immunity*
- *Poor appetite*
- *Urinary infections*

INTERNAL USE

Cranberries have long been valued for improving the appetite and enhancing the digestion and absorption of food. The sourness of the berries increases the flow of saliva and other digestive juices and thereby activates digestion. The fibre they contain also helps to keep the bowels regular. They have been best known over the last hundred years, however, as a folk remedy for treating infections of the bladder, kidney and urinary tract, as well as preventing and treating kidney stones and gravel.

It was thought that the acidity of the fruit prevented the formation of stones and inhibited infection. The acidity of cranberries is certainly inhospitable to bacteria in the urine, preventing them from reproducing. Research that has been conducted over the last 50 years has actually shown that bacteria cause damage to the urinary system by their adherence to the walls of the urinary tract. Substances in cranberries prevent bacteria from adhering to the walls in this way, and enable them to be easily flushed away out of the system. It has been shown that the regular consumption of cranberry juice can stop an infection in its tracks, even before any symptoms appear.

A daily dose of 1 or 2 glasses of cranberry juice is enough to prevent both kidney and bladder infections in susceptible people, and 2 glasses taken daily can help to treat them. It is best, however, to avoid those commercial brands of cranberry juice that have a high added sugar content. Modern research has also indicated that cranberries can certainly help in the prevention of calcium-type kidney stones. In addition to helping prevent bacteria from adhering to the walls of the urinary tract, cranberries may well perform the same action in the mouth and the digestive tract, bringing about equally beneficial results in these parts of the body. Research continues in these areas.

Further research into the beneficial properties of the cranberry indicates that it contains plenty of vitamin C and other antioxidant substances that help to prevent damage to the body by free radicals. Thus cranberries help to prevent degenerative diseases such as arthritis, heart disease and cancer and to slow the effects of the ageing process. The bioflavonoids contained in cranberries, notably a substance known as anthocyanin, also help to protect against tumour formation and to enhance vision, particularly night vision.

HOW TO GROW

Cranberry plants require a very acid soil and wet, almost boggy, conditions in order to thrive. Add lots of well-rotted organic matter to the soil and water with rainwater, not tap water. In some regions, tap water may contain lime and this will reduce the acidity of the soil.

Cranberry plants do not like to be moved so it is best to buy container-grown specimens and plant them about 60–90 cm (2–3 ft) apart. They are best planted out in garden beds, but they can be successfully grown in containers in areas where the soil is very limey. If cranberries are planted out, spread sand on the soil around the plants to hold down their creeping branches and encourage them to root. Once rooted, they can be cut away and replanted where needed.

Cranberries should be picked in the autumn, before the first frost occurs. They are difficult to pick, so wait until most of the berries have ripened and pick them all at once. They require little pruning – only tidying up is required.

Cranberry
recipes & remedies

Cranberries are too tart to eat raw, but they blend well with apple juice, which makes a low-calorie, nutritious sweetener.

Cranberry and apple juice

Excellent for the prevention and treatment of urinary infections.

2 eating apples
175 g (6 oz) cranberries

Cut the apples into quarters, wash the cranberries and remove their stalks. Extract the juice from the fruit in a juice extractor. Make sure that the apple and cranberry juice are thoroughly mixed, and serve.

Cranberry sauce

To improve digestion, particularly that of meat and poultry.

450 g (1 lb) cranberries
225 ml (8 fl oz) water
110 g (4 oz) sugar

Wash the cranberries, remove their stalks and place them and the water in a pan. Bring to the boil and simmer until the fruit is soft. Pass the mixture through a sieve and return it to the pan. Add the sugar and heat until dissolved. Pour into a container and leave it to cool before serving.

herbs

Both the culinary uses and the medicinal benefits of herbs have been recognised for thousands of years. Versatile and rewarding to grow, herbs can be made into safe, natural preparations. Herbs' marvellous health-giving qualities can help to enhance energy and well-being, whether by a stroll through an aromatic garden, a soak in the bath or a simple herb tea.

Chives *Allium schoenoprasum*

Chives were popular as a culinary and medicinal herb in China as far back as 3000 BC, and are thought to have been brought to Europe by Marco Polo. Early European herbalists were suspicious of these pungent-tasting fresh leaves, which they thought might cause 'evil vapours' in the head. Chives did not become popular until the Middle Ages, when people used to hang the leaves and flowers in bunches from their rafters to ward off evil spirits.

Chives are the smallest member of the onion family, and like their close relatives, leeks, onions and garlic, they contain sulphur and alliin, and an enzyme allinase, that combine to form allicin. This compound has a valuable antiseptic effect, and is an efficient antibacterial, antiviral and antifungal agent. Very often the foods and herbs that were valued in the past for their ability to ward off evil spirits are those with antimicrobial properties that fight off infection. The illnesses we now know to be caused by infections were in the past believed to be the result of invasion by evil forces.

CHIVES CAN HELP TO TREAT

- *Anaemia*
- *Atherosclerosis*
- *Infections*
- *Low immunity*
- *Poor circulation*
- *Sluggish digestion*
- *Stomach and bowel infections*

INTERNAL USE
Chives enhance immunity and aid the body's fight against infection. Their pungent taste has a warming and stimulating effect in the digestive tract, improving appetite and aiding the digestion and absorption of food. The vitamin C and iron content of chives can help to combat infection as well as anaemia.

Allicin, which is found in chives and other members of the onion family, has been indicated by modern research to help to regulate blood pressure and to be of benefit in reducing low-density lipoprotein (LDL) cholesterol which contribute to atherosclerosis. Although chives contain less allicin than their relatives onions and garlic, they are still able to contribute to a healthy heart and circulation, and to support the body's immune system. They are best used fresh.

Chives look attractive in the vegetable and herb garden with their purple pom-pom flowers and bright green grass-like leaves. They make excellent edging plants and good companions for vegetables, fruit and flowers, since their antifungal and insecticidal properties help to ward off pests and diseases.

HOW TO GROW
Chives are hardy perennials that can be propagated by sowing seeds *in situ* in April or May or by planting pot-grown specimens in spring or autumn. Space the clumps about 30 cm (1 ft) apart. Chives will tolerate most soils but they prefer fertile, moisture-retentive soil and full sun. They need to be kept watered, especially in hot, dry weather, and flower heads should be removed in order to stimulate leaf growth.

Chives can be cut as required from March to October. The leaves should be cut to within 2.5 cm (1 in) of the soil.

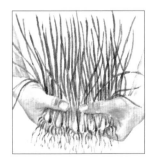

Divide chives every 2 or 3 years by hand in the autumn or early spring. Replant 30 cm (1 ft) apart in well-manured soil.

Dill *Anethum graveolens*

Dill has attractive, aromatic feathery leaves and umbels of tiny yellow flowers, looking and smelling very much like fennel but smaller in stature. Dill comes originally from the Mediterranean and can often still be found growing wild there. The leaves are delicious chopped into salads, vegetable, meat and fish dishes alike, enhancing them with their delicate flavour. The seeds are traditionally used as a pickling spice for gherkins and cucumbers.

DILL CAN HELP TO TREAT

- *Asthma*
- *Babies' sleeping problems*
- *Colic*
- *Constipation*
- *Coughs*
- *Diarrhoea*
- *Flatulence*
- *Indigestion*
- *Muscle tension*
- *Nausea*
- *Poor appetite*
- *Sluggish digestion*
- *Stress-related digestive problems*

The name dill is said to derive from the Saxon word *dilla*, meaning to lull, since dill has an ancient reputation for relaxing infants and young children into a restful sleep. It is a remedy that has particular significance for parents with fractious babies. Its tranquillising properties have been valued since the days of the ancient Greeks and Romans, and its use in this capacity is even recorded in the Bible. The seeds used to be called 'meeting house seeds' since they were chewed during long church services to stop the stomach rumbling. Dill makes an excellent remedy for problems of the digestive system.

INTERNAL USE

The pungent taste and aroma of dill stimulates the flow of digestive juices, whetting the appetite and enhancing the digestion and absorption of food. It also has a mildly warming effect, which acts to release tension and to ensure the proper movement of food and wastes along the digestive tract. Both the leaves and the seeds of dill contain volatile oils that have a relaxant effect on smooth muscles throughout the body. In the digestive tract this helps to release the tension and spasm contributing to colic and wind, indigestion and nausea, constipation as well as diarrhoea. Dill is a vital ingredient in Gripe water, which has been used by generations of mothers to

The tender young leaves of thinned dill seedlings can be used in cooking.

soothe their babies' colic. Traditional gripe water is easy to make: simply add 13 g ($\frac{1}{2}$ oz) of bruised dill seeds to 225 ml (8 fl oz) of boiling water and allow it to infuse. Strain, cool, and offer the baby 15 ml (1 tbsp) whenever it is needed. Gripe water can also be useful for cases of flatulence and indigestion in adults.

Dill's relaxant effect in the bronchial system helps to sooth harsh, irritating coughs and paroxysmal coughing, as well as asthma.

HOW TO GROW

Dill is an annual, which can be propagated by sowing seeds at intervals from April to July to ensure a plentiful supply of fresh leaves. Thin to 25 cm (10 in) apart when the seedlings are large enough to handle. Dill prefers well-drained soil and full sun and should be watered regularly in dry weather. It needs to be planted well away from fennel in order to prevent cross-pollination. Dill can grow up to about 1 m (3 ft) tall. The leaves are ready for picking approximately 2 months after sowing, but they should be harvested before the plant flowers in July or August. Some flowers should be left to go to seed, and these can be harvested when they have turned brown. They can be dried out by spreading them on a tray in a dry, warm place and can be planted in the following spring to produce that year's crop.

Chervil *Anthriscus cerefolium*

Chervil is an attractive aromatic plant, native to the Middle East, south-east Europe and Asia. It is a member of the parsley family (*Umbelliferae*) and has delicate, feathery leaves, umbels of lacy white flowers, and a sweet aniseed flavour and smell. It is often found in traditional cottage gardens, and looks lovely in summer with its pinkish red stems. The leaves are delicious in salads and sauces.

CHERVIL CAN HELP TO TREAT

- *Arthritis*
- *Fluid retention*
- *Gout*
- *Poor appetite*
- *Poor circulation*
- *Sluggish digestion*
- *Tiredness and lethargy*

Chervil is popular in French cookery and is one of the ingredients of *fines herbes*. It is delicious added to soups, fish dishes, eggs and cheese, casseroles and salads, and it can be used interchangeably with parsley. It is best used fresh and added to food or sprinkled on top as a garnish just before serving, since its delicate taste and remedial benefits are easily lost through drying and cooking. It is tasty sprinkled on nettle soup – an excellent "spring cleanser".

INTERNAL USES

Like dandelion, watercress and nettle, chervil has long been valued as a spring tonic, a cleansing herb to clear the body of toxins after the heavy food and sedentary habits of winter. In parts of Europe it is traditionally eaten as a cleansing herb on Holy Thursday as part of Easter preparations, and chervil soup is still eaten on this day in many parts.

In medieval times chervil was a popular remedy for cleansing the liver and kidneys, enhancing the elimination of water and gravel via the urinary system, stimulating the circulation and purifying the blood. It used to be given after falls or blows to disperse congealed blood and to help prevent bruising. It is still used today for its mild diuretic action, increasing the elimination of fluid and toxins. It may help people with arthritis and gout by assisting in the excretion of uric acid.

Thin plants to 15 cm (6 in) apart and water regularly in hot weather.

Chervil also has a mildly stimulating effect on the circulation and may help to enhance lymphatic drainage. By increasing blood flow to and from the tissues, it improves their uptake of nutrition and the removal of toxins – aiding its cleansing action and giving a sense of well-being. This is enhanced by its benefits to the digestive system. Its lovely, sweet and pungent taste stimulates the appetite and improves digestion and absorption. It is a good herb for people with sluggish digestion, particularly the elderly.

EXTERNAL USE

An infusion of chervil leaves used to be popular as an eyewash for sore, tired and inflamed eyes and to soothe skin problems. Traditionally, the washed leaves were applied as a poultice to bruises and haemorrhoids.

HOW TO GROW

Chervil can be grown as an annual or a biennial. It should be sown at intervals of 3 to 4 weeks from spring to early autumn. Seeds germinate in about 2 weeks and leaves are ready to be cut in 6 to 8 weeks. Seeds sown in autumn in a warm sheltered place will be ready for picking in the following spring. Plant seeds 15–20 cm (6–8 in) apart in well-drained soil; chervil seedlings do not transplant well. Chervil does best in partial shade. When cutting, leave some flower heads to encourage self-seeding.

Borage *Borago officinalis*

Borage, a native plant of the Mediterranean region, is sometimes found growing wild in other countries. It has blue, star-shaped flowers, which are much visited by bees, and makes an attractive addition to a herb garden. The young leaves of borage are nutritious and lend a refreshing cucumber taste to salads, while the pretty blue flowers can brighten summer cocktails, fruit drinks, salads and puddings. Borage flowers also look extremely decorative when candied.

BORAGE CAN HELP TO TREAT

- *Allergies*
- *Anxiety and tension*
- *Arthritis*
- *Asthma*
- *Children's infections*
- *Catarrh, coughs and colds*
- *Cystitis*
- *Fevers and flu*
- *Fluid retention*
- *Hormonal problems*
- *Low immunity*
- *Poor lactation*
- *Stress-related conditions*
- *Tiredness and lethargy*

One of the old names for borage was 'herb of gladness' as it has an ancient reputation for lifting the spirits and dispelling gloom and despondency. Its name borage, or *borago*, is said to derive from the Latin *cor-ago*: *cor* meaning heart, or courage, and *ago* meaning I carry or bring; and from *burra*, meaning woolly, a reference to the hairy stems and leaves. There is an old saying 'a garden without borage is like a heart without courage'.

INTERNAL USE

Borage has been used throughout history as a tonic to the heart, to increase strength and vitality, and to clear toxins from the system. Today, borage is still respected for its traditional uses and is added to prescriptions to relieve tension and anxiety, to strengthen the nerves, to lift the spirits and to restore vitality when feeling run down during convalescence. Borage has special significance for the adrenal glands, the organs of 'courage' that secrete adrenaline at times of stress. It helps to support the body and increases its ability to deal with stressful situations.

Borage has a cooling and cleansing effect on the body. By increasing sweat production and through its diuretic action, it clears heat and toxins from the system via the pores of the skin and the urinary tract. It makes a good detoxifying remedy for treating arthritis, gout,

Borage leaves can be dried in the oven at the lowest setting, but keep a check on them since they burn easily.

skin problems and fevers. It is useful in the treatment of such children's infections as measles and chicken pox because it helps to bring out the rash. Its decongestant and expectorant action helps to treat colds, catarrh and irritating coughs. Borage has long been used to enhance milk flow, and modern research into the properties of borage seeds indicates that they are rich in gamma-linoleic acid, a fatty acid vital to the normal function of the hormonal as well as immune system, which may make them useful for treating hormonal problems, allergies and arthritis.

HOW TO GROW

Borage is a stout, hairy annual that can be propagated by sowing seeds outdoors in April or May, 30 cm (1 ft) apart, once the danger of frost has passed. Borage does not react well to being moved, but some people have had success sowing it indoors in individual pots earlier in the year and then transplanting it. In spring, when seedlings are large enough to handle, they should be thinned to 30–45 cm (12–18 in) apart. Borage prefers well-drained soil, in sun or light shade, and it grows 60–90 cm (2–3 ft) high. Borage flowers between June and September and its leaves are ready to be picked about 8 weeks after sowing the seed. It self-seeds freely in the right soil and light conditions.

Marigold

Calendula officinalis

This brightly coloured plant with its bold, orange daisylike flowers is a native of southern Europe and parts of Asia, and has long been a favourite in cottage gardens. In its native sunny climes, the flower was said in Roman times to be seen on every calends, the first day of each month of the year – hence its Latin name *Calendula*.

Calendula has been highly valued as a medicine through the ages. The Romans recognised its ability to throw off fevers and infections and medieval monks prescribed it for bowel problems, liver complaints and insect and snake bites. Doctors in the American Civil War adopted marigolds as a styptic, to stop bleeding and speed the healing of wounds, and in the First World War, calendula flowers were used in dressings for battle wounds, both to stop bleeding and as an antiseptic.

MARIGOLD CAN HELP TO TREAT

- *Bowel infections*
- *Candidiasis*
- *Chilblains*
- *Colds*
- *Colitis*
- *Cuts and grazes*
- *Fevers and flu*
- *Fluid retention*
- *Gastritis*
- *Haemorrhoids*
- *Hot flushes*
- *Low immunity*
- *Peptic ulcers*
- *Period pain*
- *Thrush*
- *Varicose veins and ulcers*
- *Warts*
- *Wounds and skin infections*

INTERNAL USE

Marigolds have astringent and antiseptic properties, are rich in carotenoids, and are able to help the body to fight off a range of infections such as colds, the herpes virus, pelvic and bowel infections, including enteritis, amoebae and worms, and such fungal infections as candidiasis (thrush). In the digestive tract, marigolds can relieve irritation and inflammation and promote healing of the gastric and bowel mucosa, which is useful for treating gastritis and ulceration of the gut as well as colitis and diverticulitis. The bitters stimulate the appetite, enhance digestion and absorption, and improve liver and gall bladder function.

If marigolds are taken in a hot infusion, they increase circulation and promote sweating, helping to relieve fevers, improve blood and lymphatic circulation and enabling the body to expel toxins. Their diuretic action is useful here also, aiding elimination of fluid as well as toxins via the urinary system. Marigolds also have significance for the female reproductive system: they can help to regulate menstruation and ease problems associated with the uterus that can cause painful periods, excessive bleeding, endometriosis and cysts. They are also valuable during the menopause, helping to relieve symptoms such as hot flushes and heavy bleeding.

Caution: Avoid taking marigolds internally during pregnancy.

EXTERNAL USE

Marigolds help to stop bleeding and speed healing of cuts and grazes, and their astringent and antiseptic properties are excellent for helping to heal sores and ulcers, varicose veins and haemorrhoids, minor burns and scalds, chilblains, cold sores and slow-healing wounds.

Deadhead marigolds regularly for a continuous supply of flowers throughout the growing season.

HOW TO GROW

Marigold is a hardy annual propagated by sowing seeds in spring *in situ* 30–45 cm (12–18 in) apart, or by taking tip cuttings in summer and early autumn. It likes well-drained soil and full sun and can grow up to 50 cm (20 in) in height. The flowers should be harvested as soon as they are fully open, and the leaves when they are young.

Caraway *Carum carvi*

Caraway is an attractive member of the carrot family with bright green, feathery leaves and umbels of small white flowers in summer. It is a native of the northern and central parts of Africa, Asia and the Middle East and grows in many parts of North America. The seeds that follow the flowers in late summer and early autumn are deliciously aromatic and a popular spice for flavouring breads, cakes, biscuits and liqueurs. In Germany in particular, caraway seeds have long been used to flavour cheese, cabbage and sauerkraut, soups, rye bread and other baked goods.

CARAWAY CAN HELP TO TREAT

- *Catarrh, coughs and colds*
- *Colic*
- *Constipation*
- *Flatulence*
- *Hiccoughs*
- *Indigestion*
- *Poor appetite*
- *Poor circulation*
- *Sore throats*
- *Tiredness, lethargy*

Caraway seeds have been enjoyed as a food flavouring for thousands of years. Seeds have been found in Mesolithic excavations that date back about five thousand years, and we know that they were used by the ancient Egyptians, Greeks and Romans. They were popular in medieval and Tudor England, too, where the roots were cooked and served like parsnips to 'warm and stimulate a cold languid stomach', the leaves were frequently added to soups and salads and the seeds were baked in bread.

INTERNAL USE

Caraway contains an aromatic volatile oil that is responsible for the rather parsleylike smell of the leaves and the spicy pungent taste of the seeds. It has been used traditionally as a remedy for flatulent indigestion and to prevent colic and dyspepsia. It also stimulates the appetite and, by increasing the flow of digestive juices, improves digestion and absorption. A few seeds, fresh or dried, chewed before or after a meal are enough to have a beneficial effect and they make a good remedy for relieving hiccoughs. Caraway 'comfits' were traditionally made in a copper pan by covering the seeds with a syrup. They were given to children in America to stop them hiccoughing in church. Caraway seed tea can

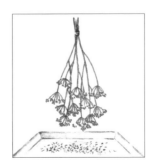

In order to preserve caraway, hang the seed heads upside down over an open container.

help to relieve colic in babies and the tannins in caraway seed have an astringent effect, which can help to curb diarrhoea.

Caraway seeds have a warming effect throughout the body as they increase the circulation. They have long been used for symptoms associated with cold, such as tiredness, lethargy, weak digestion or lowered immunity. They have an invigorating and uplifting effect and their antiseptic volatile oils can help the body's fight against infection. By enhancing digestion they ensure regular bowel function and thereby remove from the gut stagnant food and toxins. Taken in a hot decoction, they can help to relieve colds, coughs and chest infections. A gargle of the decoction will soothe a sore throat.

HOW TO GROW

Caraway is a hardy biennial which can be propagated by sowing seeds in early to late summer and thinning to 20 cm (8 in) apart when the seedlings are large enough to handle. Caraway likes rich, moderately heavy soil and full sun and can grow to 60 cm (2 ft) in height. The leaves can be harvested at any time, the root in autumn or spring of the second year and the seeds once they are ripe (brown) in late summer or early autumn. Caraway self-seeds freely.

Coriander

Coriandrum sativum

Coriander is a highly aromatic and graceful member of the carrot family, native to southern Europe and the Middle East, and is widely cultivated throughout the world for its parsleylike leaves and spicy seeds. Coriander leaves have a very individual flavour, delightful to many, though some may find it hard to appreciate. The ancient Greeks named coriander after a type of bedbug (*koriannon*) because they considered its taste and smell unpleasant.

CORIANDER CAN HELP TO TREAT

- *Allergies*
- *Arthritis*
- *Catarrh, coughs and colds*
- *Chest infections*
- *Colic and griping*
- *Fevers and flu*
- *Flatulence*
- *Gastritis*
- *Indigestion*
- *Inflammatory digestive problems*
- *Peptic ulcers*
- *Poor appetite*
- *Sinusitis*
- *Skin problems*
- *Sore throats*
- *Tiredness and lethargy*

Coriander seeds were some of the earliest to be used in cooking. They are referred to in ancient Sanskrit texts and in the Old Testament as one of the bitter Passover herbs. The ancient Egyptians, Indians and Arabs used coriander seeds, as they still do today, to flavour curries, meat dishes, vegetables and soups, as well as in medicines for the digestion. In China, coriander was believed to confer longevity, even immortality, on those who ate it.

INTERNAL USE

Coriander is useful as a mild antispasmodic and digestive. An infusion of crushed coriander seeds helps to relieve wind and indigestion, colic and griping, and the seeds are often combined with laxatives to prevent any griping the latter may cause. Simply chewing the seed stimulates the flow of digestive juices and so enhances appetite and promotes digestion and absorption of food. Coriander is a good remedy for stress-related digestive disorders, such as gastritis and peptic ulcers.

Coriander is an excellent herb to balance the flavour of hot spicy dishes as it has a cooling effect. In Ayurvedic medicine, both the leaf and the seed are added to prescriptions to remedy problems associated with excess heat, such

Coriander should be harvested in early autumn. The seed heads should be cut off and left to dry on trays in a warm place. When they are dry, the seeds can be shaken loose.

as hot inflammatory joint problems, digestive and urinary problems, conjunctivitis and skin rashes. Fresh coriander leaf tea or juice is used as a remedy for allergies such as hay fever. The fresh leaves are rich in antioxidants, vitamins A and C, as well as in calcium, niacin and iron, helping to enhance immunity and slow the ageing process – just as the Chinese claimed so many centuries ago.

Coriander has an energising effect on the system when taken regularly, which may account for its recommendation as an aphrodisiac and rejuvenative. The seeds have a reputation for lessening the effects of alcohol by their beneficial action on the liver, and for reducing the soporific effect of large meals. In China the seeds are used to break a fever and to stimulate the appetite.

HOW TO GROW

Coriander is a hardy annual which can be propagated by sowing seeds *in situ* in early spring. Thin the seedlings to 25 cm (10 in) apart when they are large enough to handle. Coriander can grow up to 45 cm (18 in) in height and does best in a sunny position in well-drained soil mixed with plenty of well-rotted manure. Water plants well in dry weather to promote the growth of larger lower leaves.

Sweet bay *Laurus nobilis*

Sweet bay, a native of the Mediterranean, is popular in gardens as an evergreen tree or bush, and its shiny aromatic leaves are vital ingredients of a bouquet garni and provide excellent flavouring for soups, stews, casseroles and marinades. Its mildly pungent taste was once used for flavouring custards and milk puddings. For many centuries sweet bay has been highly valued for its aromatic properties and mythical origins, as well as for its cleansing and antiseptic properties.

BAY CAN HELP TO TREAT

- *Arthritis*
- *Bruises and sprains*
- *Catarrh, coughs and colds*
- *Chilblains*
- *Colic*
- *Diarrhoea*
- *Fevers and flu*
- *Flatulence*
- *Fluid retention*
- *Gout*
- *Headaches*
- *Indigestion*
- *Muscular aches and pains*
- *Nausea*
- *Period pains*
- *Poor circulation*
- *Rheumatism*
- *Tiredness and lethargy*

In its native Mediterranean sweet bay can grow as high as 15 m (50 ft), bearing creamy-white blossoms and purple berries. However, in cooler climates it generally reaches no higher than 6 m (20 ft) and rarely flowers.

INTERNAL USE

The medieval herbalist Culpeper recognised the warming nature of bay, which is still valued today to stimulate the circulation and ward off the effects of cold, such as tiredness, lethargy, chilblains, cramps, rheumatism, respiratory ailments and catarrh. Bay's pungent properties are particularly recommended to those who tend to feel the cold and to those with weak digestions. Added to food or taken in a hot infusion, it stimulates the appetite and promotes digestion and absorption, easing indigestion, nausea, wind, colic and diarrhoea. The volatile oils that lend bay its characteristic taste and smell have an antispasmodic action, releasing muscle tension throughout the body and helping to relieve cramp, period pains and headaches. The volatile oils are also antiseptic, aiding the body's fight against infection, and are excellent for respiratory infections – colds, sore throats, coughs and flu. Taken hot, bay reduces fevers, and its expec-

torant properties are helpful for coughs and bronchial congestion; bay has long been used for chronic bronchitis. Bay also has a diuretic effect, enhancing the elimination of excess fluid and toxins from the system, which can help to relieve such problems as arthritis.

EXTERNAL USE

Essential oil of bay can be used diluted in a massage oil to improve circulation, for chilblains, bruises and sprains, aching muscles and cold arthritic joints. A few drops of oil added to a bowl of hot water makes an inhalant for sore throats, colds and coughs.

To achieve a ball-headed shape, the tip of the leader (see page 143) should be removed when the tree is 1.2 m (4 ft) high. The lower laterals should be pruned to 3 or 4 leaves. When the tree is mature, headers should be trimmed to 4 or 5 leaves and lower laterals removed.

HOW TO GROW

Bay can be propagated by taking 10 cm (4 in) cuttings in autumn or by layering established shrubs in late summer or early autumn, but it is easier to buy a plant from a nursery. A bay tree can either be planted in a flower bed and allowed to grow to its natural height or grown in a tub and its height kept down by pruning into a ball-headed shape (*see left*). Bay needs a sunny, sheltered site, and young plants need to be protected from wind and frost. The leaves can be harvested all year around but they are said to be at their most flavoursome in August.

Lavender

Lavandula officinalis

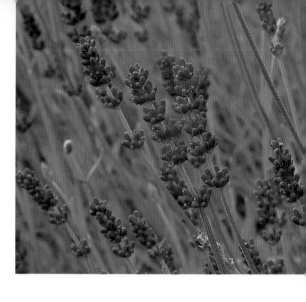

This aromatic shrub, which is a native of the Mediterranean, is one of the most popular scented shrubs in both European and North American gardens. It has been popular since the time of the ancient Greeks, and was used by the Romans to perfume their baths, which explains its Latin name which comes from *lavare*, to wash.

LAVENDER CAN HELP TO TREAT

- *Anxiety and tension*
- *Arthritis*
- *Cuts and grazes*
- *Flatulence*
- *Headaches and migraine*
- *Indigestion*
- *Insect bites and stings*
- *Insomnia*
- *Minor burns and scalds*
- *Muscular aches and pains*
- *Nausea*
- *Nervous palpitations*
- *Poor appetite*
- *Rheumatism*
- *Sinusitis*
- *Sore throats*
- *Stress-related problems*

The medicinal properties of lavender were much appreciated in the 16th and 17th centuries when one writer observed that lavender was 'of especiall use for all the griefes and pains of the head and the heart' and the Italian herbalist Mattioli said 'it is much used in maladies . . . of the brain due to coldness . . . it comforts the stomach and is a great help in obstructions of the liver and spleen.'

INTERNAL USE

Lavender is still considered an excellent remedy for the nervous system and digestion. Its essential oils have a balancing effect on the emotions, calming the mind and lifting the spirits. Taken as a tea or tincture, or by inhaling the volatile oils, lavender makes an effective remedy for anxiety and nervousness, and for all stress-related problems such as headaches, migraine, aching muscles, insomnia, tiredness, palpitations and digestive problems. Lavender also has strengthening properties, restoring energy and vitality to those feeling run down or exhausted.

The plant's relaxing properties can be felt throughout the body. In the digestive tract it releases tension and spasm and can be used to relieve flatulence, nausea, poor appetite and indigestion. The volatile oils in lavender, as in all aromatic herbs, have an antiseptic effect, helping to combat stomach or bowel infections that cause nausea, vomiting or diarrhoea. The oil used as an inhalation or in a vapour rub helps to clear congestion in the nose and sinuses and to resolve repiratory infections.

Lavender has a diuretic action and this, combined with its diaphoretic properties (enhancing sweating), makes it a good cleanser, eliminating toxins via the pores and the urinary system.

Lavender leaves can be picked at any time, but the stems should be harvested as soon as the flowers open. They can be dried by hanging in small bunches in paper bags.

EXTERNAL USE

Lavender can be used to treat cuts, sores and wounds and to soothe mild burns and scalds. It speeds healing by stimulating tissue repair and minimises scar formation. When the oil is applied undiluted it can relieve pain, and it speeds the healing of minor burns and scalds, insect bites and stings. The oil can be diluted in massage oils and rubbed into painful joints, aching muscles and bruises. The tea is a good gargle for sore throats and a mouthwash for ulcers.

HOW TO GROW

Propagate by sowing in late summer or autumn or by taking 10–20 cm (4–8 in) stem cuttings in spring or summer. Thin or transplant to 45–60 cm (18 in–2 ft) apart, or 30 cm (1 ft) apart to make a lavender hedge. Lavender can grow up to 90 cm (3 ft) high and flowers in midsummer. It likes full sun and well-drained, sandy soil and should be pruned in spring or late autumn to prevent straggly growth.

Chamomile

Matricaria recutita & *Chamaemelum nobile*

There are two types of chamomile used medicinally: the annual German chamomile (*Matricaria recutita*) and the perennial creeping Roman chamomile (*Chamaemelum nobile*). The medicinal properties of the two plants are almost identical, but German chamomile is generally preferred since it tastes less bitter.

The principal constituent of both the German and Roman types of chamomile is a blue volatile oil containing azulences, and it is these that lend chamomile its distinctive apple-like fragrance.

CHAMOMILE CAN HELP TO TREAT

- *Anxiety and tension*
- *Arthritis*
- *Babies' colic*
- *Colitis*
- *Conjunctivitis*
- *Cuts and bruises*
- *Cystitis*
- *Earache*
- *Eczema*
- *Gastritis*
- *Hyperactivity*
- *Insomnia*
- *Migraine*
- *Minor burns and scalds*
- *Nausea*
- *Neuralgia*
- *PMS*
- *Sore throats*
- *Stomach and bowel infections*
- *Stress-related digestive problems*
- *Thrush*
- *Urticaria*

INTERNAL USE

The blue volatile oil contained in chamomile has an anti-inflammatory action, helping to relieve inflammation as in for example gastritis, colitis and irritable bowel syndrome. However, chamomile is probably best known as a relaxing herb. It helps to reduce tension and anxiety, relieve insomnia, and is excellent for tense, stressed people, who tend to be over-sensitive, irritable or hyperactive and who are also prone to digestive problems and allergies. It can be used for soothing fractious or over-excited children and encouraging quiet and sleep. Chamomile relieves digestive discomfort and soothes colic in young babies and has analgesic properties that can help to relieve pain and discomfort such as teething. Chamomile's analgesic action also helps to reduce pain in, for example, migraine, neuralgia, muscle tension, arthritis and earache.

Chamomile is also used to treat a range of respiratory infections and fevers, in both adults and children. It has an antiseptic action and by helping relaxation and aiding sleep it encourages the body's natural recovery processes through rest. Chamomile can also reduce the symptoms of PMS, and can be given for mastitis and menopausal changes. During pregnancy it can help to quell nausea, and if it is taken throughout childbirth it can relieve tension and pain.

EXTERNAL USE

Chamomile can help to reduce inflammatory skin reactions such as eczema and urticaria, minor scalds and burns, cuts, wounds and ulcers. It also has the ability to speed tissue repair. Chamomile tea makes a good antiseptic lotion for the skin, a mouthwash and gargle for throat infections, a douche for vaginal problems such as thrush, an eyewash for conjunctivitis and inflamed eyes, and chamomile can also be added to bath water to soothe cystitis. The essential oil can be used in massage oils to relieve the pain of arthritis, neuralgia and muscular aches and pains.

HOW TO GROW

German chamomile is an annual plant that can be propagated by sowing the seeds in the spring or autumn in well-drained, preferably chalky soil, about 20–25 cm (8–10 in) apart. German chamomile flowers throughout the summer months and self-seeds freely. It grows best in full sun and can reach 60 cm (2 ft) in height. Pick the flowers when they are fully open.

Roman chamomile is a perennial plant that can be propagated by sowing seeds *in situ* in spring 30–45 cm (12–18 in) apart, taking 8 cm (3 in) cuttings in summer or dividing plants in the spring or autumn. It grows best if it is planted in light, well-drained soil and in full sun. The leaves can be gathered at any time, and the flowers once they are fully open. Keep it free from weeds and remove dead flowers frequently. For a chamomile lawn plant seedlings about 10–15 cm (4–6 in) apart.

Lemon balm

Melissa officinalis

Lemon balm has a delightful, refreshing scent and flavour, which is excellent for adding to cooling summer drinks and fruit cups and is delicious as a tea. The fresh chopped leaves can enhance a leafy salad and enliven jellies, jams and puddings. Lemon balm has been favoured not only for its sweet taste but also for its many medicinal virtues since at least Roman times. Lemon balm is sometimes called 'bee balm' (*Melissa* is Greek for bee), since lemon balm is loved by bees and when planted by hives will attract new members to the colony.

LEMON BALM CAN HELP TO TREAT

- *Allergies*
- *Anxiety and tension*
- *Children's infections*
- *Cuts and grazes*
- *Eczema*
- *Hay fever and allergic rhinitis*
- *Indigestion*
- *Inflammatory eye problems*
- *Insect bites and stings*
- *Muscular aches and pains*
- *Nausea*
- *Period pains*
- *PMS*
- *Viruses*

The modern use of lemon balm bears out the wisdom of the ancients. Recent research has shown that it influences the limbic system in the brain, which is concerned with mood and temperament, and explains why it has therapeutic benefits in the treatment of anxiety and depression. While having a relaxing and sedative effect, enhancing relaxation and aiding sleep, lemon balm is also rejuvenating and can be used to aid concentration and memory.

INTERNAL USE

Lemon balm has particular significance for the digestive tract, relaxing tension and soothing irritation and inflammation. Lemon balm tea will help to relieve indigestion, heartburn, nausea, wind and diarrhoea, and is excellent for stress-related digestive problems. It is an easy herb to give to babies and children since it has a lovely lemon taste, and will not only calm excitable children at night, but it can also relieve colic and stomach upsets and reduce fevers. Its antiseptic properties can help to fight off invading microbes in children's infections. Lemon balm has been shown to have an anti-viral action effective against herpes simplex

After the first year of growth, cut the stems back to approximately 15 cm (6 in) from the ground in June. They will need to be cut again in October (see right).

(cold sores), mumps and other viruses, due to the polyphenols and tannins in the leaf. The volatile oil also has an antihistamine action, which is helpful for treating hay fever. The relaxing effect of lemon balm can help to relieve period pain and PMS, and if it is taken in the weeks before childbirth it helps relax the uterus and lessen pain during the birth.

EXTERNAL USE

Lemon balm can be used for skin problems such as eczema and for inflammatory eye problems, and its crushed leaves can be applied to soothe insect bites and stings and cold sores. A lotion made from the tea speeds healing and helps to stop infection in cuts.

HOW TO GROW

Lemon balm is a hardy perennial. It can be propagated by sowing seed in April or May in moist soil and full sun and thinning seedlings to 45 cm (18 in) apart. It should be kept watered in dry weather. Lemon balm grows to 60–90 cm (2–3 ft) high and flowers in midsummer. It can be harvested throughout the summer months and plants should be cut back to just above ground level in October.

Mint *Mentha* sp.

Many of the different species of this delightfully refreshing and aromatic herb can be used interchangeably – these include peppermint, lemon mint, spearmint, apple mint and pineapple mint. Although they all have broadly similar medicinal properties and culinary virtues, the action of peppermint is the most pronounced. The mildly pungent taste and smell of this herb have been enjoyed for thousands of years all over the world, not only in the garden but also in the kitchen and the world of perfume and confectionery.

MINT CAN HELP TO TREAT

- *Asthma*
- *Back pain, neuralgia*
- *Catarrh, coughs, colds and chest infections*
- *Cold sores*
- *Diarrhoea*
- *Fevers and flu*
- *Gingivitis*
- *Headaches and migraine*
- *Joint pain*
- *Mouth ulcers*
- *Nausea*
- *Period pains*
- *Ringworm*
- *Sinusitis*
- *Skin infections*
- *Sore throats and tonsillitis*
- *Tiredness and lethargy*

The volatile oils in mint, notably camphor and menthol, have an effective antiseptic action which was valued in the past for treating infections such as tuberculosis, diphtheria and dysentery. Today, research has confirmed the antibacterial, antiviral, antifungal and antiparasitic properties of the volatile oils in mint, which make it a very good remedy for colds, flu, sore throats, tonsillitis, coughs and chest infections.

INTERNAL USE

Mint is excellent for enhancing the appetite and promoting the digestion and absorption of food. It has valuable antispasmodic properties, relaxing tension in the digestive tract that might interfere with good digestion, and easing wind and distension, colic, indigestion, nausea and heartburn, constipation and travel sickness. The astringent tannins found in mint help to protect the lining of the gut from irritation, inflammation and infection, and make it an excellent remedy for diarrhoea, bowel infections and spastic constipation.

Mint's antispasmodic action, coupled with its beneficial relaxing effect on the nervous system, means that it can be used for tension and spasm throughout the body – for asthma, period pains, headaches, muscle tension and insomnia. Its analgesic properties also help to relieve pain: migraine, back pain, sciatica, arthritis and gout all respond well when mint is taken internally. Though relaxing, mint also has a revitalising effect, dispelling tiredness. This is because of its stimulating effect on the circulation, enhancing the nutrition of every cell in the body and ensuring good blood flow to the brain. Taken in a hot tea, mint disperses blood to the surface of the body and causes sweating, making it a first-rate remedy for fevers and for cleansing the body by enhancing elimination of toxins via the pores. Its astringent and decongestant action helps to relieve complaints such as catarrhal congestion, which is why menthol is often found in chemists' shops in decongestant preparations.

EXTERNAL USE

When applied to the skin, mint can help to treat ringworm and herpes simplex (cold sores). It can be used as a gargle for sore throats, and as a mouthwash for ulcers and gum problems. In a massage oil or lotion, it can be applied to help back pain, sciatica, arthritis and headaches.

HOW TO GROW

Mint can be propagated by dividing roots and planting them 25 cm (10 in) apart in autumn or spring, or by obtaining a few pots from a nursery and planting them outdoors 15 cm (6 in) apart. Mint does best in sun or light shade, and it will grow under almost any conditions in almost any soil. It grows up to 90 cm (3 ft) high and flowers in midsummer. It can be harvested between May and October. If you are planting mint in a flowerbed, it is best contained in a pot or bottomless bucket sunk into the ground to prevent its underground runners from spreading too far.

Basil *Ocimum basilicum*

Basil, with its delicious, spicy, clovelike fragrance and flavour, needs little introduction to lovers of Italian cuisine; it is the perfect accompaniment to tomatoes and pasta. Basil is a native of India, South Asia and the Middle East, and it has also been grown throughout the entire Mediterranean region for centuries. It can flourish in temperate climates, but it should be grown either indoors in pots or out in the garden under cloches (clear plastic or glass coverings) until all danger of frosts has passed.

BASIL CAN HELP TO TREAT

- *Anxiety and tension*
- *Catarrh, coughs and colds*
- *Colic*
- *Constipation*
- *Coughs*
- *Cuts and grazes*
- *Diarrhoea*
- *Flatulence*
- *Headaches and migraine*
- *Indigestion*
- *Insect bites and stings*
- *Muscle tension*
- *Nerve pain*
- *Sinusitis*
- *Sore throats*
- *Tiredness and lethargy*

Basil was introduced to Europe from India where basil leaves were often placed in the hands of the dead to ensure a safe journey to the next world. Similarly, since ancient times in Egypt and Greece, basil has been associated with death and it was believed to have the power to open the gates of heaven.

INTERNAL USE

As a medicine, basil has long been valued for its tranquillising properties and its calming effect on the digestive system. It has been favoured as a remedy to clear nervous headaches and catarrhal congestion when taken as a snuff. In Japan, it has long been considered useful for treating the common cold and, in Jewish lore, basil was said to lend strength while fasting, even when held in the hand.

Today, basil taken in food or made into a medicine makes an excellent digestive, enhancing appetite and promoting digestion and absorption. Its flavoursome volatile oils have a relaxing effect throughout the digestive tract, relieving tension and spasm, wind and distension, nausea and indigestion, and diarrhoea as well as constipation. Basil also has a relaxing effect on the nervous system, and makes an excellent natural tranquilliser. It can be used not only for indigestion and colic but also for tight coughs, asthma, nervous headaches, migraine, muscle tension and nerve pain. It can help to relieve anxiety and tension, lift the spirits and enhance energy, and it makes a good remedy for clearing the mind and improving memory and concentration. Basil also, particularly when taken in a hot infusion, has a decongestant action, helping to clear a stuffy head, colds, catarrh, sinusitis and bronchial congestion. Its antiseptic properties enhance the body's fight against infection, whether in the digestive or respiratory system.

EXTERNAL USE

Crushed fresh basil leaves can be rubbed on to minor cuts and grazes, insect bites and stings to aid healing, and basil tea can be used as a steam inhalation for colds and catarrh.

In colder climates, basil grown outdoors should be protected by cloches.

HOW TO GROW

Basil is an annual herb. Propagate by sowing seeds under glass or indoors in spring. Transplant seedlings to a bed or to outside pots once all danger of frost has passed, planting them 30 cm (1 ft) apart. Basil does best in rich, well-drained soil in a warm, sheltered position, grows up to 90 cm (3 ft) and flowers in mid to late summer. Remove the flowers to stimulate bushy leaf growth and harvest from June to September.

Marjoram

Origanum majorana & *Origanum vulgare*

No herb garden would be complete without at least one of the members of the deliciously aromatic marjoram family. Sweet, or knotted, marjoram (*Origanum majorana*), with its white flowers growing in bundles, or knots, up the stem, is the sweetest smelling of all the marjorams, and it bears attractive grey-green leaves. Wild marjoram, or oregano (*Origanum vulgare*), has a stronger flavour than sweet marjoram, especially when it is found growing on mountainsides in warm regions, such as the Mediterranean, the Middle East and Asia.

MARJORAM CAN HELP TO TREAT

- *Anxiety and tension*
- *Catarrh, coughs, colds and chest infections*
- *Chilblains*
- *Colic*
- *Cramp*
- *Fevers and flu*
- *Headaches*
- *Insomnia*
- *Muscle tension and pain*
- *Period pains*
- *Poor circulation*
- *Stomach and bowel infections*
- *Urinary infections*

INTERNAL USE

All members of the marjoram family of herbs can be used to enhance general health and promote a sense of well-being. Their warming and relaxing properties can be felt throughout the entire body, helping to improve circulation and relieving problems such as chilblains and cramps, and releasing the tension in muscles that is responsible for such problems as abdominal pain, menstrual cramps, headaches, and tired, aching muscles.

Marjoram makes a good tonic for the nervous system, helping to reduce tension and anxiety, to lift the spirits, improve energy levels and yet induce restful sleep. It is an excellent remedy for all stress-related symptoms, particularly those associated with the digestive tract. It stimulates the appetite and promotes the digestion and absorption of food. Marjoram can also be taken to relieve indigestion, nausea, wind, spastic colon and constipation.

The volatile oils in marjoram that lend the plant its spicy, aromatic taste and smell are antiseptic in nature and so make marjoram a good medicine for stomach and bowel infections and for a wide range of other infections, whether bacterial, viral or fungal. Marjoram is well worth taking with or after antibiotics, to help to re-establish a normal bacterial population of the gut, and it makes an effective remedy to help

ward off coughs, colds, flu and fevers. Taken as a hot tea, marjoram reduces fevers and acts as an effective decongestant for treating colds, coughs, bronchial and nasal congestion, sinusitis and hay fever.

The antioxidants found in marjoram assist in protecting the body against the ravages of the ageing process, while its diuretic properties help to relieve fluid retention and promote the elimination of toxins from the system.

EXTERNAL USE

When added to rubbing oils, marjoram may be used to help to relieve stiff, aching muscles and painful arthritic joints.

HOW TO GROW

Sweet marjoram is usually grown as a half-hardy annual (one that is unable to withstand severe winter frosts) in temperate areas, but it can be grown as a perennial in warmer climates. Propagate marjoram by sowing seeds under glass and plant the seedlings out in April or May, or once all danger of frost has passed. Space plants about 25 cm (10 in) apart. As an alternative, you can take stem cuttings in summer or divide the rootball in autumn and overwinter in a frost-free area. Marjoram grows best in light, well-drained soil and if it is planted in full sun it can reach a height of up to 60 cm (2 ft).

Parsley *Petroselinum crispum*

Parsley is the most popular of all culinary herbs, not only because of its delicious refreshing taste but also for its health-giving properties. Its popularity is nothing new, for it was valued by the ancient Egyptians, who used it as a remedy for urinary problems, and it was still in favour in the 16th century, when the herbalist Culpeper wrote: 'this herbe is so well known it needs no description.' The great respect our ancestors had for parsley is understandable. It is highly nutritious, rich in vitamins A, B and C and in minerals, including iron, calcium, magnesium, manganese and sodium, as well as in essential fatty acids. To gain most benefit from its nutrients, parsley is best eaten fresh.

PARSLEY CAN HELP TO TREAT

- *Anaemia*
- *Anxiety*
- *Arthritis*
- *Bladder irritation*
- *Bruises and sprains*
- *Colic*
- *Flatulence*
- *Fluid retention*
- *Gout*
- *Headaches*
- *Insect bites and stings*
- *Period pains*
- *Poor circulation*
- *Tiredness and lethargy*
- *Vitamin and mineral deficiency*

The Greek physician Galen wrote 'there is no herb so commonly used at table' and the Roman natural historian Pliny the Younger recorded that 'parsley is in great request'. Parsley certainly stimulates the appetite and promotes digestion and absorption, particularly of protein.

INTERNAL USE

Parsley makes an excellent nutritious tonic when feeling tired and run down, when convalescing or anaemic, because its digestive properties enable those with weak digestions to benefit from its health-giving vitamins and minerals. The volatile oil that gives parsley its characteristic taste and smell has a relaxing effect throughout the body, helping to ease spasm, colic, wind and nervous indigestion as well as headaches, migraine, asthma and an irritable bladder. In addition, parsley's volatile oils, especially apiol (*see page 170*), has been shown to have antiseptic properties that help to combat infections.

Parsley has significance for the urinary system. The root, especially, stimulates the kidneys and has a diuretic action, helping to relieve urinary infections and fluid retention, and helping to clear from the system toxins which contribute to arthritis and gout. Parsley stimulates the uterus and can be used to promote menstruation, to relieve period pain and to promote contractions during labour. Parsley also helps to stimulate the circulation and acts as a warming tonic. It has a supportive action in the nervous system, and can often help to relieve anxiety and mild depression.

EXTERNAL USE

Crushed fresh parsley leaves can relieve the irritation caused by insect stings. When they are cooked in wine and applied as a poultice, parsley leaves are an old remedy for bruises and sprains. Parsley juice can also be applied on cotton wool to relieve toothache or earache.

Caution: Parsley should be avoided by sufferers of kidney disease, and during pregnancy since it may induce contractions.

HOW TO GROW

Usually treated as an annual, parsley can be slow to germinate, taking 4–6 weeks, so it is a good idea to soak the seeds for 24 hours in warm water before sowing them. Sow in March for summer use and again in midsummer for winter use. Plants should be thinned to 15–20 cm (6–8 in) apart once they are large enough to handle. Parsley prefers moderately rich, well-drained soil, in sun or partial shade. It grows 36–50 cm (14–20 in) high and bears flowers in mid to late summer. Leaves can be harvested when plants are over 15 cm (6 in) tall.

Rosemary

Rosmarinus officinalis

This culinary herb is a native of Mediterranean shores, where its aroma can often be smelt on the warm sea air. Since the times of the ancient Egyptians and Greeks, rosemary has symbolised love and loyalty, friendship and remembrance, and has played a part in rituals and ceremonies associated with both marriage and death. Rosemary has long been revered for its strengthening and tonic properties, in particular for the heart, brain and nervous system. This may be explained by the fact that rosemary improves blood flow by stimulating the circulation.

ROSEMARY CAN HELP TO TREAT

- *Anxiety and tension*
- *Arthritis*
- *Asthma*
- *Catarrh, coughs and colds*
- *Chilblains*
- *Fevers and flu*
- *Fluid retention*
- *Hangovers*
- *Headaches and migraine*
- *Indigestion*
- *Infections*
- *Minor burns and scalds*
- *Poor appetite*
- *Poor circulation*
- *Sinusitis*
- *Tiredness and lethargy*

INTERNAL USE

Rosemary has a relaxing effect on the nervous system and a stimulating one at the same time, enhancing energy and concentration. It is an excellent herb to take in the morning.

Rosemary was a favourite in old apothecaries' shops for curing hangovers. By increasing blood flow to the head and releasing tension in muscles, rosemary is a useful herb for headaches and migraines when taken on a regular basis. Its warming and stimulating properties increase the flow of digestive juices and of bile from the liver, aiding digestion and liver function and thereby helping to detoxify the system – an additional benefit when treating migraines.

Rosemary's diuretic properties enhance the elimination of toxins via the urinary system. Modern research has shown that rosemary contains antioxidant substances that may slow down the ageing process and helps prevent degenerative diseases.

Hot rosemary tea makes an excellent remedy to take at the first sign of colds, flu, and coughs and chest infections, and to bring down fevers. The pungent and stimulating properties have an excellent decongestant action which can be put to good use in helping to treat not only catarrh and congestion but also asthma, since rosemary's relaxant effect helps to relieve spasm in the bronchial tubes.

EXTERNAL USE

Rosemary oil, diluted in a base oil and rubbed on to the skin, has an invigorating effect, and by bringing blood to the surface it helps to reduce inflammation and speed healing. It can be used to heal cuts, sores, chilblains, and minor burns. The dilute rosemary oil makes an excellent remedy for soothing arthritic joints and aching muscles, and for treating local infections such as thrush. Rubbing rosemary oil on the temples or adding just a few drops to the bath makes an excellent 'pick me up' to dispel lethargy and drowsiness which is recommended for those wishing to enhance concentration.

HOW TO GROW

Rosemary is a hardy, evergreen perennial, which makes an attractive hedge. Propagate by sowing seeds in early spring, pricking out individual seedlings into pots when they are large enough to handle, and transplanting in May and June. They should be planted about 1 m (3 ft) apart. Alternatively, take hardwood cuttings from June to September. These should be 15–20 cm (6–8 in) long and can be planted in autumn. Rosemary does best in a slightly alkaline, well-drained soil, full sun and a sheltered position, since some forms are slightly tender. Rosemary grows up to 2 m (7 ft) high and flowers from April to May. It can be harvested all year around.

Sorrel *Rumex acetosa*

The young leaves of sorrel, a relative of rhubarb and dock, have a tangy, refreshing taste and make a piquant addition to salads. Sorrel soup is delicate and delicious, and puréed cooked sorrel makes a fine sauce for eating with fish. The name sorrel derives from the old French word *surele*, meaning sour, and the French variety, *R. scutatus* or buckler-leaf sorrel, has long been popular in French cuisine; it is slightly less sharp than the garden sorrel, *R. acetosa*. French sorrel is native to the mountains of central and southern Europe, Turkey and northern Iran, while garden sorrel is the cultivated form of the wild variety, with smaller leaves, that is native to Britain and Europe.

SORREL CAN
HELP TO TREAT

- *Acne*
- *Anaemia*
- *Boils and abscesses*
- *Eczema*
- *Fluid retention*
- *Skin problems*
- *Vitamin C deficiency*

In 1629, the herbalist John Parkinson wrote: 'sorrel is much used in sauces both for the whole and the sicke . . . procuring unto them an appetite unto meat when their spirits are almost spent . . . and is also of a pleasant relish for the whole in quickening a dull stomacke that is overloden with every daies plenty of dishes.'

INTERNAL USE

When eaten before a meal, sorrel leaves stimulate the appetite and aid the digestion of the food that is to follow. They have a laxative effect and a cooling action throughout the digestive tract. These cooling properties were put to good effect in the past as a remedy for fevers and for 'cooling the blood'. They have detoxifying properties, mainly through their diuretic action, aiding the elimination of toxins and wastes via the urinary system. In this way they help to cleanse the blood to remedy skin problems and other toxic conditions. Sorrel leaves are an old-fashioned spring cleansing remedy, like nettles and dandelions, helping to invigorate the system after the sedentary habits and heavy food of the winter months. A decoction of sorrel leaves was also an old remedy for cooling such skin problems as eczema, acne, boils and abscesses. Traditionally, a hot sorrel poultice was often applied to help heal abscesses.

Due to its high vitamin C content, sorrel was once a popular remedy for scurvy, which is caused by a deficiency of vitamin C. It is also used for anaemia since it is rich in iron. Sorrel is a good source of carotenoids, chlorophyll, potassium and magnesium. Carotenoids and vitamin C are antioxidants, which help to prevent damage caused by free radicals and to protect against degenerative diseases and possibly cancer.

Caution: Sorrel is rich in oxalates and should not be eaten regularly by those suffering from kidney disease or stones, arthritis, gout or irritation of the stomach.

HOW TO GROW

Sorrel is a perennial which can be propagated by sowing seeds *in situ* in April. Germination takes approximately 10 days, and seedlings can be thinned to 25 cm (10 in) apart when they are large enough to handle. Sorrel should be divided and replanted approximately every 5 years. Keep sorrel watered in dry weather and remove any flower heads that appear. Leaves can be taken from established plants from March to November, but choose small ones, since the larger leaves may have a bitter taste. Dried sorrel has little flavour, so freezing is probably the best way to preserve it.

Sage *Salvia officinalis*

Sage is a handsome shrub with highly aromatic velvety leaves and whorls of violet-blue flowers. The ancient Greeks called it 'the immortality herb' because it was believed to increase longevity. Sage has long been popular as a culinary herb, famous for the taste it imparts to sage and onion stuffing, and for easing digestion when eaten with rich and fatty foods such as goose. This traditional culinary use can be explained by its first-rate digestive properties.

SAGE CAN HELP TO TREAT

- *Bronchial congestion*
- *Colic, griping*
- *Cuts and grazes*
- *Flatulence*
- *Fluid retention*
- *Gingivitis*
- *Gout*
- *Hot flushes and night sweats*
- *Indigestion*
- *Minor burns and scalds*
- *Mouth ulcers*
- *Nausea*
- *Period pains*
- *Poor concentration*
- *Respiratory infections*
- *Sore throats and tonsillitis*
- *Urinary infections*
- *Vaginal infections*
- *Vomiting*

Modern research has discovered the presence of antioxidant substances in sage, which may explain its beneficial action on the nervous system and its ancient reputation as a brain tonic and longevity herb. By helping to slow the effects of ageing, and by its beneficial effect on the nerves, sage makes an excellent remedy to improve memory and alertness.

INTERNAL USE

Sage can help to treat indigestion, nausea, wind, bad breath and excessive salivation. Its antispasmodic properties relax muscle tension throughout the body, and in the digestive tract this eases colic, stomachache, wind and constipation. The astringent tannins in sage protect the gut lining from inflammation and help to relieve diarrhoea.

Sage's powerful antiseptic properties make it an excellent remedy for a wide range of respiratory infections – for sore throats, colds, flu, coughs, tonsillitis and bronchitis – and a good decongestant at the same time, dispersing catarrh and bronchial congestion accompanying coughs and asthma. It used to be a popular remedy for tuberculosis and other debilitating infections accompanied by profuse perspiration and night sweats, since it can help to reduce secretions, such as mucus and sweat.

Its relaxing properties can be helpful during childbirth and to expel the placenta. Sage's hormone-balancing and diuretic properties are useful during the menopause for hot flushes and night sweats.

Sage makes an excellent cleansing remedy. Its bitter constituents enhance liver function, while the diuretic action aids elimination of toxins via the urinary system.

EXTERNAL USE

Sage's antiseptic and astringent properties can be put to good use as first aid for cuts, scalds and burns, sores and sunburn. Sage also makes an excellent gargle for sore throats, and a mouthwash for ulcers and inflamed gums. Sage can be used as a douche for thrush.

Caution: Although helpful in labour, sage is not recommended during pregnancy or when breastfeeding, as it can inhibit lactation. Sage should not be taken over long periods.

HOW TO GROW

Sage is an evergreen perennial shrub which can be propagated by sowing seeds in trays in early spring. Prick out the seedlings when the first leaves show and transplant them in April or May. Sage grows best in well-drained soil and a sunny sheltered position. It grows up to 75 cm (30 in) tall and flowers in early summer. It can be harvested all year around.

Heeled cuttings of sage can be taken between June and September. Rooting time is approximately 1 month in summer.

Dandelion

Taraxacum officinale

This familiar plant with its bright yellow flowers is often considered a weed when it is found growing in lawns, flower borders and meadows. In Europe it commands a deserved respect and is popular as a spring vegetable. A variety of cultivars are grown in gardens and blanched like endive to create more tender and less bitter leaves. Wild dandelions are found all over the world, comprising about 600 species; they are incredibly resilient plants, partly because they produce so many winged seedheads that they can reproduce without fertilisation.

DANDELION CAN HELP TO TREAT

- *Boils and abscesses*
- *Constipation*
- *Fluid retention*
- *Gall bladder infections*
- *Kidney stones*
- *Liver problems*
- *Mastitis*
- *Poor appetite*
- *Prostate problems*
- *Skin problems*
- *Tiredness and irritability*
- *Urinary infections*
- *Vitamin and mineral deficiency*
- *Warts*

INTERNAL USE

Young dandelion leaves are highly nutritious, rich in antioxidant vitamins A and C, as well as vitamin B, potassium, and iron, while the long milky taproots have long been roasted and ground to make a pleasant caffeine-free coffee substitute. Young dandelion leaves are delicious in salads, and when included in cooked dishes they can be mixed with an equal quantity of spinach leaves to improve their bitter taste.

The French name for dandelion, *pissenlit*, and the old English name, piss-a-bed, inform us in no uncertain terms of the dandelion's renown as a diuretic. The leaves are particularly effective, and make the dandelion an excellent detoxifying remedy, useful for fluid retention, urinary infections and prostate problems. A decoction of both the root and the leaves is an old folk remedy for dissolving kidney stones and gravel.

The bitter taste of the leaves and roots stimulate the bitter receptors in the mouth, which in turn send signals to the rest of the digestive tract and the liver to secrete digestive enzymes and bile. This stimulates the appetite and enhances the digestion and absorption of food. By helping to increase the flow of bile from the liver, the dandelion cleanses it. The young leaves have been eaten in spring for centuries as a cleanser, and a decoction of the root is sometimes used by herbalists to treat liver problems, hepatitis, gall bladder infections, constipation and for symptoms associated with a sluggish liver, such as tiredness, headaches, irritability and skin problems. In China, dandelion root is used specifically to treat mastitis.

EXTERNAL USE

The milky juice of the dandelion stalks can be applied daily over several weeks to cure warts. Applying the leaves as a poultice is a traditional Chinese remedy for treating boils and abscesses. Tea made from the leaves and flowers has long been used as a wash for skin problems such as eczema and acne.

Caution: If sucked excessively by children, the milky juice from the dandelion stalk may cause nausea, vomiting or diarrhoea. Dandelions grown on a lawn which has been treated with chemicals should not be eaten.

HOW TO GROW

Dandelion will seed itself easily in the garden, but it can be propagated by sowing seeds in April. The plants prefer full sun, but they will grow in almost any soil. They can grow up to about 30 cm (1 ft) high and flower from late spring to early autumn. Harvest the young leaves before they grow too large and bitter. Roots are best dug up in the autumn.

Thyme *Thymus vulgaris*

Thyme is native to the western Mediterranean and southern Italian regions, where the smell of wild thyme growing in the heat of the sun is wonderfully pungent. It is the essential oil in thyme that gives it this smell and its rich taste. For years, the main constituent of thyme's essential oil, thymol, has been used as an ingredient in antiseptic throat lozenges, cough remedies, vapour rubs and mouthwashes.

THYME CAN HELP TO TREAT

- *Anxiety and tension*
- *Arthritis*
- *Asthma*
- *Bowel infections*
- *Catarrh, coughs, colds and chest infections*
- *Croup*
- *Cystitis*
- *Diarrhoea*
- *Fevers and flu*
- *Gastro-enteritis*
- *Gingivitis*
- *Irritable bladder*
- *Low immunity*
- *Mouth ulcers*
- *Poor circulation*
- *Sinusitis*
- *Sore throats and tonsillitis*
- *Thrush*

INTERNAL USE

Thyme's antiseptic properties can be put to good use in treating all sorts of infections: coughs, colds, sore throats, tonsillitis, flu, chest infections and gastroenteritis, for example. Taken as a tea, a tincture, or an inhalation of the essential oil, thyme enhances immunity and aids the body's fight against infection. Its expectorant action, combined with its antispasmodic effect, is excellent for moving phlegm out of the chest and easing tight, irritating and hacking coughs.

In the digestive tract, thyme's antispasmodic action releases tension and can be used for treating irritable bowel syndrome and spastic colon. The tannins in thyme have an astringent action which helps to dry up secretions and to protect mucous membranes throughout the body from irritation, inflammation and infection. The astringent action, combined with thyme's antiseptic properties, makes it worth using to treat diarrhoea and bowel infections, and to re-establish a normal bacterial population in the gut after taking antibiotics or in the treatment of systemic candidiasis.

Thyme is a particularly effective remedy for those suffering from poor circulation, and hot thyme tea is an excellent revitalising tonic when taken on a cold day. Recent research has discovered that the volatile oils in thyme have antioxidant properties, protecting the body against damage from free radicals and the onset of degenerative diseases such as arthritis and possibly cancer.

Thyme may help to relieve arthritis by other means as well. It has a generally cleansing effect, since it aids the elimination of toxins via the lungs, bowel, skin and urinary system. Its diuretic and antiseptic properties are useful for treating cystitis when combined with soothing herbs such as marshmallow (*Althaea officinalis*) and for aiding the elimination of uric acid and toxins that contribute to arthritis.

EXTERNAL USE

Thyme's warming and stimulating effects can also be put to good use in liniments for arthritis and muscle pain. As an antiseptic, it can be applied in lotions to cuts, grazes and infections, used in gargles for sore throats, in mouthwashes for ulcers and bleeding gums, and in douches for vaginal infections such as thrush. Using thyme oil in a rub for the chest will help to clear coughs, colds and sinusitis.

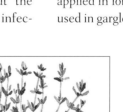

If cuttings are difficult to root, try layering the plant to encourage new sections to root. You can do this by pegging down one stem so that its underside is touching the soil.

HOW TO GROW

Sow seeds in pots in spring and transplant in September. Heeled cuttings can be taken in early summer and rooted in a cold frame. Thyme prefers well-drained soil and a sunny position and grows prostrate or upright to 30 cm (1 ft). Harvest as needed and clip back after flowering and in autumn to encourage bushy growth.

This chapter outlines the principles and processes of organic growing.

the natural kitchen garden

Working with, not against, nature to develop a truly 'green' garden isn't all digging and forking. A union of traditional husbandry and modern technology helps to remove the drudgery and allows gardeners to see their seedlings grow and fruit, knowing that they are producing tasty, chemical-free foods for themselves and their families.

Organic gardening

Growing a kitchen garden is a way to establish a natural connection to the land, and organic gardening makes that connection a positive, creative one. For example, natural pesticides can be made from garlic, onion, seaweed and even from slugs, which can be killed by leaving out a saucer of beer for them to drown in. Crop rotation and companion planting can make the soil rich and productive. Tough perennial weeds can be controlled by covering a plot with mulch.

Organic gardening allows you to feed the land that is feeding you. Vegetable peelings, tea leaves, coffee grounds, mown grass and more can all be composted to make rich fertiliser. Healthy gardens produce robust vegetables, fruits, and herbs that, in turn, help make people healthy.

PLANNING YOUR GARDEN

Before planting your garden, take a pencil and some paper and make a rough plan of your planting design. Every garden is unique, and planning a successful growing area is is not just a matter of personal preferences – a plan must also take into account the type of soil, the aspect of the site, shade from buildings and trees, the space available, and how much of it you wish to devote to fruits, vegetables, and herbs and how much to ornamentals. Plans have been included throughout this section for guidance.

SOIL

Healthy soil is an essential prerequisite for productive growth. Soil, however, is not inert. Rather, it is a living entity composed of sand, stones, clay, mineral nutrients, organic matter and trace elements. Bear in mind, too, that there is also a wealth of micro-organisms contained in soil and that these contribute to its fertility. Anything that destroys these micro-organisms, such as chemical pesticides, renders the soil less fertile.

Healthy soil

The key to maintaining soil fertility and structure is a good supply of humus. This is decaying vegetable matter provided by plants that have died, and adds nutrients and bulk to the soil. Humus can also be applied manually in the form of compost or manure, and its presence encourages the activity of bacteria, fungi and the other micro-organisms and invertebrates in the soil. The action of these micro-organisms releases the nutrients from the decomposing matter, which then dissolve in the soil water and are absorbed by the tiny hairs at the root tips of plants.

The best way to keep soil healthy is by continually growing plants in it. The roots of the plants keep the soil broken up, allowing air and moisture to circulate freely, which is vital for the supply of nutrients to the roots. If left fallow (uncultivated), clay soils will dry hard or become muddy, while sandy soils will either dry out, with a consequent danger of soil erosion, or rain will dissolve nutrients in the soil and leach them away. It is crucial not to walk or drive equipment on the soil as much as possible; compacted

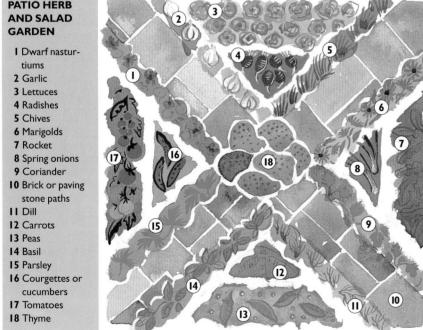

PATIO HERB AND SALAD GARDEN

1 Dwarf nasturtiums
2 Garlic
3 Lettuces
4 Radishes
5 Chives
6 Marigolds
7 Rocket
8 Spring onions
9 Coriander
10 Brick or paving stone paths
11 Dill
12 Carrots
13 Peas
14 Basil
15 Parsley
16 Courgettes or cucumbers
17 Tomatoes
18 Thyme

soil will form a crust, preventing oxygen from reaching the roots of plants.

UNDERSTANDING YOUR SOIL
Soil types

To get the best from your garden, it is important to learn what kind of soil you have. As you get to know your soil, you will be able to feed and plant it appropriately. There are four main types:

1 *Clay soils* are heavy, rich in nutrients that are locked up because of lack of air and freely moving water. Plant roots find it difficult to penetrate. It takes a long time to heat up in the spring and has poor drainage. It is very difficult to dig both when it is wet and when it is hard and dry (and best not attempted). Clay soil needs plenty of humus and some sand to improve its structure and release its nutrients. Humus can be dug into the soil or added in the form of an organic mulch – a layer of garden compost or other organic matter spread over the soil surface (*see pages 124–5*).

Clay soil tends to be acid (*see below*) and, if it is, will benefit from a light spreading of lime over the surface in autumn before planting the following spring. Never apply lime at the same time as manure, as they react chemically and disperse the nitrogen. Lime should not be dug in, and plants should not be planted directly into soil that has just been spread with lime. Heavy soils (when cultivated) are suitable for plants that need rich soil: leafy crops including beans, brassicas, peas and potatoes.

To prepare: Dig in late autumn or early winter so that frost can break up the lumps over the winter. Incorporate plenty of humus to lighten its structure and allow air in; the addition of garden compost, manure, leaf mould or sharp sand will, over several years, improve drainage.

2 *Sandy soils* are easy to work and warm up quickly in spring but they dry out easily and tend to be deficient in nutrients, particularly potassium, which are easily

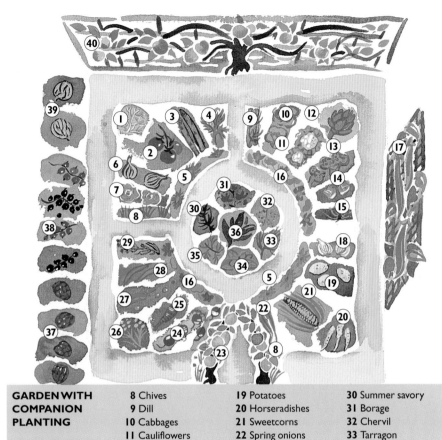

GARDEN WITH COMPANION PLANTING

1 Wormwood	**8** Chives
2 Tomatoes	**9** Dill
3 Asparagus	**10** Cabbages
4 Parsley	**11** Cauliflowers
5 Marigolds	**12** Artichokes
6 Onions	**13** Broccoli
7 Lettuces	**14** Brussels sprouts
	15 Anise
	16 Nasturtiums
	17 Runner beans
	18 Garlic
19 Potatoes	**30** Summer savory
20 Horseradishes	**31** Borage
21 Sweetcorns	**32** Chervil
22 Spring onions	**33** Tarragon
23 Apples	**34** Basil
24 Radishes	**35** Southernwood
25 Carrots	**36** Sage
26 Tansies	**37** Raspberries
27 Peas	**38** Red/blackcurrants
28 Dwarf beans	**39** Gooseberries
29 Hyssop	**40** Apples

washed out of the soil. They also tend to be slightly acid and require humus to help retain water. The addition of garden compost and/or well-rotted manure will add nutrients to the soil.

To prepare: If the soil is too acid, add lime in autumn, as for clay soils. Dig in the late winter or early spring in order to prevent winter rains leaching out the nutrients. Add garden compost and/or well-rotted manure at the same time. Once the ground is planted, mulch all crops well to preserve moisture in the soil.

3 *Chalk soils* are alkaline. They tend to dry out easily and benefit from mulching (apply over well-watered ground). They are fairly fertile but may lack nitrogen.

To prepare: Dig in garden compost or well-rotted manure and peat (or peat substitute) in early spring. To increase nitrogen, dig in a 'green manure' (*see pages 128–9*) of peas, annual lupins or comfrey.

4 *Loam* is the type of soil all gardeners aim to achieve: a well-balanced mixture of clay, silt and sand with a good structure, a high fertility and humus content, good water retention and drainage, easy to work and perfect for most crops. Almost any soil can reach this ideal state if it is worked well over a long period.

Testing for pH

As well as understanding what type of soil you have, you will also need to know

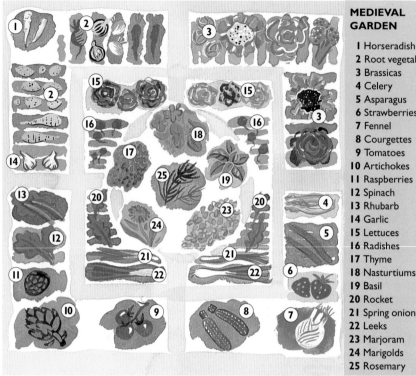

whether your soil is acid, alkaline or neutral, and this may vary from one part of the garden to another. A pH (potential of Hydrogen) test is available from all garden stores and is easy to use. Soil acidity is measured from 0 to 14. An average-to-normal (neutral) soil has a pH of 7; lower indicates an acid soil; higher an alkaline one. Acid soils will suit potatoes, strawberries and raspberries; slightly acid to slightly alkaline soils suit such plants as beetroot, broccoli and cauliflower.

If your soil is very acid or alkaline, you may find it deficient in certain nutrients. Acid soils can be corrected by adding a top-dressing of lime. Mushroom compost is suitable for this because of it lime content. Alkaline soils are harder to correct, but benefit from well-rotted manure. Mushroom compost and lime should obviously be avoided.

Nutrients in the soil

Healthy plants need certain essential elements that should naturally be present in the soil. Any lack or imbalance of these can cause deficiency diseases. The three main requirements for healthy plants are nitrogen, phosphorus and potassium. Nitrogen is required for healthy green leaves and stem growth; phosphorus for good root growth and for the production of fruits and seeds; and potassium protects plants from diseases and helps to maintain healthy growth.

Plants also require calcium, magnesium (needed for the production of chlorophyll) and sulphur, as well as trace elements (or micronutrients) such as manganese, iron, zinc, copper, and molybdenum, all of which should exist in minute quantities in the soil. They can all be obtained from garden compost or well-rotted manure.

Deficiencies in the soil

Deficiencies are usually caused by a lack of good organic matter in the soil and the use of chemical fertilisers, which upsets the natural balance of minerals. A lack of nitrogen leads to stunted growth, while a lack of potassium leads to an increased

susceptibility to disease as well as to discoloration of the edges of leaves.

In order to avoid or remedy deficiencies, it is important to adopt a good regime of composting and adding organic matter to the soil. In extreme cases, wood ash will supply potassium and comfrey liquid will supply nitrogen. Excesses of potassium, calcium or nitrogen bring their own problems, since they create deficiencies of other nutrients, so it is important to aim for a healthy balance.

Plants may also fail to thrive because the soil you plant them in has the wrong pH. Blueberries like very acid soil (pH 4.5 to 5.2). Potatoes like acid, too, doing well in soil with a pH of 5.3 to 6.0. Strawberries, raspberries and asparagus like it slightly acid, and broccoli prefers a pH of 6.4 to 7.0, slightly acid to neutral. Beets, on the other hand, like slightly alkaline soils with a pH of 7.5 to 7.8.

Too much water can be worse than too little, and some plants like full sun while others prefer partial shade. Pay attention to your plants' individual needs and they will do well for you.

Drainage

Poor drainage can be a problem where there is heavy clay soil. This problem will be compounded if the soil is often trodden on, since this causes compaction. Signs indicating poor drainage include horsetail on neglected sites, puddles left after rain, and moss. Poor drainage is bad for plants because excess water deprives the roots of oxygen and the necessary bacteria cannot thrive. As a result, plants will fail to grow well and may wither and die. (See page 127 for information on how to improve soil drainage.)

IMPROVING YOUR SOIL
The purpose of digging

The general purpose of digging is to improve the texture of the topsoil by breaking up heavy soils, improving aeration and drainage, adding humus in the form of garden compost and/or well-rotted manure, digging out perennial weeds and digging in annual weeds before they run to seed. Digging is particularly necessary on poor soil and on soil that is being prepared for cultivation for the first time.

It is essential when digging to avoid mixing the infertile subsoil with the fertile topsoil (the colour of the subsoil will be noticeably lighter). You should also avoid digging when the soil is dry, since any moisture that is present will be lost in the process. Roughly dig heavy clay soils in late autumn or early winter so that the frost can cause the water in the earth to freeze, expand and, thus, break up large clumps. Dig light soils in early spring, incorporating lots of organic matter.

The no-dig system

A debate rages about whether to dig at all, and there are a number of good reasons for not digging once the ground has been initially prepared. After one thorough double digging, with large amounts of garden compost or well-rotted manure incorporated, further organic matter can be provided annually as a mulch or top-dressing. A mulch laid on the surface (*see below*) will be taken down into the soil by earthworms and decomposed by micro-organisms to add humus to the soil and so increase its fertility; it will also protect the soil from drying out. A no-dig system is certainly better for light soils, where it is important to retain moisture, and it is obviously ideal for permanent crops (such as fruit bushes or asparagus) where

the surrounding soil can be forked over and watered before a mulch is laid on the surface. It also obviates the necessity of walking or driving equipment on the soil and so risking compaction.

Raised beds fulfil the same purpose and are particularly useful where there is poor drainage. They are constructed so that even the centre can be reached from an adjacent path: the maximum width should be 1.2 m (4 ft) and they should be 30–75 cm (12–30 in) high. The walls can be built of any suitable building material – anchored railway sleepers, for example, bricks or stone. They must be well constructed so that they do not collapse if you lean on them or give way under the weight of the soil they are retaining. If drainage is a particularly bad problem, it is best to make the walls slightly higher and put a good layer of sand, gravel and stones on the bottom. Top up with good soil, lots of organic matter (garden compost or well-rotted manure), and sharp sand if this is needed for extra drainage.

Organic mulches

As an alternative to digging garden compost or very well-rotted manure into the soil in order to maintain its fertility, it can be laid on the surface in the form of a mulch to a depth of 5–10 cm (2–4 in). You can also use leaf mould, grass cuttings or mushroom compost to add humus to the soil (*see the following list*).

This system relies on the activity of earthworms to do the digging for you. The worms take the humus down into the topsoil and their little tunnels provide drainage and allow access for oxygen, while the worm casts provide extra nutrients. The ground should be wet before a mulch is applied, since mulching helps to conserve moisture. A mulch also keeps the soil warm, provides nutrients and controls annual weeds by depriving them of light. It will not, however, control perennial weeds, which need to be dealt with by hand.

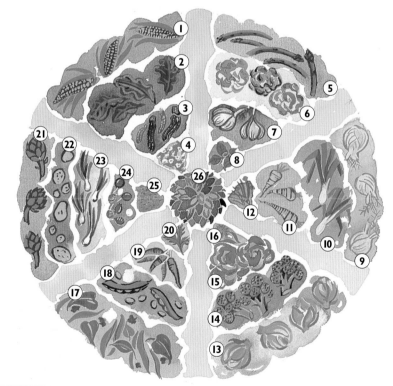

WHEEL-SHAPED POTAGER	6 Lettuces	14 Broccoli	22 Potatoes
	7 Garlic	15 Cabbages	23 Spring onions
	8 Basil	16 Marigolds	24 Radishes
1 Sweetcorns	9 Fennel	17 Runner beans	25 Thyme
2 Spinach	10 Leeks	18 Broad beans	26 Bay tree
3 Courgettes	11 Parsnips	19 Carrots	
4 Chamomile	12 Chives	20 Parsley	
5 Asparagus	13 Brussels sprouts	21 Artichokes	

Good organic mulches:
- Garden compost (*see page 127*).
- Well-rotted farmyard manure (cow or horse dung mixed with straw or hay). Horse manure with wood shavings can also be used as a mulch, but this must not be dug into the soil since the shavings inhibit plant growth.
- Mushroom compost, which tends to have a high lime content and so should be avoided near lime-hating plants. It should not be used year after year.
- Leaf mould, which is excellent for improving the soil texture but is deficient in nutrients.
- Composted straw and hay. Layers of uncomposted straw can also be used to protect plants from frost.
- Commercial forest bark.
- Coir compost, which is made from coconut fibre.
- Seaweed, which is very rich in nutrients. It can be collected from beaches where there is no pollution.

Digging

Single digging to one spade's depth – or one 'spit', which is about 30 cm (1 ft) – is done to incorporate garden compost or well-rotted manure in ground that has previously been cultivated.

Standard double digging to two spades' depth – or two 'spits', which is about 60 cm (2 ft) – is best suited to previously uncultivated plots in order to break up compacted soil, improve drainage, remove deep roots of perennial weeds, such as bindweed and horsetail, and improve fertility by incorporating garden compost or well-rotted manure. Double digging breaks up the soil to a deeper level and is, therefore, appropriate where deep-rooted crops are to be grown, but it is mainly useful because it provides a good preparation of uncultivated soil for planting. However, some experts do not recommend double digging because there is a danger of the valuable topsoil, which contains most of the soil bacteria, earthworms and organic matter, becoming mixed with the less fertile subsoil (*see pages 124–5*). Careful double digging, following the instructions shown below and opposite, ensures this does not happen.

Single digging

1 *Dig a trench to a depth of one spit across the width of your plot, and reserve the soil in a wheelbarrow or on some plastic sheeting.*

2 *Scatter compost evenly in the bottom of the trench.*

3 *Dig an adjacent trench, filling the first trench with the soil from the second, forking it well to mix it with the compost. Do not leave any compost on the surface.*

4 *Scatter compost evenly in the bottom of the second trench.*

5 *Dig a third trench and repeat the process until the allotted space has all been composted. Fill the last trench with the soil reserved from the first trench.*

Double digging

1 *Dig a trench one spit deep across the width of your plot and reserve the soil in a wheelbarrow or on some plastic sheeting.*

2 Using a fork, break up the soil at the bottom of the trench to the depth of another spit.

3 Add a layer of compost evenly on top of the broken soil.

4 Dig an adjacent trench, using the soil from the second trench to fill the first.

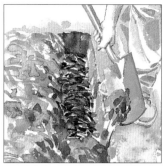

5 Repeat the process until the allotted space is dug and composted. Fill the last trench with the soil reserved from the first trench.

Preparing an uncultivated or neglected plot

When taking over a new patch, the soil will probably lack nutrients and a good structure. It will first need double digging, incorporating lots of garden compost and/or well-rotted manure. You should test for acidity and ascertain the type of soil in order to determine how best to improve it.

If there are lots of perennial weeds, covering the whole area with old carpet or thick black plastic for one growing season should get rid of most of them, except perhaps bindweed and horsetail, which may need two growing seasons – their roots can go down 60 cm (2 ft) or more. Otherwise, double dig (*see opposite and above*), carefully removing as many roots as possible as you go.

Improving drainage

To improve drainage on an unprepared site, use standard double digging, adding sharp sand or coarse grit to the garden compost or well-rotted manure that is forked into the second spit. Drainage should gradually improve as organic matter is added to the soil over a period of time. If this has no effect and the soil remains waterlogged, there is a clear need to construct a drainage ditch or lay pipes. An easier alternative is to make raised beds (*see page 125*).

Garden compost

The decomposed organic matter provided by garden compost is an invaluable source of nutrients and humus for the soil. It is also a marvellous means of recycling kitchen waste and all manner of greenery from the garden.

Ingredients that are good to add to the compost heap include vegetable and fruit peelings from the kitchen, dead cut flowers from the house, tea leaves and coffee grounds, thinnings and prunings, spent annual plants, grass cuttings, cut nettles, cow parsley, bracken, rhubarb leaves and annual weeds.

Grass cuttings serve a particular purpose on a compost heap – if the heap is well constructed, then the heat generated by the decomposition of the cuttings (caused by bacterial activity) will be high enough to kill the roots of bindweed and other perennial weeds (such as couch-grass, ground elder and dock) and weed seeds. If you are not able to construct a compost heap in such a way that these high temperatures are achieved – in the range of 65–70°C (150–158°F) – then avoid including weed seeds and the roots of perennial weeds in the heap.

Concentrated poultry, goat and rabbit manure, or chopped comfrey can be added in layers to activate the compost.

Avoid putting woody material on the compost heap. Instead, shred it and use it as a mulch for roses, strawberries and raspberries. Don't put cooked food of any type on the heap (since this may attract rats and other animals), or soil (shake it out of the roots of weeds) or sawdust. Diseased plants should be discarded.

How to construct a compost heap

There are several ways to achieve a well-built compost heap. You can construct or buy a wooden compost box, and a variety of good plastic compost bins is also available. These have lids to retain moisture and heat, but are open at the bottom to allow air to circulate and worms to work their way up from the ground; their activity is important in the process. Since the worms also take the compost down into the soil, a portable bin has advantages. It can be moved annually and the nutrient-rich soil underneath planted up.

Ideally, you should have two bins – one with compost ready for use, and the other left with new waste material to compost down. While this second one is being used, the first can be refilled, covered and left to compost in turn.

First, decide on the type of bin you want. Whether you buy or make a bin, bear in mind that a good compost pile needs to be about 90 cm (3 ft) across and the same deep. If it is smaller than this, it will not generate enough heat to kill weed seeds and harmful bacteria. At the bottom of the bin, make a layer of woody material, such as twigs or bush clippings. Over this, make a second layer, about 15–20 cm (6–8 in) thick, of green material – grass cuttings mixed with vegetable trimmings and green garden waste, for example. Then put down a layer of brown material, such as dead leaves. Ideally, chop up the dead leaves first by running them through a shredder or even running over them with a mower. Sprinkle on some mature compost or well-rotted manure and then repeat the green and brown layers until the pile is at least 90 cm (3 ft) deep.

Don't bother with so-called compost activators – all the micro-organisms that are needed exist naturally in the material of the heap. Do not add lime, since this will upset the essential carbon-nitrogen balance of the heap. If you leave it undisturbed, the compost will be ready to use in 6 to 12 months. However, if you turn it frequently (once a week, for example), you can have usable compost in as little as 8 to 12 weeks.

Manures

Manures, another form of decomposed organic matter, also help to maintain the fertility of the soil, as well as providing humus. Manures will improve the condition of the soil, add nutrients and help to protect against drought. By supplying decomposing organic matter they, as with compost, provide food for the micro-organisms living in the soil, which, in turn, release nutrients for the plants to take up through their roots. However, an excess of manure in the soil will cause it to become too acid – requiring an application of lime to compensate.

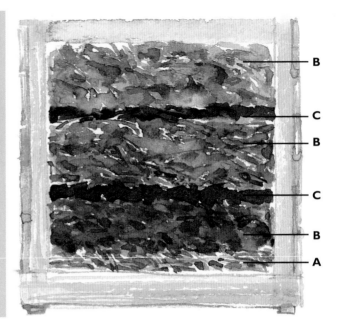

COMPOST HEAP

A Woody material such as twigs and bush clippings.

B Green material such as lawn mowings, green garden waste and vegetable trimmings.

C Brown material such as dead leaves.

Green manures are quick-growing leafy crops, such as mustard, lupins, borage, comfrey and buckwheat, that can be raised over a short season and then dug back into the soil in order to enrich and condition it. These manures can also be used to help retain nutrients in fallow ground, which is often susceptible to leaching. The sappy stems and leaves of the plants break down quickly, adding extra humus and nutrients to the soil and encouraging the activity of earthworms. Winter crops such as winter tares and Hungarian grazing rye will help to protect the soil so that it is not left open to the elements, when nutrients can be washed out of the soil.

All green manures will prevent the loss of nitrogen from the soil, while decomposing lupins and winter tares add valuable extra nitrogen thanks to the nitrogen-fixing bacteria found in their roots. However, these crops must always be cut before they go to seed – usually at a height of about 20 cm (8 in). They are useful when grown on areas that would otherwise be left bare after the main food crops have been harvested. They will deter, or even kill, annual weeds by starving them of light.

Green manures for spring sowing

Mustard is very good for new plots and recently cleared allotments, but it should not be grown year after year as it can encourage clubroot. Seeds should be sown thickly between April and July, and plants dug in when they reach 30 cm (12 in) in height (in about 4–5 weeks).

Mustard will deter wireworms (the larvae of click beetles), which attack the roots of carrots and potatoes, and will also ward off snails. However, as with cabbage, mustard is a crucifer, and may increase the incidence of clubroot if this is already a problem.

Lupins are a good crop to cultivate before planting a strawberry bed, since their roots have phosphorus-gathering fungi. Sow seeds between April and July. Dig in the plants before they flower and before they become too stemmy.

Vetches are all members of the pea family and they add valuable nitrogen to the soil. Purple vetch (*Vicia atropurpurea*), common vetch (*V. sativa*) and hairy vetch (*V. villosa*) choke out weeds as well as feed beneficial insects. They also yield substantial amounts of organic matter. Seeds should be sown in the early autumn or spring.

Buckwheat (Fagopyrum esculentum) is principally used to attract to the garden bees and hoverflies, which then feed on aphids. Buckwheat is a particularly suitable crop for heavy clay soils and has attractive white flowers, which look decorative in the garden. Sow seeds between April and July.

Green manures for winter sowing

Hungarian grazing rye (Lolium perenne) is a good crop for sandy soils because it has an extensive root system that will help to hold water and nutrients in the soil. It is a useful crop to plant before planting potatoes or members of the cabbage family. Sow seeds between early August and the end of October. Dig in the plants in April.

Winter tares (Vicia sativa) are a member of the pea family and add nitrogen to the soil. These plants are frost-resistant but because they are soft they rot down easily. Sow seeds between August and October and chop them down when they are 30–40 cm (12–16 in) high (in March or April). Alternatively, sow seeds between March and May, to dig in in July.

Animal manures

These contain faeces, urine and bedding materials from animals and poultry, and are rich in nitrogen and phosphorus. They also supply trace elements and bacteria as well as humus, which helps to provide good soil texture.

Horse manure is usually available from a local stable or a friendly horse-owning neighbour, and consists of a mixture of horse dung and straw. It tends to be wet and heavy to move but has the advantage of being mainly free from pesticides. If it is well rotted, it can be dug straight in, but it often requires rotting down for at least a year. It should be stacked on top of a plastic sheet to collect the liquid that will drain out. Position it against a wall or mound it up, and compress the heap as much as possible by treading it down in

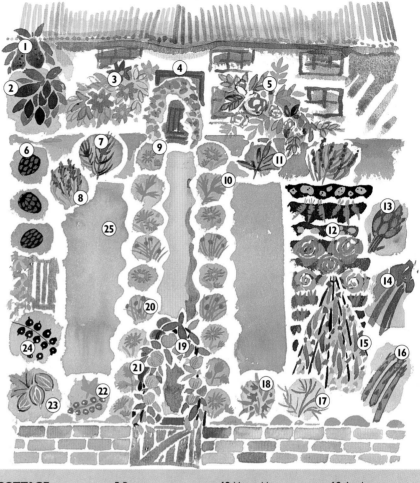

COTTAGE GARDEN			
1 Pears	5 Roses	12 Vegetables	19 Apples
2 Plums	6 Raspberries	13 Artichokes	20 Chives
3 Clematis	7 Rosemary	14 Rhubarb	21 Coriander
4 Nasturtiums	8 Lavender	15 Beans	22 Redcurrants
	9 Marigolds	16 Asparagus	23 Gooseberries
	10 Parsley	17 Fennel	24 Blackcurrants
	11 Sage	18 Borage	25 Lawn

order to exclude air. Hose it down if it is dry, and cover it with plastic or a corrugated sheet in such a way that the rain will drain off, to prevent nutrients being leached out from the heap. Covering it will also prevent nitrogen leaking out in the form of gas and will trap in bad smells. If the manure is dung and wood shavings (not straw), this should not be dug in, but can instead be used as a surface mulch once it is well rotted.

Poultry manure, if you can obtain it from a poultry breeder, usually comes in the form of deep litter incorporated with straw, and is rich in potassium, nitrogen and phosphorus. It is normally dry and easy to transport. It is rich and concentrated so you should only use a 10-litre bucket per m² (2-gallon bucket per square yard), dug into the soil in autumn or spring. Poultry manure that is not from deep litter is even more concentrated and should be used very sparingly – only as a top-dressing or as a compost heap activator. If possible, avoid poultry manure from factory farms because it may contain traces of antibiotics and hormones. Free range is best.

VERTICAL GARDEN

1 Raspberries	8 Tomatoes	17 Chamomile	27 Pears
2 Peas	9 Red/ Black currants	18 Rosemary	28 Plums
3 Nasturtiums	10 Marigolds	19 Damsons	29 Rhubarb
4 Lettuces	11 Blackberries	20 Carrots	30 Artichokes
5 Radishes	12 Thyme	21 Potatoes	31 Pumpkins/squash
6 Spring onions	13 Parsley	22 Dill	32 Strawberries
7 Rocket	14 Coriander	23 Sage	33 Climbing squashes
	15 Basil	24 Cherries	34 Runner beans
	16 Trailing nasturtiums	25 Marjoram	35 Ballerina apples
		26 Peaches	

check this at the source. Stack pig and cow manure as you would horse manure. *Goat and rabbit manures* are both good compost activators. Goat manure is rich in potassium and nitrogen; rabbit droppings in nitrogen and phosphorus.

Leaf mould

Leaf mould provides wonderful humus and generally improves soil fertility. It is an excellent mulch and also an environmentally friendly peat substitute. This material contains fewer nutrients than compost or manure but can either be used as it is or combined with grass cuttings or chopped comfrey leaves to increase the nutrient content of the soil.

Leaf mould kept for one year is good enough to dig into soil and after two years it can be used as potting compost. Oak and beech are the best leaves for making leaf mould. The leaves of holly, holm oak, laurel and conifers should be avoided because they do not rot down well.

How to make leaf mould

Leaf mould is made through the action of fungi, which need no oxygen. To speed up the rotting process and enrich the compost you can mix it up with grass cuttings, equal parts of chopped comfrey or urine. Construct a frame for a leaf mould heap with stout posts at the corners and wire netting to make the sides. The main object is to stop the leaves blowing about, though it also helps if they are kept damp. You can make smaller quantities of leaf mould in plastic rubbish bags, which can be kept in a shed or a corner of the garden (make sure there are no weeds mixed in). This is the best method for making comfrey leaf mould for potting compost (*see page 146*). It breaks down more quickly than if left in the open, and should be ready to use in a few months.

Mushroom compost

This is compost that has been prepared and used by commercial mushroom

Pigeon manure is another possibility, and it is usually dry and easy to transport. It should not be put directly on to the garden, but used on the compost heap as an activator. It is best stored in a plastic (not metal) dustbin and sprinkled on top of a layer of green kitchen waste or grass cuttings (*see pages 127–8 for how to build a compost heap*). Avoid breathing in the dust, since it can cause lung disease.

Pig and cow manures, as with poultry manure, is best obtained from an organic farm, since manure from factory farms may contain antibiotics and pesticides. Farmers sometimes add copper sulphate to pig feed, which is toxic to the soil – so

growers, who sell it off, either in bulk or in small bags, after they have harvested their crop of mushrooms. It is usually based on horse manure, with a mixture of lime, peat and straw with dried blood added to it. The mushroom grower will probably also have added pesticides or other chemicals – these may possibly be organic, but it is always best to check before buying. Mushroom compost provides humus that tends to be lacking in nitrogen because it has been used up by the mushrooms. It is not advisable to use mushroom compost year after year because of its lime content; nor should it be used on alkaline soil or anywhere near lime-hating plants.

Peat substitutes

Peat is sterile (contains no weed seeds), rich in humus, helps to lighten heavy soils, and plant roots readily find a way through it. It is also light and clean to transport, is a good base for seed and potting composts and is useful for storing vegetables. However, peat is a finite resource and to continue to use it would cause irrevocable damage to the environments from which it is extracted. As a result, much work has recently gone into finding good substitutes.

For improving the soil, you can substitute well-rotted manure, garden compost or leaf mould; you can also buy shredded bark, mushroom compost, composted and dried animal manures, and coir compost (or coconut fibre). (*For alternatives to peat for use as a mulch, see pages 125–6, and for alternatives to peat used as a homemade seed or potting compost, see page 146.*)

WEED CONTROL

PERENNIAL WEEDS

It is best to attempt to remove deep-rooted perennial weeds before planting; once the garden is planted, the weeds

CITY GARDEN

1 Peas
2 Bush basil
3 Peppers
4 Chillies
5 Tomatoes
6 Rocket
7 Radishes
8 Coriander
9 Mint
10 Ballerina apple tree
11 Peach tree
12 Strawberries
13 Lettuces
14 Chives
15 Parsley

will be far harder to get rid of, although continual cutting down will eventually weaken and kill them. Perennial weeds include couch grass, bindweed, ground elder, nettle, creeping thistle, creeping buttercup, horsetail, dock and dandelion.

There are several ways of clearing persistent weeds from a new site:

1 You can double dig and remove all the roots you can by hand. In fine weather you can leave them on the surface to dry, then rake them up and discard them, or compost them if your compost heap gets hot enough to kill them.

2 You can rotovate the site if you have the space and time. This chops up the weed roots, and if you do this regularly over a period of time most weeds will gradually become exhausted and die. However, the chopped roots of bindweed, ground elder and couchgrass, will not die – each piece will resprout.

3 You can cover the plot with old carpet or black plastic, making sure that it is well buried, or held down with stones at the edges to stop it lifting in the wind. This method kills weeds by light starvation. The covering is best put down in very early spring and left for one whole growing season. A thick mulch of newspaper between soft-fruit bushes, held down with stones or about a 15 cm (6 in) layer of straw, will deter couch grass and creeping buttercup.

4 Nettles are weeds but they make excellent fodder for the compost heap, where they work as an activator, and they can also be turned into an excellent liquid manure (*see page 136*). In addition, nettles provide a good habitat for caterpillars, and also for aphids, which provide food for ladybirds. For all these reasons it is worth keeping a corner of the garden for nettles – and the young shoots make a delicious and nourishing soup.

5 Ground elder, introduced to Britain by the Romans as a cure for gout, can be killed by growing Mexican marigold (*Tagetes minuta*) alongside; the exudations from its roots are poisonous to ground elder.

6 Weeds with long, anchoring taproots, such as docks and dandelions, can be lifted out with a spade. The easiest time to do this is in February or March, when the soil is moist and when they have less

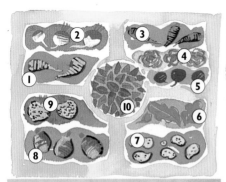
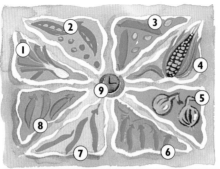
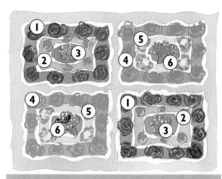

CROP ROTATION Bed 1		
1 Parsnips	5 Beetroots	9 Celeriac
2 Turnips	6 Spinach	10 Bay tree
3 Carrots	7 Potatoes	
4 Lettuces	8 Swedes	

CROP ROTATION Bed 2		
1 Leeks	5 Onions	8 Mange tout
2 Peas	6 Dwarf beans	peas
3 Broad beans	7 Runner	9 Sun dial
4 Sweetcorn	beans	

CROP ROTATION Bed 3		
1 Red	3 Calabrese	6 Broccoli
cabbages	4 Green	
2 Brussels	cabbages	
sprouts	5 Cauliflowers	

hold on the soil. If the root breaks, however, it will sprout again. They will also be weakened by continual cutting. Docks can be cut back in the first week of June and then again in September.

ANNUAL WEEDS

Annual weeds appear in succession from early spring. Learn to recognise them and deal with them as soon as they appear. Groundsel, chickweed and speedwell can all be hoed or hand-weeded. Meadowgrass is best hand-weeded because it will resprout from the root.

GENERAL MAINTENANCE

- Mulching helps to prevent the growth of weeds by depriving them of light.
- Always deal with weeds before they flower and seed. Hand-weed or hoe while they are still small.
- When preparing soil for planting, dig in annual weeds by turning them under the soil and burying them, or pull them up and add them to the compost heap.
- Between shrubs, fork weeds into the ground or hoe.
- Between tender plants, vegetables and herbs, hoe or hand-weed.
- Try to keep the soil in cultivation so that weeds have nowhere to grow.
- Hoe only 1.5 cm ($\frac{1}{2}$ in) deep to prevent damage to roots of nearby plants.

- If possible, hoe in warm weather when the weeds will quickly wilt on the surface. Avoid hoeing if it looks as if it might rain.

CULTIVATION

CROP ROTATION

Crop rotation means growing different crops in different parts of the vegetable plot in annual succession. Crops benefit and deplete the soil in lots of ways, and crop rotation helps to prevent the soil becoming exhausted as well as discouraging disease.

Crop rotation depends on grouping vegetable crops as 'families', according to their type and also to the demands they make on the soil. Different plant families require different elements from the soil, or the same elements but in different quantities. A crop rotation can be organised over a 3-, 4- or even a 5-year period, depending on how many crops you want to rotate. A 3-year rotation is most common in small gardens, but a 4-year rotation is preferable if space allows.

Vegetables for rotation are categorised into root crops and tubers; brassicas; alliums; and legumes. Roots and tubers are usually divided into early and main crop potatoes in one plot and all other roots

(and tomatoes) in another, though it is perfectly possible to grow them in one plot. Members of the allium family (onions, shallots, leeks, garlic) and courgettes (which are usually grown with the allium family) will be in another, brassicas in a third and legumes in a fourth.

Crop rotation is a good, balanced organic approach to vegetable gardening. It prevents the depletion of the same nutrients year after year (which can result in a need for chemical fertilisers), and improves the general fertility of the soil. For example, potatoes will help to break up the ground on a new plot during the first year, and will grow well even in poor soil. These can be followed in the second year by legumes, which have nitrogen-fixing nodules on their roots. These legumes – cut down after cropping, with the nitrogen-fixing roots left in the ground to rot, and extra compost or well-rotted manure added – prepare the way for the 'hungry' brassicas in the third year. In a 4-year rotation, these can then be followed by planting other root crops that are less nitrogen-hungry. Lettuces as well as other quick-growing crops such as salad onions, spinach, French beans, peas and radishes, can be grown as follow-ons or fill-ins (catch-crops) after the main crop has been harvested so that land is always under cultivation.

Crop rotation helps to control soil-borne pests and diseases, which tend to run in families. Cabbage family clubroot spores, for example, can live in the soil for 20 years, but even a 4-year rotation will help to check them. White rot found on onions and scab on potatoes are kept in check by rotation, which also helps to protect against eelworms on potatoes.

When using crop rotation you need to apply common sense. Plant what you enjoy eating and what grows well in the conditions that prevail in your garden, and choose disease-resistant varieties that are suited to your soil. You will also need to leave room for permanent crops such as rhubarb and asparagus. Crops all mature at different times, so plan for a planting succession: spring cabbage, kale and leeks can be put in after main crop potatoes have been harvested in late summer; early carrots, leeks and celery can be put in to follow early potatoes in June or July. Catch-crops, such as radishes or spinach, can fill in anywhere.

Crop families

Brassicas: broccoli, Brussels sprouts, cabbages, cauliflowers, kale, radishes, and turnips.
Legumes: beans (broad, French, haricot, scarlet runner) and peas.
Root crops: beetroots, carrots, celery, parsnips, swedes, Jerusalem artichokes, turnips and potatoes.
Alliums: garlic, leeks, shallots and onions.

Rotation plans

Three-year plan: The rotation is as follows: in the 2nd year, Bed 1 moves on to the plot previously occupied by 3, Bed 3 moves on to the plot previously occupied by 2, Bed 2 moves on to the plot previously occupied by 1, and so on (*see below*).
Bed 1 Root crops – such as beetroots, carrots, potatoes, parsnips, Jerusalem artichokes – can be followed by spinach or lettuces to fill in
Bed 2 Legumes – such as beans, peas – and also celery, onions, leeks

Bed 3 Brassicas – such as Brussels sprouts, cabbages, cauliflowers, broccoli

Four-year plan: The rotation is as follows: in the 2nd year, Bed 1 moves on to the plot previously occupied by 4, Bed 4 moves on to the plot previously occupied by 3, Bed 3 moves on to the plot previously occupied by 2, Bed 2 moves on to the plot occupied by 1, and so on (*see below*).

Plan A
Bed 1 Roots – celery, carrots, parsnips, potatoes, swedes, turnips – as well as peppers, celeriac and tomatoes
Bed 2 Legumes
Bed 3 Brassicas
Bed 4 Leeks, onions, shallots, garlic
Plan B
Bed 1 Early and main crop potatoes
Bed 2 Brassicas
Bed 3 Legumes
Bed 4 Other roots – beetroots, carrots, parsnips, Jerusalem artichokes, salsify – as well as onions

THREE-YEAR PLAN

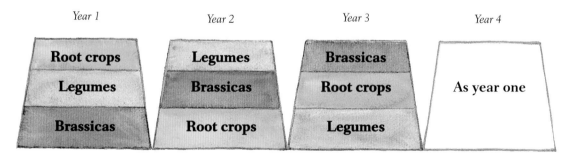

Year 1 — Root crops / Legumes / Brassicas
Year 2 — Legumes / Brassicas / Root crops
Year 3 — Brassicas / Root crops / Legumes
Year 4 — As year one

FOUR-YEAR PLAN

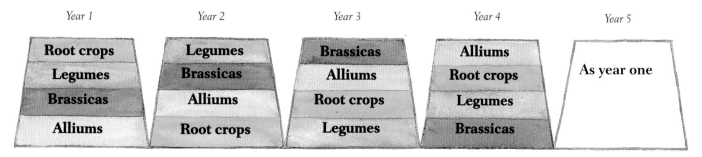

Year 1 — Root crops / Legumes / Brassicas / Alliums
Year 2 — Legumes / Brassicas / Alliums / Root crops
Year 3 — Brassicas / Alliums / Root crops / Legumes
Year 4 — Alliums / Root crops / Legumes / Brassicas
Year 5 — As year one

Courgettes and pumpkins can either be planted with the onion family or with the root crops.

COMPANION PLANTING

Companion planting is a great addition to crop rotation. It is based on the simple principle that all living things are interdependent and that several plants are mutually beneficial to each other. This interrelationship can be beneficial in different ways: plants used for hedges provide warmth and shelter to others nearby; some plants attract pollinators and predators such as ladybirds and lacewings to the area; highly scented vegetables and herbs, and flowers rich in essential oils, deter pests by confusing the scent. For example, onions planted in a bed adjacent to carrots deter carrotfly and French marigolds help to prevent eelworm on potatoes. Aromatic herbs such as lavender, tansy and sage deter ants; rosemary, thyme and peppermint deter cabbage butterflies and slugs – as do French marigold, garlic and onions. Artemisias discourage moths and insects that attack brassicas and carrots, and rue's unpleasant smell keeps away most pests. Tall plants such as sunflowers and sweetcorn can provide support for crops like peas, beans and squashes; those with leafy ground cover will keep the ground cool and moist for others that require those conditions. There are beneficial influences that are provided by plants underground as well as above ground: some have exudations from the roots that inhibit weeds; some fix nitrogen in the soil, which is beneficial to other plants; root channels made by root hairs and larger roots provide pathways through the soil for other plants, and once the original plant dies it provides nutrients that line these passageways.

Companion planting tends to help most where there is a high density of plants in the soil, thus increasing yields and deterring the presence of weeds

Plants	Good companions	Poor companions
Apples	chives, garlic, horseradishes, nasturtiums, tansy	
Apricots	basil, horseradishes, tansy	
Asparagus	anise, basil, parsley, tomatoes	
Beans	anise, brassicas, calendulas, carrots, celeriac, celery, cucurbits, potatoes	fennel, garlic, onions
Brassicas	anise, beetroots, celeriac, celery, dill, French beans, garlic, nasturtiums, onions, peas, potatoes	radishes, strawberries, tomatoes
Carrots	anise, coriander, chives, garlic, leeks, lettuces, onions, peas, rosemary, sage, tomatoes	dill
Celery	anise, beans, brassicas, dill, leeks, tomatoes	
Cucurbits	anise, beans, chives, marjoram, nasturtiums, peas, radishes, sunflowers, sweetcorns	potatoes
Currants	tansy	
Gooseberries	tomatoes	
Leeks	carrots, celeriac, celery, garlic, onions	
Lettuces	anise, calendulas, carrots, cucurbits, onions, radishes	
Onions and garlic	beetroots, lettuces, parsley, strawberries, summer savory	beans, peas
Parsnips	anise, garlic	
Peaches	garlic, nasturtiums, tansy	
Peas	beans, carrots, cucurbits, potatoes, radishes, sweetcorns, turnips	garlic, onions
Potatoes	beans, brassicas, calendulas, horseradish, peas, sweetcorn	curcubits, tomatoes
Radishes	anise, chervil, lettuces, mustard, nasturtiums, peas	brassicas
Raspberries	calendulas, tansy	
Spinach	most things, particularly strawberries	
Strawberries	beans, borage, garlic, leeks, lettuces, onions, sage, spinach	brassicas
Tomatoes	anise, asparagus, basil, calendulas, carrots, chives, dill, garlic, marigolds, nasturtiums, onions, parsley	brassicas, kohlrabi, potatoes
Turnips	peas	

through light starvation. It enables you to create a beautiful garden in which the plants live together in harmony and reciprocity – a garden full of colour, when marigolds or nasturtiums are interplanted with vegetables, and beds are surrounded by aromatic herbs.

Companion planting can be approached in two ways: either by planting crops in rows (rows of carrots interplanted with rows of onions, for example); or in adjacent beds. It is important to space plants so they all get adequate light and nutrients and can be harvested with ease. There are some minor problems that can occur when using companion plants with different soil preferences. Herbs, for example, tend to prefer a light sandy soil while most vegetables need rich soil with plenty of humus. Cropping times can differ, meaning that harvesting one crop must be done carefully so as not to damage the companion crop. A good plan needs to be made if this system is to be undertaken methodically and work well.

Vegetables in an ornamental planting

For thousands of years, flowers have been grown alongside food crops or medicinal plants – for adorning altars, for their beauty, to combat smells, or, most commonly, because they had medicinal or other virtues themselves. It is possible to change this emphasis in a small garden so that some food plants are grown in an otherwise ornamental border. This is easily done by leaving a small area in the front of the border which can be prepared for smaller vegetables, such as the ornamental cabbages, lettuces, French beans, basils and so on. Larger plants (broad beans, scarlet runner beans, climbing French beans or tomatoes) can be grown on supports further back along with globe artichokes, which are themselves attractive, tall plants.

There are several advantages to mixed gardening in this way. It not only protects

POT PLANTS			
1 Lavender	5 Thymes	10 Dandelions	15 Trailing nasturtiums
2 Sorrel	6 Parsley	11 Rocket	16 Basil
3 Chamomile	7 Chervil	12 Lettuces	17 Coriander
4 Variegated mint	8 Wild strawberries	13 Garlic	18 Chives
	9 Radishes	14 Marigolds	19 Fennel

vegetables from pests and diseases, but it is also convenient in very small gardens or where few vegetables are needed.

Container planting

Growing foods and herbs in containers is another and quite feasible way of dealing with a small space – even a patio garden, roof terrace or a balcony. Pots should be placed in a sunny position, near a warm wall or house that will protect the plants from cold and wind. Herbs are often

grown in this way, but many fruits and vegetables can also be grown like this: lettuce, cucumbers, rocket, tomatoes (such as 'Gardener's Delight'), French beans – for which the pot must be at least 25 cm (10 in) deep – early dwarf peas, strawberries (in strawberry pots), squashes (for which the soil must be loam-based) and peppers. Most herbs are ideal, except for the really large ones such as angelica or borage. A bay looks most attractive in a terracotta pot, and even fruit trees can be grown in containers: dwarf apple trees can be grown outside, while dwarf peaches and even lemon trees can be kept in a greenhouse in winter and taken outside in the summer. Most bush and cane fruits can be grown in containers if necessary. All like sheltered, sunny places in which to grow.

Use pots filled with organic compost and you will need to make sure that the plants are watered regularly. It is also a good idea to use water-retaining granules in the compost, since pots and grow bags dry out surprisingly quickly in summer if the weather is hot.

Pots need to be free-draining, with crocks or stones placed in the bottom, and are best elevated a little, on bricks or stones, to allow the free circulation of air.

ORGANIC FERTILISERS
These fertilisers are good for 'quick fixes' for your plants; they will not improve the soil in the way that garden compost or well-rotted manure will, since they provide no bulky material, no humus, and are easily washed out of the soil. They come in the form of liquid manures or powdered concentrates.

Liquid manures
Comfrey (Symphytum officinale) or Russian comfrey (*Symphytum uplan-dicum*), which is richer in minerals, makes an excellent weekly feed for potatoes and tomatoes. Roughly fill a plastic or fibreglass water butt with cut comfrey (you can get 3–4 cuttings a year from your plants), and fill the butt with water. A butt with a tap at the side is best. After 2–4 weeks you will get a very black, slimy (and smelly) mess. Strain this liquid off to provide a very concentrated feed rich in potassium. Dilute it to 20 parts water:1 part liquid comfrey before use. *Nettle liquid* is so nutritious (only low in phosphorus) that it is nearly a complete fertiliser. It is made by the same process as for comfrey, using about 1 kg nettles

A TRADITIONAL VEGETABLE GARDEN

1 Lavender	15 Sorrel	27 Vegetable bed for rotation I (brassicas)	37 Rhubarb
2 Lawn	16 Lemon balm		38 Fennel
3 Bay tree	17 Mint	28 Raspberries	39 Rosemary
4 Runner beans	18 Sorrel	29 Black- and redcurrants	40 Pumpkins and marrows
5 Bush Basil	19 Caraway		
6 Purple Basil	20 Knotted Marjoram	30 Gooseberries	41 Asparagus
7 Chervil	21 Thyme	31 Blackberries	42 Strawberries
8 Chives	22 Garlic	32 Cucumbers and tomatoes	43 Spring onions
9 Dill	23 Sage		44 Pears
10 Fennel	24 Chamomile	33 Compost heaps	45 Cloches
11 Coriander	25 Vegetable bed for rotation I (roots)	34 Apples	46 Potatoes
12 Parsley		35 Horseradish	47 Lettuces
13 Oregano	26 Vegetable bed for rotation I (legumes)	36 Artichokes	48 Rocket
14 Borage			49 Chicory

to 10 litres water (2 lb nettles to 2 gallons water). Nettles collected in the spring are best. Strain off the liquid after 2 weeks and dilute 10:1. If it is used to water in when transplanting, diluted nettle liquid will boost growth and further applications during the growing season will encourage abundant fruiting.

Seaweed liquid is good for tomatoes and also where plants are showing signs of any sort of deficiency. It contains all the trace elements and can be sprayed on to the leaves or fed directly into the soil.

Powdered concentrates

Soft rock phosphate should be used in preference to the 'superphosphates'. This provides slow-release phosphorus where it is lacking in the soil. It is unlikely to be needed in most gardens – only those in acid areas of high rainfall, on deep peat, on exceptionally heavy clay soil or soil that has been damaged by the overuse of chemical fertilisers. It is generally applied in the autumn at a rate of 240 g per m² (8 oz per square yard). It is not, however, ideal because it is expensive and from finite sources. Bonemeal can be used as a substitute.

Bonemeal provides slow-release phosphorus, plus calcium and various trace elements, and makes a good top-dressing for strawberries. However, do not use it with calcium-hating plants.

Dried blood provides long-lasting, slow-release nitrogen to help boost plant growth. It is useful in the spring and summer and can either be added to water and used as a liquid feed or mixed into the topsoil at a rate of 30 g per m² (1 oz per square yard).

Hoof and horn provides slow-release nitrogen to be taken up by plant roots and can be added to potting compost – 30 g to a 9-litre bucket (1 oz to a 2-gallon bucket) – and applied as a mulch.

PESTS AND DISEASES

An organic garden provides a habitat for both pests and their predators. It is important to remember that if the soil is healthy the plants will usually have fairly good resistance to pests and diseases.

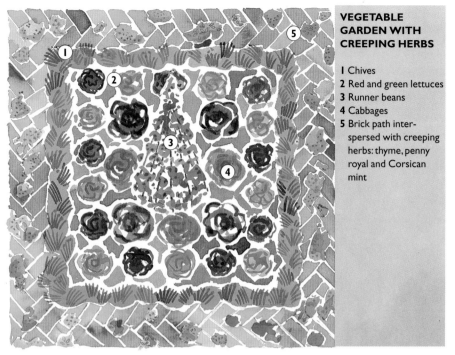

VEGETABLE GARDEN WITH CREEPING HERBS

1 Chives
2 Red and green lettuces
3 Runner beans
4 Cabbages
5 Brick path interspersed with creeping herbs: thyme, penny royal and Corsican mint

When buying seed, always choose resistant varieties, and when buying plants, make sure there is no discoloration of the leaves or sign of disease.

Attacking pests with chemicals kills not only the pests but also a good many of their predators. It destroys the delicate ecology of the environment, restricting the food supply of natural predators. In the long run, chemical pesticides only exacerbate the pest problem; they also drench our food and the soil in poisons.

There are some general preventive measures that can be taken against pests that will help keep a good, natural ecological environment in the vegetable garden:
1 Keep the soil healthy with good garden compost or manure, and always remove and discard any diseased plant material.
2 Practise crop rotation (*see pages 132–4*), which prevents soil-borne pests, spores and fungi from getting a real grip on the crops. If you do not have room for a formal crop rotation, make it a general principle not to plant the same crop in the same place two years running.
3 Practise companion planting (*see pages 134–5*), using other plants to deter pests.

4 Avoid growing large areas of any one plant (monoculture), since this promotes a tendency to insect infestations.
5 Grow plants that attract predators that feed on aphids. Nasturtiums and poached egg plants, for example, attract hoverflies; sunflowers attract bees, lacewings and predatory wasps; and dill attracts wasps and hoverflies.
6 Avoid treading on ground beetles, which like to live under stones. They will usefully eat eelworms, cutworms (a species of caterpillar that attacks vegetables) and leatherjackets (larvae of daddy-longlegs that feed on plant roots).
7 If you have a pond and a wild area of the garden, this will encourage frogs, toads and hedgehogs, which will, in turn, eat snails, woodlice and wireworms.
8 Birds can be a help or a hindrance, but blue tits will pick off greenfly eggs and others will eat slugs and snails. So, encourage birds to the garden by providing food and water in winter, but protect young crops with wire netting.
9 Pick up caterpillars by hand and throw them to the birds. Wear gloves as some may give you a rash.

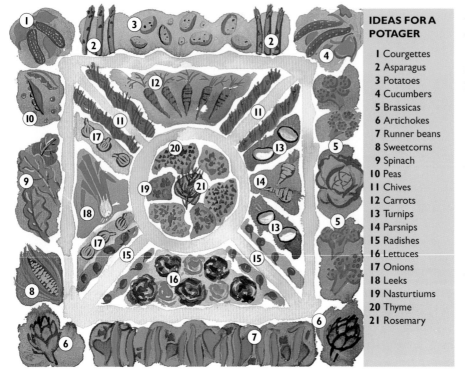

affect such other vegetables as cauliflowers, turnips and tomatoes.

20 If there is a really persistent problem, simply avoid growing that particular crop for a year or two.

NATURAL PESTICIDES AND FUNGICIDES

Garlic or onion spray is effective against blackfly, carrot fly, wireworms, pea and bean weevil, slugs and onion fly. Chop about 115 g (4 oz) of garlic or onion and leave it to macerate in a little oil overnight. Press and strain, reserving the oil. Add the oil to a pint of water in which you have dissolved 10 g (¹/3 oz) of soft soap and then dilute 30 ml (1 fl oz) in 570 ml (1 pint) of water as a spray.

Tansy spray is a useful pesticide for use against aphids, cabbage worms, Colorado beetles, Japanese beetles and squash bugs. Make a double-strength infusion (*see page 158*) and use neat.

Slug and snail water will deter just about everything. After several days, filter the water in which the slugs and snails were killed, and use the liquid as a general garden spray.

Soft soap will dissolve the waxy shell of aphids and kill them, but does no harm to their predators such as ladybirds and hoverflies. It also kills red spider mites and whiteflies. Soft soap can be bought from your local hardware shop or garden centre. Dissolve 25 g (1 oz) in 3.5 litres (6 pints) of rainwater, or follow container directions, and use as a spray.

Derris-pyrethrum will kill greenfly, blackfly, thrips and aphids. This product can be applied as a liquid spray (dilute as specified on the bottle) or as a dusting powder. ***Caution:*** This bio-degradable plant-derived powder is a poison and must be used carefully, wearing protective clothing. It is toxic to fish, as well as to bees, although it is not harmful to plants.

Bordeaux mixture is a copper-based mixture, useful for cases of potato blight and leaf spot. Purchase it as a powder, mix it

10 Sink a jam jar of beer in the ground to attract slugs and snails, or go out at night with a torch and capture them by hand, then put them into strongly salted or boiling water to kill them (*see right for use as garden spray in 'Natural Pesticides and Fungicides'*). If you are squeamish take them to a field well away from the garden and dump them there.

11 Learn to tolerate a few bugs and holes in your lettuces, as long as they leave enough for you. Just wash your vegetables thoroughly or soak them briefly in salted water.

12 Carrot fly (whose larvae not only eat the roots of carrots but also those of parsley, parsnips and celery) cannot fly very high. A very close mesh, at least 75 cm (30 in) high around the vegetable patch will keep them away, and so will horticultural fleece laid over the plants and anchored at the sides.

13 Old carpet or cardboard placed on the ground around the stalks of young brassicas will prevent cabbage root flies from laying eggs. Cut 10–15 cm (4–6 in) squares and make a slit in the centre.

14 Put plastic collars around the base stems of courgettes to protect them from cutworms and slugs. You can make collars from tins with the tops and bottoms removed, or from plastic drinks bottles or yoghurt pots, topped and tailed.

15 Holly leaves scattered between rows of crops will help to deter mice. So will summer savory, mint and narcissi planted near beans.

16 Sow vegetable seeds at a time most likely to avoid pests: for example, carrots in early summer rather than late spring, to avoid carrot fly.

17 Place tomato leaves between rows of vegetables to drive away flea beetles.

18 Ensure that conditions are suitable (light or shade, soil type, etc.) to produce hardy plants.

19 Avoid planting brassicas in summer if clubroot is a problem. Crop rotation will also help with this problem. If your vegetables are affected, use a heavy dressing of lime on the plot in autumn, before sowing the following year. Beware of a build-up of excess lime in the soil, which can predispose to canker in beetroot and

according to the instructions, and use it as a spray. You should, however, remove and then discard the infected parts of any affected plants. **Caution:** Be careful when using the Bordeaux mixture because it is poisonous to humans.

Seaweed solution helps control aphids, potato scab, leaf curl virus, damping off in seedlings and tomatoes, and potato eelworms. Use a weak solution at two-week intervals.

Rhubarb or elder spray is used for killing greenfly and other aphids as well as small caterpillars. Boil 450 g (1 lb) of rhubarb or elder leaves in 2.8 litres (5 pints) water and simmer for 30 minutes. Leave to cool. Strain and use as a spray.

PLANTING FRUIT TREES AND BUSHES

Fruit trees and bushes can be decorative, utilitarian and productive. You can plant fruit bushes such as blackcurrants to make hedges, and espalier or fan-shaped fruit trees can decorate walls, separate areas of the garden, or hide an unsightly compost heap or garden shed.

When buying fruit trees or bushes, make sure you choose healthy specimens from a reputable nursery or garden centre, and choose varieties that are suitable for your purposes, the space available, your soil type and general conditions.

Fruit trees and bushes should ideally be planted out during their dormant season in early winter. November is best the time. They then have time to become established before putting their energy into new spring growth. If that is not possible, plant them no later than early spring. Never plant in frosted ground and try to avoid planting in a frost pocket.

Before planting, the ground should be well prepared and cleared of all perennial weeds (*see page 124–7*). Dig in good organic matter and remember that the ground near a brick or masonry wall is usually drier than in other parts of the garden, as the wall absorbs moisture, so mulch this area extra well. You will need to put up support wires for cordons, fans or espaliers (*see below*). For these, use vine eyes available from garden centres and mail-order sources to attach the wire to the wall, and make sure it is tightened sufficiently. You may also need to erect sturdy posts strung with wire for growing raspberries.

If you decide to grow fruit trees or fruit bushes as fans, espaliers or cordons against a wall, certain varieties grow best in different situations:

Against an east-facing wall: pears, cherries, redcurrants and gooseberries.
Against a west-facing wall: plums, cherries, apples and pears.
Against a south-facing wall: blackberries and, in the more protected parts of the country, peaches and apricots.
Against a north-facing wall: redcurrants, gooseberries.

FRUIT TREES

These can be grown as standards (traditional orchard trees), half standards, dwarf pyramids (free-standing, and somewhere

(continued on page 142)

Training fruit trees and bushes

Stepover

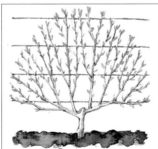

Fan trained

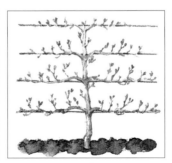

Espalier

Standard dwarf

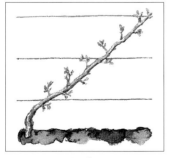

Cordon

Two types of tree supports: wires and vine eyes against a wall (right), and wires and posts in an open garden (far right).

Planting a bare-rooted fruit tree or bush

1 *Soak the roots well for several hours before planting. Check for damage and cut away damaged roots or any that are much longer than the others with a clean cut that will point downwards when the tree or bush is planted.*

2 *Dig a hole deep and wide enough to accommodate the roots without cramping them. Hold the plant in the hole to check that it is large enough; if not, make it bigger. Trees should be planted at the same level as they were in the nursery, so look for the soil mark on the stem. Lay a cane across the hole to ensure you are planting to the correct depth.*

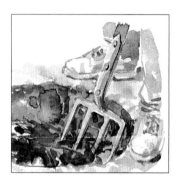

3 *Break up the soil at the bottom of the hole with a fork to allow the circulation of air and water. Fork in some compost and cover it with a layer of soil.*

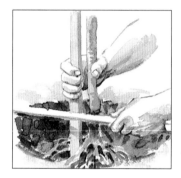

4 *If the tree or bush is to be staked (see left), hammer the stake firmly into the ground to the windward side of the plant before planting. If it is put in afterwards, the roots may be damaged. If a newly planted tree or bush moves in the wind, the tiny hairs on the roots will break and the plant will be damaged. Hold the tree in the hole, spread out the roots and gently shovel fine soil back over them.*

5 *Fill the hole with soil and tread it down gently to avoid damaging the roots. Level the soil to prevent puddles forming, and water it well. Check over the next few days to see if the soil has settled. If it has, top it up and firm it down again.*

Your support must be able to take the weight of a fully developed plant, which may be considerable, particularly when it is subjected to rain, snow or wind. Attach the tree or bush to its stake. Use an adjustable tie (above left), *available from garden centres, or protect the stem with hessian or sacking and use garden twine tied firmly to the stake and then tied loosely round the tree (above right). Don't use plastic-covered wire as it may cut into the plant.*

Planting a container-grown tree or bush

1 *Dig a hole wide and deep enough to accommodate the plant's root ball.*

2 *Loosen the soil at the sides and bottom with a fork. Incorporate some compost and cover it with a layer of soil.*

3 *If the tree or bush needs to be staked, hammer the stake very firmly into the ground to the windward side of the plant before planting.*

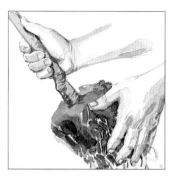

4 *Ease the plant gently out of the pot and gently separate any tangled roots without breaking up the root ball.*

5 *Hold the plant next to the stake in the hole and distribute soil around the roots with your fingers. Lay a cane across the hole to ensure that you are planting to the correct depth, indicated by the soil mark.*

6 *Fill the hole with soil and tread it down very gently to avoid damaging the roots. Level the soil so that no puddles can form and water well. Check over the next few days to see if the soil has settled. If it has, top it up and firm it down again.*

Fruit cages and nets

You may need to protect fruit trees and bushes from frost, mice, deer and birds. Cover them with sacking, horticultural fleece or fine mesh netting to protect them from the cold. To protect against birds, use a fine mesh netting or things that flutter in the wind. A fruit cage is best for soft fruit bushes such as blackcurrants and others that are particularly favoured by birds. Wrap the base of tree trunks with plastic tree tape to keep mice away from the tender bark. Sturdy fences are required to keep deer away.

Taking hardwood cuttings

1 *Choose a firm, ripe stem and take cuttings of at least 25cm (10in). Cut straight across the stem beneath a node.*

2 *Cut away all the leaves and trim to approximately 15cm (6in), cutting at an angle directly above a node.*

3 *Dig a narrow trench, which should be 3–5cm (1–2in) shallower than the length of your cuttings.*

4 *Sprinkle a little sand into the bottom of the trench to improve drainage.*

5 *Place the cuttings in the prepared trench at intervals of about 10–15cm (4–6in). Bear in mind that the straight-cut end is the bottom of the cutting and the angled end is the top.*

6 *Fill in the trench and firm the soil around the base of the cuttings. Water well and label the cuttings clearly.*

(*continued from page 139*)

between a bush and a cordon) or cordons. New varieties of Ballerina apples with single stems that fruit on spurs are particularly suitable for container growing and small spaces, but they must have plenty of light.

All fruit trees are now grafted on to rootstocks of other varieties, and it is the rootstock that determines the eventual size of the tree. If the tree is for a small space, check that a dwarfing rootstock has been used or you may end up with an enormous specimen. Many types of tree can also be trained to be used as screens, or to go against a wall.

Cordons take up the least space and consist of a single stem with short spurs. They are either trained on wires against a wall and usually grown obliquely, or are planted free-standing, supported with posts, which should be buried in the ground 60 cm (2 ft) deep and spaced approximately 2.75 m (9 ft) apart. The support wires should be spaced about 45–60 cm (18–24 in) apart.

Espaliers can be grown against a wall, or as a screen on a good support structure of posts and wires, as for a cordon (*see page 139*). They are trained to rise in a series of horizontal tiers (usually four) from a single central stem.

Fans radiate out against a wall or screen, and new growth is trained to fill in any spaces. Support wires should be spaced 15 cm (6 in) apart.

Stepovers, a form of espalier suitable for apples and pears, grown as low as 30 cm (1 ft), make a lovely edging for paths. If you buy trees that have already begun to be trained (espaliers with two tiers; fan-shaped with four ribs) this will save you a lot of trouble.

Since most fruit trees require a pollinating partner, you will need to buy two trees that flower simultaneously. When buying plum or pear trees, you will need to check that they are compatible.

When planting soft fruit it is best to try to avoid frost pockets, since the blossoms are fragile and easily damaged. Any damage means that you will not get fruit later in the season from those flowers. When buying plants, try to find varieties that are frost-resistant, and check that they are free of viruses. When growing blackberries and raspberries, you will need posts and wires to support them (*see page 139*) – three wires strung in parallel lines between posts 1.2 m (4 ft) apart will support raspberries, while five-wire supports are better for growing blackberries. Blueberries, black-, red- and white currants and gooseberries can all be grown as free-standing bushes. Red- and white currants and gooseberries can also be grown as cordons against a wall or well-built fence, or supported by free-standing posts and wires.

PRUNING FRUIT TREES

Before pruning fruit trees of any type, it is essential to check the requirements of each variety so that you know exactly when it fruits before you pick up your secateurs. A good general principle of pruning is: 'to stimulate new growth, cut out old wood.' Use sharp secateurs and cut cleanly when pruning. Although some pruning should be done in winter, it must never be attempted during frosts.

Correct pruning will control the size of the tree, improve its shape and encourage new growth. However, you must check the flowering times of the different varieties and know the fruiting habits of each species: if the tree fruits on new growth, you can cut out the previous year's growth, but if the fruit grows on the previous year's growth, you must be careful not to remove growth on which fruiting will take place. Free-standing trees seldom need to be pruned vigorously – it is often enough just to remove diseased stems and to thin out stems that are overcrowded or overlapping.

The correct and rigorous pruning of trained fruit trees is, however, essential. With these, any outward-growing shoots are cut off, but other training will depend on the style chosen. Pruning will strengthen the root system, allow more air and light to circulate (reducing the incidence of disease) and rain to penetrate, and improve the size and quality of the fruit. When pruning, thin out the weaker branches, removing lateral stems that may damage the tree by rubbing against other stems.

Winter pruning is undertaken to encourage new growth in the following spring. It consists of cutting out dead wood and thinning overcrowded stems. Leaders are best shortened to a strong, upward-facing bud, which will then spring to vigorous life as soon as the warmer weather begins. Most plants and trees are pruned in winter, but in some very cold parts of the country pruning is best delayed until March or April.

Summer pruning is used especially for cordons, espaliers, dwarf pyramids and fans. It aims to reduce leaf growth and so stimulate the tree into making fruit buds. It should be done in July and

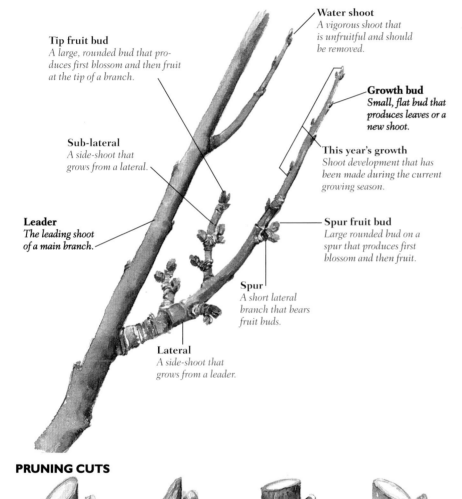

Tip fruit bud
A large, rounded bud that produces first blossom and then fruit at the tip of a branch.

Sub-lateral
A side-shoot that grows from a lateral.

Leader
The leading shoot of a main branch.

Water shoot
A vigorous shoot that is unfruitful and should be removed.

Growth bud
Small, flat bud that produces leaves or a new shoot.

This year's growth
Shoot development that has been made during the current growing season.

Spur fruit bud
Large rounded bud on a spur that produces first blossom and then fruit.

Spur
A short lateral branch that bears fruit buds.

Lateral
A side-shoot that grows from a leader.

PRUNING CUTS

✔   ✗   ✗   ✗

August. The leaders should be shortened by a quarter of their new growth and the laterals by a third of their new growth. In the following winter, take off all the new growth that has occurred since the summer pruning and remove one further bud of the old growth. Aim to improve the shape of the tree, and if lopping a branch to remove it completely, make sure that the cut is completely even, leaving just a small collar to aid healing. At the same time, tie in loose branches.

Pruning soft fruit bushes

This is done in October or November when the leaves have dropped and it is easy to see any dead or crossing wood. Either remove dead or unwanted stems entirely, or cut them down to a new, strong sideshoot. Cut the healthy stems down to a third or fourth outward-facing bud. Bushes should be cut into what is known as the 'goblet' shape, working on the principle that the centre should be open to allow light to penetrate.

Redcurrants and white currants live up to 25 years and require no drastic pruning. The fruit grows on spurs made on old wood. When pruning redcurrant or blackcurrant, set healthy pruned stems aside. Make a trench in your vegetable garden and plant a row of cuttings – about 20 cm (8 in) long – with only 5 cm (2 in) of the cutting showing above the ground. Firm the earth around the cuttings, water them in, and leave them until the following spring. With any luck you should have a row of fresh, new plants ready for planting out.

PROPAGATION

BUYING AND SAVING SEED

Most vegetables are raised from seed, which is either bought or saved from the previous year's harvest. When choosing seeds for your garden, you need to consider the geographic location of the area, the location of the plot and the type of soil you have to work with. Choose appropriate varieties that are disease-resistant and reliable varieties that you know will grow in your garden; but you may also want to experiment with others.

In general, allow the seeds to ripen on the plant and then gather the pods just before the seeds fall. You may need to use a paper bag to catch smaller seeds. Otherwise, pick the whole stem and hang it upside down in a warm, airy place over a sheet of paper to collect the falling seeds. Store the seeds in clearly labelled envelopes for use in the following season. Do not attempt to save seeds from hybrid varieties since they will not grow true to type. Concentrate instead on what are known as 'heritage' varieties for successful seed-saving. Don't save seeds from brassicas since they interbreed very easily.

SOWING SEED

Seed packets give basic directions about when to sow and how deep seeds should be planted. The actual time of sowing, however, will be subject to some local variation, depending on where you live and weather conditions at the time. If in doubt, it is better to wait a week or two for better conditions than to sow when instructed if it is too wet, too dry or too cold. Seeds sown 'late' will soon catch up and will then do better than those sown under less-ideal conditions.

Most vegetables can be successfully sown out of doors, either in seed beds (like the brassicas, which will be transplanted into a plot in the autumn once the summer crops are over), or in the place in which they are to grow to maturity. However, seeds sown indoors will give you an early start, especially with

Sowing smaller seeds in seed trays or other containers

1 Fill a seed tray with well-watered compost and firm gently with a board or the base of another tray.

2 Sprinkle seeds over the surface, cover with a shallow layer of compost and water them gently.

3 Label the tray with the name and date of sowing. Cover the tray with glass, polythene or newspaper to

keep in the moisture. Shade the tray if it is in direct sunlight. Some seeds germinate best in the dark (check the instructions on the seed packet). Check every day that the glass or polythene has not collected too much condensation; seeds may go mouldy if they are too damp. As soon as the seeds have started to germinate, remove the covering to give the seedlings air and light.

Sowing larger seeds in pots

1 *Fill a pot with well-watered compost. Press the surface down gently, using the base of another pot.*

2 *Push 4–5 seeds into the compost about 1.5–2.5 cm (¹/2–1 in) deep.*

3 *Gently sprinkle and firm a layer of compost over the seeds.*

4 *Water gently, using a watering can preferably fitted with a rose. Label with the name and date of sowing.*

Pricking out and potting on

1 *Fill a pot, compartmented pack or other container with well-watered potting compost and make small round holes with your finger or a stick.*

2 *Ease the seedlings up gently, using a small knife or spatula, and gently separate them. Take care not to damage their roots.*

3 *Hold a seedling by a leaf (avoid touching the stem if possible) and place it in a hole in the new pot so that the roots fall easily into the hole.*

4 *Gently firm the soil around the seedling and water, using a watering can preferably fitted with a rose.*

the more tender plants, and they can then be planted out after the danger of frosts has passed – usually the last week of May, but this depends on the prevailing weather conditions in any particular year, the location of your garden in the country, and any factors that may be specific to your garden.

Suitable plants for optional indoor sowing include French and scarlet runner beans, courgettes and marrows. Some plants, such as cucumbers, tomatoes and peppers, require the higher temperatures found indoors or in the greenhouse in order to germinate.

Sowing seeds in seed trays indoors is fairly labour-intensive, since seedlings will need to be pricked out, potted on and then hardened off (*see above and page146*). There are various types of growing mediums you can use. Most proprietary seed and potting composts contain loam, sand and peat as well as chemicals; it is worth looking for organic ones.

You can make your own homemade seed and potting compost (*see page 146*), but never use garden soil.

Sowing seeds indoors

You can sow your seeds in either shop bought or homemade seed compost, in seed trays, seed modules, pots, or plastic tubs from the kitchen (with holes made in the bottom for drainage), following the instructions found on the back of all seed packets. Smaller seeds are usually sown

Planting out or transplanting young plants

1 *Use a length of string tied to two sticks, a hoe handle or a plank to form a straight line, and use a dibber or trowel to make a row of holes in the soil.*

2 *Carefully holding each seedling by a leaf, lower it into a hole and gently firm the soil around each one.*

3 *Tender young plants can be protected from wind, slugs and snails, and from drying out for the first few days by covering them with cloches. These can easily be made by cutting the bottom off a plastic drinks bottle and placing the top part over the plant. Remove the screw top to allow for ventilation. Young plants should also be protected from birds (see page 147).*

---

in seed trays; larger seeds, such as beans, should be sown 2–3 to a pot.

Homemade seed compost
If you want to make your own seed compost, it is recommended to use fine leaf mould 2–3 years old, either on its own or with some sifted loam from turf stacked upside down and left for about a year.

Alternatively, you could use 4 parts comfrey leaf mould (*see page 130*) to 1 part sharp sand, or 2 parts peat moss and 1 part horticultural sand soaked in liquid seaweed (*see pages 126 and 137*).

Homemade potting compost
Seedlings come up very thickly and must be pricked out and potted on in larger containers filled with more nutrient-rich compost before they become leggy from insufficient light, air and growing space.

Potting compost, like seed compost, can be bought or homemade. Here are two recipes you could try yourself.

1 4 parts loam, 2 parts peat (or peat alternative, such as 2–3-year-old leaf mould or coir), 225 g (8 oz) seaweed meal, 115 g (4 oz) bonemeal, and 55 g (2 oz) calcified seaweed.

2 In a dustbin, mix 3 parts peat (or alternative), 1 part sharp sand, and 1 part compost. Add 85 g (3 oz) calcified seaweed to every 45 litres (10 gallons) of mixture.

Hardening off
Young plants ready for planting out should first be hardened off. This will protect them from the shock of going into direct sun, cold soil, cold night air or poor weather conditions after the protected environment indoors or in the greenhouse. Hardening off can be done in several ways. The pots can be put under cloches or in a cold frame outside, or put out in the open during the day and brought in at night or if the weather conditions become poor.

PLANTED PATIO

1 Lettuces
2 Courgettes
3 Sage
4 Peas
5 Carrots
6 Rosemary
7 Thyme
8 Onions
9 Beetroots
10 Dwarf beans

Planting out or transplanting young plants

The best time for planting out or transplanting young plants is the evening. If you plant out in the middle of a hot summer day the plants will wilt. Make sure that the soil is moist and well prepared, that the plants are already well watered, and that the holes you make are deep enough to accommodate the roots without cramping them. Tomatoes, squashes and sweetcorns are better planted with a trowel because it is important that the rootball is left intact.

You can, of course, buy seedlings for planting out. Make sure that you buy plants that have healthy dark green leaves, and check for signs of disease. Reject any that are not strong, as well as brassicas with swelling roots, which is a sign of clubroot disease.

Each seedling should be handled carefully so as not to disturb the root system. Always make sure that seedlings are well watered before planting and that the ground is well prepared. When planted in rows, seedlings can be staggered, thus allowing you to fit more into any given space and with enough leaf space for each. This also helps to suppress weeds by depriving them of light.

Sowing seed out-of-doors in seed beds and in situ

Ideally, having dug garden compost and/or well-rotted manure into the soil the previous autumn, fork the soil over lightly in the spring prior to planting and break up any large lumps of earth. Tread the soil down to break up the lumps further, then rake it over gently with a backwards and forwards motion. Repeat these stages until the soil is fine and crumbly.

Always remember to label rows of seeds and protect them from birds by using wire netting, pieces of string tied to sticks and zig-zagging 15–25 cm (6–10 in) off the ground, or fluttering bits of kitchen foil or brightly coloured plastic as a bird scarer.

Thinning out

Seeds sown in rows usually come up far too close together and the seedlings will then need to be thinned out in order to allow room for the young plants to develop (*follow the instructions given for transplanting young plants on page 146*). This will probably need to be done more than once. The first thinnings can be discarded since the seedlings will be too small to transplant or eat. Never leave thinnings lying on the soil as they attract pests; this is especially true of onions and carrots, which may attract onion and carrot flies. Thin the seedlings carefully, and gently press the soil back around the remaining plants.

The second thinning often produces miniature vegetables that are very sweet and delicious to eat. Some of these thinnings may even be worth transplanting to another site. Young plants can be harvested as they are needed from the rows, thus leaving increased space for the remaining crop to develop.

Sowing

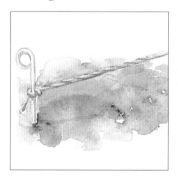

1 *Use a length of string tied to two sticks to mark out where you are to sow your seeds. Alternatively, use a hoe handle or a plank to mark a straight line.*

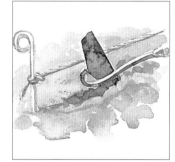

2 *Make a drill along this line, either with a stick or with the corner edge of a hoe, to a depth suitable for the particular seeds (see the instructions for individual plants on pages 144–145).*

3 *Gently water the drill using a watering can, preferably fitted with a rose, then trickle fine seeds through your fingers to distribute them evenly along the drill. It may help to mix very small seeds with fine, dry sand first. Cover with soil.*

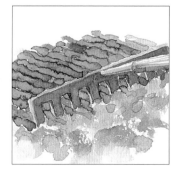

4 *Draw the rake carefully across the drill and gently tread down, aiming to get the soil as flat as possible and so avoid any dips where water can collect.*

storing produce

Preserving and storing your own home-grown produce is worthwhile and satisfying on many different levels. Apart from following in a tradition that stretches back for thousands of years to a time when preserving food was essential for survival, the range of different storing and preserving techniques gives you the opportunity to enjoy your produce at any time of the year, in or out of season, and to create tastes and flavours that make food a positive pleasure.

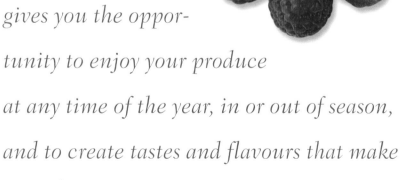

Preserving food

The traditional kitchen gardener has always aimed to grow produce to provide a tasty and interesting selection of fresh, organic food for as much of the year as possible. By storing and preserving the harvest, the garden's bounty can be enjoyed all the year round.

The availability of freezers has led to a decline in the use of such traditional preserving methods as bottling, pickling and drying, but there is satisfaction in having shelves loaded with gleaming bottled fruits, preserves and pickles, and storage areas filled with fruits and vegetables. There is also the additional benefit that stored in these ways, your produce is safe against power cuts that would affect a freezer and its contents.

Produce will not improve from being stored, canned or dried, so start with the pick of your crop. Avoid bruised or damaged items, or anything that shows even the slightest sign of mould or insect damage. One bad piece can spoil the whole batch.

BOTTLING

When bottling, bear in mind that dangerous moulds and bacteria can grow and thrive in improperly preserved produce. It is really easy to do it the right way, so why take chances?

EQUIPMENT

In addition to regular kitchen equipment, the tools for safe bottling are few and mostly inexpensive. You may already have some in your kitchen. You will need:

- A preserving pan, or any large saucepan as long as it has a tight-fitting lid, with a wire rack or special preserving rack with handles, which the jars or bottles stand on to keep them off the base of the pan.
- Metal tongs or long-handled wooden spoons – for removing jars, bottles, lids and so on from boiling water.
- Ladle – for filling jars.
- Bottling funnel – makes filling easier, and helps to keep jar tops clean.
- Narrow plastic spatula – to remove air bubbles from the produce.
- Pressure cooker – an expensive item to buy just for preserving unless you already own one, but it is an essential piece of equipment if you want to bottle low-acid foods.

CONTAINERS

Bottling jars come in several styles and sizes. Straight-sided, wide-mouth jars can be used for bottling or freezing; jars with shoulders, however, may burst if they are frozen. 500 ml (1 pint) and 1 litre (2 pint) sizes are convenient for most home-bottling purposes.

Do not be tempted to use old mayonnaise or jam jars that have been made for

one-time use only, or old-fashioned bottling jars with spring closures. To ensure a safe seal, buy new, sturdy bottling jars (often called Mason jars) with separate lids and screw bands.

The jars themselves (if they are undamaged) and the screw bands (if they are free of corrosion) may be reused. But do not reuse bottling lids – the rubbery compound that provides a safe seal may not work the second time. Jars, lids and caps need to be very clean or the produce is likely to spoil. Wash jars and lids in warm soapy water and rinse thoroughly. Do not use any kind of abrasive cleaner. Place the jars in a saucepan, half fill it with water, and bring it to a boil for 15 minutes. Reduce the heat to a slow simmer and leave the jars in the hot water until you are ready to use them. Place the lids in a saucepan of hot (but not boiling) water until you are ready to use them. Dry the screw bands and set them aside.

FILLING JARS

It is best to deal with one jar at a time – fill it and immediately fit its lid before moving on to the next one. This reduces the possibility of bacteria infecting the produce. Using tongs or wooden spoons, remove a jar from the simmering water, empty the water out (let it drain for a couple of seconds) and place it on a clean towel on a clean worktop. Then immediately fill the jar with the prepared hot produce.

Using a bottling funnel helps to keep the top of the jar clean as you fill it. Even so, you should wipe the top of the jar with a clean paper towel before placing the lid in position.

To ensure a proper seal, it is important to leave the correct space between the top of the food (or its liquid) and the lid of the jar. This is called the headspace. A general rule of thumb is to leave 2.5 cm (1 in) headspace for low-acid foods and vegetables; a 1.25 cm (½ in) headspace for high-acid foods, tomatoes, and fruit; and a 65 mm (¼ in) headspace for jams, jellies and pickles.

After filling a jar, use a narrow plastic spatula to push the contents down to remove any air bubbles that may have become trapped in the produce. Do not use a metal knife to do this, since its hard edges could scratch or otherwise damage the hot glass of the jar.

Carefully remove a lid from the hot water and centre it on the jar. Centring the lid ensures that the rubber composition seal will work properly. Then fit the screw band.

PROCESSING

Different foods require different processing techniques. A saucepan or preserving pan with a tight-fitting lid is fine for high-acid foods. A pressure cooker reaches a higher temperature, however, which is needed for foods with a low-acid content. These two methods of preserving are not interchangeable, so follow the recipe instructions.

Using a saucepan or preserving pan
Pour enough warm water into the pan to reach half way up the sides of the jars. After lowering the filled and capped jars onto the wire rack in the water, put the lid on and turn up the heat to high. Bring the water to a full boil. Adjust the heat to keep the water at a gentle rolling boil. Start timing the processing period called for by the recipe at this point.

When the time is up, turn off the heat and remove the lid. Wait until the jars are cool enough to handle, then gently remove them and place them on a clean towel on your worktop. Allow about 5 cm (2 in) of space between the jars. Leave them there to cool, undisturbed, for 12 to 24 hours. Avoid draughts that might crack the hot jars. Do not tighten the screw bands.

Using a pressure cooker
Put 5–7.5 cm (2–3 in) of water in the bottom of the cooker and heat it to a fast simmer. Using jar-lifting tongs, place the filled, capped jars on a wire rack. When the rack is full (but the jars should not be touching), lock the cooker lid securely in place. Following the manufacturer's instructions, raise the heat to medium high and allow the steam to vent for 10 minutes. Close the valve and allow the pressure cooker to come up to the correct pressure.

Preserving acid fruit

1 Place the jars in a pan half filled with warm water and boil for 15 minutes.

2 After boiling, remove one of the jars, drain it and place upright on a clean paper towel.

3 Using a ladle and a bottling funnel, fill the hot jar with the prepared produce.

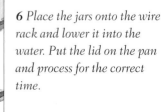

4 With a plastic spatula, gently pack the fruit down to dislodge any air bubbles.

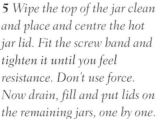

5 Wipe the top of the jar clean and place and centre the hot jar lid. Fit the screw band and tighten it until you feel resistance. Don't use force. Now drain, fill and put lids on the remaining jars, one by one.

6 Place the jars onto the wire rack and lower it into the water. Put the lid on the pan and process for the correct time.

Once the desired pressure has been reached (see individual recipes), start timing the processing period. When processing is finished, turn off the heat and let the cooker cool. *Do not open the valve until the canner has depressurised to zero.* Then wait for at least 2 minutes before removing the lid, and remember to protect yourself against the escaping steam. Leave the jars in the cooker until they are cool enough to handle. Then, gently remove the jars and place them on a clean towel on your worktop, allowing about 5 cm (2 in) of space between the jars. Leave them there to cool, undisturbed, for 12 to 24 hours. Avoid draughts that might crack the hot jars. Do not tighten the screw bands.

When the jars have cooled, check the lids for a good seal. A slight vacuum should have formed and the lids should be concave. If you press the centre of the lid and it moves up and down *the jar is not sealed*. If this happens you can store the jar in the refrigerator and use the contents soon (within a week) or you can empty the jars, reheat the produce, repack it in clean, sterilised jars and reprocess it. If a jar did not seal, it is probably because the headspace was incorrect or the top of the jar was not clean – some food or moisture may have interfered with the seal.

STORING BOTTLED PRODUCE

Label the jars with their contents and date and store bottled produce away from direct sunlight. An old-fashioned country larder is ideal for this – cool, dark and dry – but a cupboard may provide similar conditions. Bottled produce, pickles, jams and preserves will usually last, if prepared and stored properly, for a year or more. Once opened, they must be kept with a lid on in the refrigerator.

Caution: Botulism can be fatal! If you open a jar of bottled produce and the contents have a bad colour or odour, or

if the contents spurt out under pressure, throw them away immediately. Then thoroughly wash and sterilise the jar and thoroughly wash your hands and anything else that has come in contact with the spoiled produce.

RECIPES

Foods for bottling are divided into two groups: acid and low-acid. Acid foods include most fruit (including tomatoes), jams, jellies, pickles and relishes. Low-acid foods include greens, green beans, root vegetables, peas, peppers, potatoes and squash. Acid foods are processed in a saucepan or preserving pan, while low-acid foods *must* be processed in a higher-temperature pressure cooker.

When bottling fruit, it will darken unless you dip it into a commercial antioxidant solution – a mixture of ascorbic and citric acids which should be used according to the manufacturer's directions – or a mixture of 240 ml (8 fl oz) of lemon juice to 1 litre (2 pints) water.

Fruit should be peeled, cored or stoned. It can be sliced so that more of it fits in each jar. You will need to use a syrup, juice or water when bottling fruit. A simple syrup can be made from 0.5 kg (1 lb) of sugar dissolved in 1 litre (2 pints) of water. Whichever liquid you prefer, it must be heated and kept hot until you are ready to use it.

Apples

Peel, core and quarter (or slice) the apples. Boil them gently in syrup for 5 minutes. Fill the hot jars with hot fruit and syrup. Leave 1.25 cm (½ in) headspace. Remove air bubbles, cap and process in a pan for 20 minutes.

Beans (green or French)

Use fresh, tender beans. String, trim and cut them into 5 cm (2 in) pieces. Pack them tightly into hot jars. Fill the jars with boiling water. Leave 2.5 cm (1 in) headspace. Remove air bubbles,

cap and process in a pressure cooker at 5 kg (10 lb) pressure (or 'high' setting) for 25 minutes.

Berries

Rinse the berries in cold water and drain them. Measure 120 ml (4 fl oz) hot syrup into each hot jar, and then fill and cap each in turn. Leave 1.25 cm (½ in) headspace. Top up with hot water. Remove air bubbles, cap and process in a pan for 20 minutes.

Carrots

Peel and rinse the carrots. Either slice them or leave them whole, and pack them tightly into hot jars. Fill each jar with boiling water. Leave 2.5 cm (1 in) headspace. Remove air bubbles, cap and process in a pressure cooker at 5 kg (10 lb) pressure (or 'high' setting) for 30 minutes.

Kale (also spinach or any greens which become dense and compact when cooked.)

Remove any tough stems and wash the greens thoroughly under running water. Chop coarsely into pieces about 2.5–4cm (1–1½ in) across. Place the pieces in a saucepan with just enough water to cover. Heat, stirring gently, until they wilt. Drain quickly and pack them into hot jars. Fill each jar with boiling water, leaving 2.5 cm (1 in) headspace. Remove air bubbles, cap and process in a pressure cooker at 5 kg (10 lb) pressure (or 'high' setting) for 70 minutes (for 500 ml/ 1 pint jars) or 90 minutes (for 1 litre/2 pint jars).

Parsnips and turnips

Peel and slice the vegetables and place them in a pan. Cover them with cold water and bring to a boil for 2 minutes. Drain them quickly and pack them into hot jars. Fill each jar with boiling water. Leave 2.5 cm (1 in) headspace. Remove air bubbles, cap and process in a pressure cooker at 5 kg (10 lb) pressure (or 'high' setting) for 35 minutes.

Peaches

Remove the skins by dipping the peaches in boiling and then cold water. The skins will slip off. Cut the peaches in half, remove the stones and scrape out the flesh. Pack the hot jars with overlapping slices and fill with hot syrup. Leave 2.5 cm (½ in) headspace. Remove air bubbles, cap and process in a pan for 30 minutes.

Pears

Peel, core and quarter the pears. Boil them gently in syrup for 5 minutes, then pack the hot fruit into hot jars. Fill each jar with syrup, leaving 2.5 cm (½ in) headspace. Remove air bubbles, cap and process in a pan for 25 minutes.

Peas

Shell fresh-picked peas and loosely pack them into hot jars. Fill each jar with boiling water. Leave 2.5 cm (1 in) headspace. Remove air bubbles, cap and process in a pressure cooker at 5 kg (10 lb) pressure (or 'high' setting) for 40 minutes.

Tomatoes

Remove the skins by dipping them in boiling and then cold water. The skins will slip off. Cut the tomatoes in half, saving any juice. Measure 1 tablespoon of lemon juice into each hot 500 ml (1 pint) jar or 2 tablespoons for a 1 litre (2 pint) jar. Pack the jars with the tomatoes and juice, fill each one with boiling water and leave 2.5 cm (½ in) headspace.

Remove air bubbles, cap and process in a pan for 90 minutes.

PICKLING

Pickling dates at least from the time of the ancient Greeks and Romans, who preserved perishable foods for winter or times of shortage in this way. There are now whole books filled with recipes for every imaginable kind of pickle, chutney and relish.

Vegetables that are suitable for pickling include broccoli, carrots, cauliflower, small cucumbers, green beans and courgettes, as well as white pickling onions and green or red peppers.

For the best flavour and appearance, use canning salt, not regular table salt.

Pickling in vinegar

1 Peel the vegetables and leave them in heavily salted ice-cold water for at least 12 hours.

2 Place the vinegar solution (see p.154) in a non-corrosive pan and boil for 5 minutes.

3 Thoroughly rinse and drain the vegetables and add them to the boiling vinegar.

4 Pack the vegetables into hot jars and top up with the vinegar solution.

5 With a plastic spatula, gently pack the vegetables down to dislodge any air bubbles.

6 Wipe the jar top clean and centre the hot jar lid. Fit and tighten the screw band.

7 When the wire rack is full, lower it into the water and process for 15 minutes.

Even if you are making a lot of pickles, work in small batches – about 3 kg (6 lb) of vegetables is an easily manageable quantity and will make 3–3.5 litres (6–7 pints) of pickles.

Prepare your bottling jars, lids and screw bands following the instructions on page 150.

Wash and thinly slice 3 kg (6 lb) of vegetables (or, in the case of broccoli and cauliflower, divide them into small florets) and then place them in heavily salted, ice-cold water and leave them for at least 12 hours, or overnight. If they tend to float, weigh them down with a heavy plate. Drain, thoroughly rinse in cold water and drain again.

In a large pan, combine 720 ml (24 fl oz) of white distilled vinegar with 480 g (1 lb 1oz) of sugar and 2 tablespoons of salt. Bring to a boil. If you wish, this mixture can be seasoned with herbs and spices such as garlic, ginger root, mustard seeds, peppercorns, rosemary, tarragon, dill, coriander, chilli peppers or oregano. Tie the herbs or spices in muslin before you put them in the jar and remove them before filling the jars. Fresh herbs are best; dried herbs will cloud the vinegar.

Add the vegetables to the boiling vinegar, return it to the boil, then reduce the heat and simmer for 5–15 minutes, depending on the size of the produce – just make sure it is thoroughly heated all the way through. Pack the hot vegetables into hot jars, and top up with the vinegar mixture. Leave 65 mm (¼ in) headspace. Remove air bubbles, cap and process in a pan for 15 minutes.

After processing and cooling, leave the pickled vegetables in a cool, dark place for a month or six weeks to cure and develop their full flavour.

JAMS, JELLIES, CONSERVES AND BUTTERS

Most soft fruits start to deteriorate soon after they are picked. As a result, they have long been preserved in jams, jellies, conserves and butters. All of these are made by boiling fruit or fruit juice with sugar until the mixture sets when cooled.

Jams can be made with most types of fruit, including apples, pears, plums, greengages, strawberries, apricots, blackcurrants, redcurrants, blackberries, raspberries and gooseberries. Blackcurrant and redcurrant jellies are particularly popular – the latter to accompany game and holiday fare.

The pectin content of soft fruit is important when making preserves, and it largely determines the consistency of the finished produce. Acid is also important, since it helps to release the pectin; hence the addition of lemon juice in some recipes. Some fruits contain more pectin than others, and pectin is more abundant in under-ripe than over-ripe fruit. Fruits rich in pectin and acid include cooking apples, sour blackberries, currants, sour plums, concord grapes and gooseberries. Less pectin is found in blueberries, cherries, peaches and strawberries. To avoid using a lot of sugar, you can add commercial pectin.

Fruit butters and cheeses are made with puréed fruit and these tend to use less sugar than jam. This makes them more attractive from a health viewpoint, although they do not keep as long. Some individual fruit recipes can be found between pages 70–97.

FREEZING

Most fruits, herbs and vegetables can be frozen. There are advantages to this method of storage: freezing is quick and easy and it preserves the produce in good condition with its texture and flavour largely intact. All produce should be frozen straight from the garden. Adjust your freezer so that it maintains a temperature of -18° C (0° F).

Vegetables that are suitable for freezing include asparagus, beans, broccoli, Brussels sprouts, carrots, cabbage, cauliflower, kale, leeks, parsnips, peas, peppers, spinach, tomatoes and turnips.

Garden produce can be stored in the freezer in rigid plastic containers or polythene freezer bags. Containers are especially useful when the food is fragile, such as asparagus spears, but bags take up less space. Make sure that when you seal the bags you extract as much air as possible. Always label and date the contents of containers and bags using a permanent marker pen. Freeze the food as rapidly as possible to prevent the formation of ice crystals.

Vegetables should first be prepared by shelling, peeling or slicing, as required. They must then be blanched in boiling, lightly salted water for 2–5 minutes, drained, plunged into iced water, drained and thoroughly dried before being put into containers or freezer bags. *Note:* The exceptions are peppers, which should be cut into sections and frozen without blanching, and tomatoes, which can be cored, dipped in boiling water, then cold water, skinned and frozen.

When using vegetables from the freezer, the best way is to defrost them slowly in the refrigerator. If you are in a rush, immerse the frozen food in cold (but never hot) water, or use the defrost cycle on a microwave oven. Greens, such as kale or spinach, which freeze into a solid block, should be defrosted and separated before cooking, or the outside will overcook before the inside is even warm.

Fruit can often be put straight into the freezer, or it may need washing and careful drying first. Some fruits will need topping and tailing, peeling or having the stones removed before freezing. Fruits suitable for freezing include apples, blackberries, blueberries, cherries, cranberries, currants, gooseberries, pears, plums, raspberries, rhubarb and strawberries.

Fruit can be frozen in various ways: mixed with sugar (1 part sugar to 4 parts fruit), puréed, dry frozen on trays or frozen in a sugar syrup (600 g [1lb 5 oz] of sugar dissolved in 1 litre [2 pints] of water). Raspberries or blackberries, for example, can be put straight into the freezer on trays; once they are frozen hard, they can be sealed in freezer bags or boxes. Fruit may go mushy once it is thawed; defrosting it slowly in the refrigerator, in unopened containers, will help to prevent this.

WINTER STORAGE

It is important that produce picked for storage is in perfect condition – anything that is bruised or diseased will cause rotting, which will spread rapidly from one item to another. Look out for onion softness, especially around the necks, or for black areas on the bulbs. Check for maggots in carrots, canker in parsnips which causes soft dark patches, and bruising on apples. Do not store any root vegetable that has been damaged by digging or any fruit if the skin has been nicked.

Root vegetables, including carrots, kohlrabi and turnips, can be stored in deep boxes lined with 2.5 cm (1 in) of slightly damp sand or peat; they will last well in a cool, dark place. A layer of clean vegetables, with 5 cm (2 in) or so of the leaf stalk left on, should be placed in the box and covered with another layer of peat or sand. Repeat this process until the box is full. The idea is to prevent the produce from drying out and shrivelling, so make sure that the sand or peat is damp but not wet. Too much moisture will encourage rotting. Place the box in a dry, cool, dark, frost-free place – an unheated cellar is ideal, but a garage may serve just as well.

Winter squashes can be stored for up to several months on a shelf in a well-ventilated, frost-free area. They can also be hung up in bags made from string or netting or any other material that allows the free circulation of air around them. Onions and shallots can be placed on wire or slatted wooden trays and racks, but not too close together since they require the free circulation of air between them. They can also be strung up from a beam or hook by tying the necks with strong twine or raffia. Either way, they should last a whole winter and into the spring, but inspect them at least weekly and remove any spoiled items.

Parsnips can be left in the ground in some areas and dug up as they are required throughout the winter if you mulch the soil with a thick layer of straw to stop the ground freezing. If space is needed in the garden, parsnips can be dug up and left in a pile where a mild frost will sweeten them and the rain will wash them clean. If several days of hard frost are forecast, cover them with straw and sacking.

Potatoes can be stored in any convenient dark, frost-free place on slatted trays and covered with hessian, paper or other material to prevent their exposure to light, *which will cause them to turn green and become poisonous.* They can also be placed in boxes lined with straw and covered, layer by layer, with straw or newspaper, or stored in paper or hessian sacks with the top closed. Before being stored, newly dug potatoes should be left to dry off for a couple of days, and they need to be checked fairly regularly for any signs of rotting and the unwanted attention of mice.

Some varieties of apple will keep for several months in cool, dry conditions, especially the old-fashioned russet varieties that have tough skins. They need to be picked carefully in order to avoid bruising them; traditional kitchen gardeners used to pick apples on a clear, dry day and put them carefully into straw-lined baskets to prevent any damage to the fruit. Windfalls or blemished fruit should be cut up, cooked and frozen. Sound apples can be stored in straw-lined baskets or boxes, in dry sand or in paper bags; they can be wrapped in tissue paper, placed on wooden trays, or in any container that allows the free circulation of air and protects them from sudden temperature changes. They need to be checked regularly and any rotting fruit removed.

Pears should be picked unripe and will ripen slowly while being stored. They can be placed on shelves, in drawers or shallow boxes or packed in paper, straw or dry sand. They need to be kept in a frost-free area and inspected regularly.

DRYING

Many fruit crops, such as apples, apricots, blueberries, cherries, grapes, peaches, pears, plums, strawberries and tomatoes, can be dried. Grapes, plums and blueberries should be dipped in boiling water for 30 seconds to remove their natural waxy coating. To prevent darkening, apples, peaches and pears should be dipped in a commercial antioxidant solution or a mixture of 240 ml (8 fl oz) of lemon juice to 1 litre (2 pints) water.

In the right climate – sunny and dry with a light breeze and few insects – you can dry fruit outdoors on wooden or plastic racks. Many people prefer the convenience of an electric dehydrator, which, if you like dried fruit and would normally buy a lot of it, can soon pay for itself. Children enjoy nutritious dried fruit snacks, too. Fruit can be rehydrated for use in pies, salads and so on by soaking it in boiling water for 10 minutes.

Produce needs to be picked carefully. Avoid any with bruises or signs of mould. Slice produce into 1.25 cm (½ in) slices. Once the produce is completely dry, it can be stored in airtight containers in a cool, dark, dry place.

Most herbs can be dried by hanging them in bunches in a well-ventilated place. Once they are bone dry, spread sheets of clean newspaper on the floor and crumble the leaves. Separate the leaves from the twigs and store the herbs in labelled, dated, airtight containers away from direct sunlight.

To provide health benefits, some of the foodstuffs in this book need simple home-processing into basic medicines. These remedies do not have any unpleasant

preparing home remedies

side-effects, and many of the herbs, such as peppermint and chamomile, make refreshing, delicious beverages in their own right. Of course, some foods do not need even the simple preparations described in this chapter – you can get the best out of an apple simply by biting into it.

Natural remedies

Natural remedies are easy to make at home and can be prepared for both internal and external use. They range from the simple application of fruit, vegetable or herb leaf to the skin (as for an insect bite), to the addition of the ingredient to a meal (mint with lamb, for example) and to the preparation of an infusion, decoction or tincture for internal use or as the basis for an ointment or salve.

Fresh herbs, fruit and vegetables picked straight from the garden, or those which you have grown, harvested and preserved, can be used to make home preparations which are not only far cheaper than products bought from shops, but also provide the additional satisfaction of being homemade and containing only good quality natural ingredients which have been grown organically.

INTERNAL USE

Taken internally, in whatever form, the therapeutic constituents of plants enter the bloodstream via the digestive tract. The two most popular forms of internal remedies are infusions and decoctions.

Infusions

Infusions, which can either be taken as remedies or as relaxing or revitalising teas, are made by steeping the leaves and flowers of either fresh or dried plants in boiling water. Fragrant herbs such as chamomile and peppermint have traditionally been used in this way, and many other leaves, like Indian or China tea, are prepared similarly. However, plants which contain a high percentage of mucilage such as borage should be made up with cold water and left to infuse for 10–12 hours, as the hot water may destroy their therapeutic constituents. It is best to make fresh infusions each day, but provided that they are stored in airtight containers, homemade infusions can keep for up to 2 days in a refrigerator.

Herbal infusions can also be used as mouthwashes, gargles and hair rinses, as well as in foot baths and on compresses.

Infusions and decoctions are usually taken hot for treating fevers, catarrh or congestion, colds and skin problems; they are taken lukewarm or cold for problems associated with the kidneys and urinary tract such as cystitis and urethritis, and can be enjoyed in the same way as cooling drinks in the summer. If you find that certain herbs are too bitter, try combining the herbs required for the remedy with more palatable ones, such as lemon balm, peppermint or lavender, or you can use honey, unrefined sugar or liquorice as a sweetener.

TO MAKE AN INFUSION

50 g (2 oz) fresh plant or
25 g (1 oz) dried leaves or
    flowers
570 ml (1 pint) boiling water

Dosage: A normal adult dosage, for both infusions and decoctions (opposite) is 1 cup, taken 3 times a day in the case of chronic problems, and 6 or more times a day in the case of acute illness.

1 Warm the jug or pot with hot water and add the plant.

2 Pour the boiling water over the plant. Cover the container and leave to infuse for 5–10 minutes.

3 Strain and drink, adding honey or sugar to taste, or cover and store in a refrigerator for use within 2 days.

Decoctions

Decoctions are similar to infusions but involve a boiling process to break down the harder woody parts of a plant – the stalks, seeds and roots – before their therapeutic constituents can be absorbed by the water. Some plants can be bought ready-powdered, or they can be broken up by pounding with a pestle and mortar (if the roots are fresh) or ground up in a coffee grinder. Decoctions, which taste stronger than infusions, can be drunk as teas or incorporated into syrups, gargles, compresses and douches.

TO MAKE A DECOCTION

50 g (2 oz) fresh plant or
25 g (1 oz) dried leaves
650 ml (22 fl oz) cold water

Dosage: If a double-strength infusion or decoction is required, simply double the amount of plant used for the same amount of water.

1 Place plant in a stainless steel or enamelled pan (not aluminium) and cover with water.

2 Bring to the boil, cover and simmer for 10–20 minutes.

3 Take off the heat, strain and drink, or store in a sterilised jar in a refrigerator for up to 2 days.

Tinctures

Tinctures are taken in small doses; they can be taken internally or externally, added to bath water and used in ointments and lotions. The fresh or dried herb is soaked in a mixture of alcohol and water, which should be measured according to the ratios laid down in a herbal pharmacopoeia. This ratio varies from plant to plant: for many herbs, the liquid comprises 25% alcohol and 75% water, but for some resinous herbs the amount of alcohol needs to be increased in order to extract the therapeutic constituents, often to 45% alcohol and sometimes even 90%. A standard recipe is 1 part fresh herb to 2 parts fluid or 1 part dried herb to 5 parts fluid. Brandy or vodka, which are 60–70% proof (i.e. 45% alcohol), provide a good alcohol solution, and both can be used in the recipe below. For those who require a sweeter taste, you can prepare syrup-like tinctures using equal parts of water and glycerol. For more watery fresh plants, such as lemon balm, use 80% glycerol.

TO MAKE A TINCTURE

500 g (1 lb) fresh or
200 g (7 oz) dried plant
1 litre (1³/4 pints) 45% alcohol solution or glycerol solution (*see above*)

Dosage: Normal dosage is 1 teaspoon for adults or 10 drops–¹/2 teaspoon for children, 3 times a day with or after meals. Take every 2 hours for acute illness. Dilute with water.

1 Place plants in a jar with an airtight lid and cover with alcohol or glycerol solution. Seal and leave in a refrigerator for 2 weeks, shaking daily.

2 Strain the mixture into a jar or jug through a muslin bag.

3 Pour into a dark, labelled bottle and store in a refrigerator.

Syrups

Syrups incorporating infusions, decoctions or tinctures can be used to make natural remedies more palatable to both children and squeamish adults.

The standard dosage is 2 teaspoons for children, 3–4 times a day for chronic problems and 6–8 times a day in acute illness. If you have no infusion, decoction or tincture prepared, 1 teaspoon of herbs or finely chopped fruit or vegetables can be mixed with honey and given to children (1 teaspoon 3 times a day for chronic problems and 1 teaspoon every 2 hours in acute illness).

TO MAKE A SYRUP USING AN INFUSION OR DECOCTION

350 g (12 oz) 1:1 mixture of thin honey and unrefined sugar

300 ml (½ pint) double strength infusion or decoction of your choice

 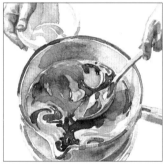 

1 Heat infusion or decoction with honey/sugar mixture in a stainless steel or enamelled pan.

2 Stir mixture as it starts to thicken and skim off foam from surface.

3 Leave to cool before pouring into a cork-topped bottle. Drink required dose immediately or store in a refrigerator for up to 3 days.

TO MAKE A SYRUP USING A TINCTURE

300 ml (½ pint) boiling water
360 ml (13 fl oz) thin honey or 600 g (1 lb 5 oz) unrefined sugar
120 ml (4 fl oz) tincture of your choice

1 Pour boiling water over the honey or sugar and stir over a low heat until the sugar dissolves and the water boils.

2 Remove from the heat and add the tincture to the mixture. If placed in a sterilised airtight container, this syrup can be stored indefinitely.

Herb and Fruit Vinegars

Some tinctures can be made with neat cider or wine vinegar, producing vinegars such as garlic or rosemary vinegar for culinary use, bay or sage vinegar for use as skin and hair preparations or raspberry vinegar for treating children's coughs and sore throats.

TO MAKE HERB OR FRUIT VINEGAR

Enough fresh herbs or fruit to fill your chosen container loosely
Enough cider or wine vinegar to cover the herbs or fruit

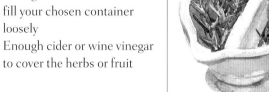

1 Bruise the freshly picked herbs or fruit using a pestle and mortar, and place in the sterilised container.

2 *Pour on the vinegar, seal with an airtight lid and leave for 2 weeks in a sunny position, shaking daily. If at the end of this time a stronger taste is required, strain the vinegar and repeat with fresh herbs and fruit.*

3 *For culinary uses, either store as it is or strain and re-bottle. If it is for use as a hair rinse add 30 ml (1 fl oz) vinegar to 220 ml (8 fl oz) of water just before use.*

EXTERNAL USE

There are several external pathways by which plant constituents can be introduced into the bloodstream: through the skin, through the rectum or vagina, through the nasal passages by means of inhalation, and through the conjunctiva of the eye. Remedies can take the form of gargles and mouth-washes, inhalants and eyewashes, hair rinses and herbal baths, suppositories, salves, creams, poultices and compresses. Infusions, decoctions and tinctures are all used in these remedies, as well as infused and essential oils.

Gargles and mouthwashes

These can be made from infusions or decoctions, or from tinctures: dilute 5 ml (1 teaspoon) of tincture in 50 ml (2 fl oz) of water, or use half a cup of infusion or decoction. Gargle 2–3 times a day for chronic problems, and every 2 hours if the infection is acute. If you are using the mixture as a mouthwash, use 2–3 times daily.

Poultices and compresses

Both poultices and compresses are applied to areas of pain and swelling. The difference between them is that while poultices use the plant or foodstuff itself, compresses use an extract of it. Bread poultices can be used for bringing boils to a head and cabbage-leaf poultices are good for relieving the pain of arthritic joints and for mastitis. Plants such as cabbage leaves can be applied directly to the skin. For painful joints, simply remove any hard ribs and outer leaves, warm the leaves in hot water or by placing them over a radiator, apply to the affected part and bandage.

Compresses can also be applied to painful joints, and they are useful for soothing skin irritations. Cold compresses are sometimes used to help relieve headaches and migraines, and to bring down fevers.

TO MAKE A WARM
POULTICE

Plant, fresh or dried, sufficient to cover the affected area
2 pieces of gauze
A light cotton bandage

1 *If using fresh herbs, bruise them using a pestle and mortar, or soak in hot water for several minutes to soften them. If using dried herbs, add hot water to make a paste.*

2 *Place sufficient plant to cover the affected area between two pieces of gauze.*

3 *Use a light cotton bandage to bind the poultice to the affected area. Keep it warm with a hot water bottle. Leave for 2–4 hours or overnight, depending on the severity of the problem.*

TO MAKE A COMPRESS

Hot or cold infusion or
    decoction of your choice or
    a few drops of essential oil
    in water
Face cloth or small towel

*1 Soak face cloth or towel
in a bowl of the chosen preparation, and wring out excess
liquid.*

*2 Apply to affected area,
repeating several times.*

Herbal baths

Herbal baths can provide relaxation,
clear blocked noses and soothe aching
limbs. Infusions and decoctions may be
strained and poured into the water, a
muslin bag filled with fresh or dried
aromatic herbs may be hung beneath
the hot tap, or a few drops of infused or
essential oils may be added to the bath
water. Warm water has the effect of
opening the pores of the skin, so that
when herbal preparations are added to a
bath, the plant constituents are quickly
absorbed via the skin. In the case of
volatile oils, they are absorbed via
inhalation through the nasal passages
and mouth into the lungs and thus into
the bloodstream. Add about 570 ml
(1 pint) double-strength infusion or
decoction and soak in the bath for 15 to
30 minutes for the best effect. You can
also add essential oils to your bath.
These, because they are extracted from
plants by steam distillation, cannot be
prepared at home, but they can be
obtained from health-food shops and
other stockists of natural products. Note
that they should always be diluted in a
base oil for babies, young children and
people with sensitive skins (2 drops of
essential oil per 5 ml [1 tsp] of base oil).

Hand and foot baths

Baths are an excellent way to give
remedies to babies and children; they
are an easy way of introducing plant
constituents into the bloodstream,
since both the hands and the feet are
sensitive areas which are fairly
absorbent, despite some thickening of
the skin. Use either 1 litre (1¾ pint)of
double-strength infusion or decoction,
several teaspoons of tincture or a few
drops of dilute essential oil in a bowl of
hot water (warm for babies and
children). Foot baths should be taken in
the evening (8 minutes for adults and 4
for children), and hand baths in the
morning, for the same length of time.

Salves and creams

Salves can be made by macerating
plants in oil. Creams can be made by
stirring tinctures, infusions, decoctions
or a few drops of essential oil into
aqueous (water-based) cream, which is
available from most pharmacists.

TO MAKE A SALVE

425 ml (¾ pint) olive oil
55 g (2 oz) beeswax
Fresh or dried herb

*1 Mix oil and beeswax
together in a heatproof bowl.*

*2 Add as much of your chosen
herb as the mixture will cover,
and mix together.*

*3 Heat gently over a pan of
boiling water for 2–3 hours.*

4 *Press out through a muslin bag, discard the herb, and pour the warm oil into a sterilised jar. Leave to solidify.*

5 *Use or store in a cool place. It will keep for up to 3 months.*

2–3 drops essential oil
55 g (2 oz) aqueous cream

Mix together thoroughly and smooth into the skin. Made with chamomile oil, this recipe is especially good for eczema.

Infused oils

Both diluted essential oils and infused oils can be used for inhalations and as massage oils for inflamed and painful joints, or for neuralgia, bruises and swellings. They can also be used as bath oils, and as a base for suppositories, ointments or liniments. There are two methods of preparing infused oils, hot and cold, and both can be easily done at home (*see below*).

TO MAKE A COLD INFUSED OIL

1 litre (1¾ pints) cold-
  pressed safflower, walnut or
  almond oil to fill chosen jar
Enough fresh or dried plant
  to pack chosen jar

1 *Pack the sterilised jar with the plant and cover with oil. Seal with an airtight lid. Leave in a sunny place for 2 weeks, shaking daily.*

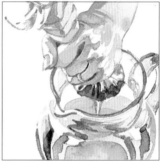

2 *Squeeze the oil through a muslin bag into a jug.*

3 *Pour the strained oil into sterilised, dark-coloured, airtight storage bottles and label.*

TO MAKE A HOT INFUSED OIL

1 litre (1¾ pints) cold-
  pressed safflower, walnut or
  almond oil
Enough fresh or dried plant,
  chopped, to pack a
  heatproof glass bowl

1 *Place the chopped plant in the heatproof bowl and cover with the oil.*

2 *Place the bowl over a pan of water and simmer for 2–3 hours.*

3 *Leave to cool, then strain into sterilised, dark-coloured, airtight storage bottles and label.*

Treatment Chart

	Acne	Alcoholism	Allergies	Anaemia	Anxiety & tension	Arteriosclerosis	Arthritis	Asthma	Atherosclerosis	Babies' colic	Babies' sleeping problems	Back pain	Bedwetting	Bladder infections	Bleeding gums	Boils & abscesses	Bowel disorders/infections	Bronchial congestion	Bronchitis	Bruises & sprains	Burns & scalds, minor	Candidiasis	Cardiovascular problems
Apple							●																
Apricot				●	●												●						
Artichoke	●					●	●		●														
Asparagus							●																
Basil					●																		
Beans, dried																							
Beans, green				●			●																
Blackberry				●					●						●		●				●		
Blackcurrant							●		●														
Blueberry/bilberry													●		●		●						
Borage			●		●		●	●															
Brassicas		●		●			●									●							
Caraway																							
Carrot				●			●									●		●					
Celery							●																
Chamomile					●		●			●							●			●	●		
Cherry				●			●																
Chervil							●																
Chicory							●																
Chives				●					●														
Coriander			●				●																
Courgette																	●						
Cranberry																							
Cucumber							●							●									
Dandelion																●							
Dill										●	●												
Fennel							●											●					
Garlic								●															
Gooseberry									●								●						
Horseradish							●									●							
Lavender					●		●									●	●				●		
Leek									●							●	●						
Lemon balm				●	●																		
Lettuce					●																		
Marigold																	●					●	
Marjoram					●												●						
Marrow																	●						
Mint										●		●											
Onion				●			●												●				
Parsley				●	●		●							●						●			
Parsnip																							
Pea																							
Peach					●												●						
Pear							●																
Pepper, hot																							
Pepper, sweet			●																				●
Plum				●			●										●						
Potato						●	●														●		
Pumpkin																	●						
Radish																		●					
Raspberry				●	●										●								
Redcurrant							●		●														
Rhubarb																							
Rocket				●																●			
Rosemary					●		●	●													●		
Sage																		●			●		
Sorrel	●			●												●							
Spinach				●																			
Squash																	●						
Strawberry	●																						
Sweet bay							●													●			
Thyme					●		●	●					●				●						
Tomato				●																			
Turnip	●						●							●		●	●						
White currant							●		●														

	Cataracts	Catarrh	Chest infections	Chilblains	Children's infections	Circulatory disease	Colds	Cold sores	Colic	Colitis	Colour & night vision problems	Conjunctivitis	Constipation	Coughs	Cramp	Croup	Cuts	Cystitis	Depression, mild	Diarrhoea	Digestive problems	Diverticulitis	Earache
Apple		•					•					•	•				•			•			
Apricot													•								•		
Artichoke																							
Asparagus	•											•											
Basil		•					•		•			•	•				•						
Beans, dried												•										•	
Beans, green												•											
Blackberry							•					•	•							•			
Blackcurrant		•					•					•								•			
Blueberry/bilberry		•					•						•				•			•			
Borage		•			•								•					•					
Brassicas				•			•			•		•					•						
Caraway		•							•			•											
Carrot											•	•					•	•		•			
Celery												•						•			•		
Chamomile									•	•	•						•	•			•		•
Cherry		•					•					•	•							•			
Chervil																					•		
Chicory												•											
Chives																					•		
Coriander		•	•				•		•				•								•		
Courgette										•													
Cranberry									•			•						•					
Cucumber																							
Dandelion												•											
Dill									•			•	•							•	•		
Fennel									•				•										
Garlic		•	•	•	•		•						•										
Gooseberry												•											
Horseradish		•		•			•					•	•										
Lavender																	•						
Leek		•	•										•				•		•				
Lemon balm					•															•			
Lettuce		•					•					•											
Marigold				•			•			•		•					•						
Marjoram		•	•	•			•		•					•	•								
Marrow										•													
Mint		•	•				•	•					•							•			
Onion		•					•					•	•					•					
Parsley									•														
Parsnip												•											
Pea												•											
Peach													•					•		•			
Pear										•			•							•	•		
Pepper, hot		•		•			•						•										
Pepper, sweet																							
Plum												•											
Potato				•						•		•					•						
Pumpkin										•													
Radish		•					•						•							•			
Raspberry		•					•					•	•							•			
Redcurrant		•					•													•			
Rhubarb													•							•	•		
Rocket		•					•						•										
Rosemary		•		•			•						•										
Sage									•								•						
Sorrel																							
Spinach												•									•		
Squash										•													
Strawberry								•				•											
Sweet bay		•		•			•		•				•							•			
Thyme		•	•				•							•		•	•			•			
Tomato					•							•											
Turnip		•		•			•					•											
White currant		•					•					•	•							•			

Treatment Chart

	Eczema	Fevers	Flatulence	Flu	Fluid retention	Gall bladder problems	Gastritis	Gastro-enteritis	Gingivitis	Gout	Grazes	Griping	Haemorrhoids	Hangovers	Hay fever	Headaches	Heart & arterial disease	Heartburn	Heat rash	Heavy periods	Hiccoughs	High blood pressure	High cholesterol
Apple		●			●	●	●									●							
Apricot																							
Artichoke	●				●					●								●					
Asparagus					●																		
Basil			●							●						●							
Beans, dried												●										●	
Beans, green					●					●													
Blackberry		●		●			●			●										●			●
Blackcurrant		●		●	●					●													
Blueberry/bilberry		●		●						●		●											
Borage		●		●	●																		
Brassicas							●			●	●							●					
Caraway			●																		●		
Carrot			●		●					●	●			●									
Celery										●												●	●
Chamomile	●						●																
Cherry					●					●													
Chervil							●			●													
Chicory					●	●				●						●		●					
Chives																							
Coriander		●	●	●			●					●											
Courgette							●									●							
Cranberry																							
Cucumber	●	●			●					●									●				
Dandelion					●	●																	
Dill			●																				
Fennel			●		●													●					
Garlic																						●	●
Gooseberry																	●					●	
Horseradish		●		●	●					●				●									
Lavender			●								●					●							
Leek			●								●												
Lemon balm	●										●			●									
Lettuce							●																
Marigold		●		●	●		●				●	●											
Marjoram		●		●												●							
Marrow							●																
Mint		●		●					●							●							
Onion			●	●	●					●												●	●
Parsley			●		●					●						●							
Parsnip																							
Pea																						●	
Peach					●													●					
Pear										●								●					●
Pepper, hot		●						●															
Pepper, sweet																							
Plum			●		●					●													
Potato							●				●										●		
Pumpkin							●									●							
Radish	●				●	●				●													
Raspberry		●		●	●																		●
Redcurrant		●		●	●					●													
Rhubarb																●							
Rocket																							
Rosemary		●	●	●											●	●							
Sage		●			●				●	●	●	●											
Sorrel	●				●																		
Spinach					●																		●
Squash							●									●							
Strawberry		●			●															●			
Sweet bay		●	●	●	●					●						●							
Thyme		●		●				●	●														
Tomato					●													●					
Turnip	●				●					●													
White currant		●		●	●																		

	Hormonal problems	Hot flushes	Hyperacidity	Hyperactivity	Indigestion	Infections	Inflammatory eye problems	Inflammatory problems	Insect bites & stings	Insomnia	Intestinal infections	Irritable bowel syndrome	Joint pain	Kidney stones	Liver problems	Low energy	Low immunity	Mastitis	Menopausal problems	Migraines	Mouth ulcers	Muscle tension	Muscular aches & pains	Nausea
Apple			•		•						•			•										
Apricot					•																			
Artichoke					•																			•
Asparagus																•								
Basil					•				•											•		•		
Beans, dried																								
Beans, green																								
Blackberry																					•			
Blackcurrant						•			•												•			
Blueberry/bilberry							•														•			
Borage	•															•								
Brassicas					•										•									
Caraway					•																			
Carrot								•			•				•									
Celery																								
Chamomile				•						•										•				•
Cherry																								
Chervil																								
Chicory					•										•									
Chives						•										•								
Coriander					•																			
Courgette					•																			
Cranberry												•			•									
Cucumber							•	•	•															
Dandelion												•		•			•							
Dill					•																	•		•
Fennel					•													•						•
Garlic																•								
Gooseberry																•								
Horseradish					•																			
Lavender					•				•	•										•			•	•
Leek									•															
Lemon balm					•	•			•														•	•
Lettuce										•	•													
Marigold		•														•								
Marjoram										•												•		
Marrow					•																			
Mint													•							•	•			•
Onion																								
Parsley									•															
Parsnip															•									
Pea																								
Peach					•																			
Pear					•						•													
Pepper, hot																								
Pepper, sweet																								
Plum																								
Potato					•																			
Pumpkin					•																			
Radish														•										
Raspberry					•															•				•
Redcurrant						•			•											•				
Rhubarb																								
Rocket																•								
Rosemary					•															•				
Sage		•			•																•			•
Sorrel																								
Spinach																•								
Squash					•																			
Strawberry						•	•																	
Sweet bay					•																		•	•
Thyme																•					•			
Tomato								•																
Turnip																•								
White currant						•		•												•				

Treatment Chart

	Nerve pain	Nervous palpitations	Neuralgia	Night sweats	Overheating	Pain in childbirth	Peptic ulcers	Period pains	Pharyngitis	PMS	Poor appetite	Poor circulation	Poor concentration	Poor lactation	Prostate problems	Respiratory infections	Rheumatism	Rhinitis	Ringworm	Sinusitis	Skin problems	Sore throats	Stomach infections
Apple						●										●					●		
Apricot											●												
Artichoke											●												
Asparagus																					●		
Basil	●																			●	●		
Beans, dried																							
Beans, green																							
Blackberry											●									●	●	●	
Blackcurrant											●									●	●	●	
Blueberry/bilberry																					●	●	
Borage														●									
Brassicas														●						●	●		
Caraway											●	●									●		
Carrot															●								
Celery																							
Chamomile			●							●											●	●	
Cherry																							
Chervil											●												
Chicory																							
Chives												●											●
Coriander							●				●								●	●	●		
Courgette					●		●							●									
Cranberry											●												
Cucumber					●																		
Dandelion											●	●		●							●		
Dill											●												
Fennel								●			●			●									
Garlic												●										●	
Gooseberry																							
Horseradish											●	●							●	●			
Lavender		●									●						●		●	●		●	
Leek											●												
Lemon balm				●						●								●					
Lettuce							●				●												
Marigold							●	●													●		
Marjoram								●			●												●
Marrow					●		●							●									
Mint		●						●										●	●	●	●	●	
Onion									●			●						●		●			
Parsley								●				●											
Parsnip																							
Pea																							
Peach																					●		
Pear																							
Pepper, hot			●					●				●								●			
Pepper, sweet															●								
Plum																					●		
Potato																							
Pumpkin					●		●							●									
Radish											●						●	●		●			
Raspberry			●																			●	
Redcurrant											●									●	●		
Rhubarb																							
Rocket											●												
Rosemary											●	●								●			
Sage				●				●					●		●						●		
Sorrel																					●		
Spinach											●										●		
Squash					●		●							●									
Strawberry																					●		
Sweet bay								●			●						●						
Thyme											●									●		●	
Tomato																							
Turnip																							
White currant											●								●	●	●		

168

Food	Stomach ulcers	Stress/stress-related problems	Sunburn	Swollen joints	Thrush	Tiredness & lethargy	Tonsillitis	Ulcers (open sores)	Urethritis	Urinary infections	Urinary stones	Urticaria	Vaginal infections	Varicose veins	Viruses	Vitamin & mineral deficiency	Vomiting	Warts	Worms	Wounds
Apple																				•
Apricot						•										•				
Artichoke												•								
Asparagus						•				•						•		•		
Basil						•														
Beans, dried																				
Beans, green		•				•										•				
Blackberry										•										
Blackcurrant				•																
Blueberry/bilberry					•									•						
Borage		•				•														
Brassicas														•		•				
Caraway						•														
Carrot																•				
Celery		•								•										
Chamomile					•							•								
Cherry						•				•						•				
Chervil						•														
Chicory						•														
Chives																				
Coriander						•														
Courgette																			•	
Cranberry										•										
Cucumber			•									•								
Dandelion						•				•						•		•		
Dill																				
Fennel																				
Garlic						•													•	
Gooseberry											•									
Horseradish						•														
Lavender		•																		
Leek										•										
Lemon balm														•						
Lettuce																				
Marigold					•			•						•				•		
Marjoram										•										
Marrow																			•	
Mint						•	•													
Onion																			•	
Parsley						•										•				
Parsnip						•										•				
Pea						•										•				
Peach						•			•							•				
Pear						•										•				
Pepper, hot																				
Pepper, sweet																				
Plum						•										•				
Potato	•			•				•												
Pumpkin																			•	
Radish											•									
Raspberry										•										
Redcurrant				•																
Rhubarb																				
Rocket						•														
Rosemary						•														
Sage							•			•			•				•			
Sorrel																•				
Spinach						•										•				
Squash																			•	
Strawberry			•													•				
Sweet bay						•														
Thyme						•	•													
Tomato																•				
Turnip																•				
White currant				•																

GLOSSARY

Amino acid One of the building blocks of protein.

Analgesic Substance that relieves pain.

Apiol Constituent of volatile oil in celery.

Arteriosclerosis Hardening of the arteries.

Antioxidant Prevents cell damage by free radicals.

Atherosclerosis Build-up of plaque on the inner lining of the arteries.

Betacarotene Precursor of vitamin A.

Bioflavonoids Plant chemicals that enhance the action of vitamin C and have an antioxidant action.

Carcinogen Substance associated with tumour formation, such as cancer.

Chlorophyll Green colouring in leaves that traps the energy of sunlight for photosynthesis to occur.

Cholecystitis Inflammation of the gall bladder.

Cholesterol Type of lipid and the most abundant steriod in the body. In excess, can cause arterial disease.

Coxsackie Virus that occurs in the intestinal tract.

Earthing up To build up earth around the base of a plant such as fennel.

Enzyme Protein molecules that act as catalysts for chemical reactions in the body.

Folic acid One of the B vitamins.

Free radicals Molecules formed by oxygen metabolism that can damage the body's cells.

Haemoglobin Pigment found in red blood cells that carries oxygen.

Hypertension High blood pressure.

Indole Nitrogen compounds thought to protect against cancer by enhancing the elimination of oestrogen.

Mucilage Gel-like substance from certain plants used as a laxative.

Nephritis Inflammation of the kidneys.

Oxalic acid Substance that inhibits the absorption of some minerals and can predispose to kidney stones.

Pectin Soluble fibre that helps to regulate the bowels and lower the level of blood cholesterol.

Peristalsis Muscular movements of the gut, enabling the passage of food and fluid.

Pharyngitis Inflammation of the pharynx (throat).

Phenolic acid Naturally occurring substance with antiseptic and disinfectant properties.

Phytochemicals Plant-derived chemicals.

Phyto-oestrogens Substances found in plants that have effects similar to oestrogen.

Protease Enzyme that digests proteins.

Purines Compounds, often found in high-protein foods, that form uric acid when metabolized.

Rhizome Creeping underground stem of some plants.

Sulphites Sulphur compounds used in food preservatives that can trigger asthma attacks.

Tannins Yellow or brown compounds derived from plants and used in medical astringents to prevent infections or reduce inflammation.

Triglycerides Fats found in the body, high levels of which may indicate coronary artery disease.

Vertical Garden Space-saving garden with upward-growing plants.

Volatile oils Compounds with an antiseptic action in highly scented herbs.

USEFUL ADDRESSES

HERB NURSERIES

Hollington Nurseries, Woolton Hill, Newbury, Berkshire RG20 9XT

Jekka's Herb Farm, Rose Cottage, Shellard's Lane, Alveston, Bristol, Avon BA12 2SY

Suffolk Herbs, Monks Farm, Pantlings Lane, Kelvedon, Essex CO5 9PG

HERBAL SUPPLIERS

Brome and Schimmer Ltd, 25 Abbey Enterprise Centre, Premier Way, Romsey, Hampshire SO51 9AQ

G. Baldwin & Co, 173 Walworth Road, London SE17 1RW

Cathay of Bournemouth Ltd, 32 Cleveland Road, Bournemouth, Dorset BH1 4QJ

Culpeper Ltd, 21 Bruton Street, London W1X 7OA

The Herbary, Prickwillow, Ely, Cambridgeshire CB7 4SJ

Napier & Sons, 18 Nicholson Street, Edinburgh, Scotland EH8 9DJ

Neals Yard Remedies, 5 Golden Cross, Cornmarket Street, Oxford, Oxfordshire OX1 3EU

Neals Yard Apothecary, 2 Neals Yard, London WC2H 9DP

Potters Herbal Supplies Ltd, Leyland Mill Lane, Wigan, Lancashire WN1 2SB

Salley Gardens, Sminkins Farm, Abbolton Lane, Westbridgeford, Nottingham, Nottinghamshire NG2 5AS

HARDY FRUIT TREES
Deacon's Nursery, Godshill, Isle of Wight PO38 3HW

SEEDS AND INFORMATION
Biodynamic Agricultural Association, Woodman Lane, Stourbridge, West Midlands DY9 9PX

British Nutrition Foundation, High Holborn House, 52–54 High Holborn, London WC1 V 6RQ

Cancer Research Campaign, 10 Cambridge Terrace, London NW1 1JC

Chase Organics, Coombelands House, Addlestone, Weybridge, Surrey KT1 5HY

Chelsea Physic Garden, 66 Royal Hospital Road, London SW3 4HS

Chiltern Seeds, Bortree Stile, Ulverston, Cumbria LA12 7PB

Friends of the Earth, 26–28 Underwood Street, London N1 7JQ

Henry Doubleday Research Association, Ryton-on-Dunsmore, Coventry, West Midlands CV8 3CG

The Herb Society, 134 Buckingham Palace Road, London SW1 9AS or 34 Boscobel Place, London SW1 W 9PE

Imperial Cancer Research Fund, PO Box 123 Lincoln's Inn Fields, London WC2 A 3PX

The National Council for the Conservation of Plants and Gardens, The Pines, Wisley Garden, Woking, Surrey GU23 6QB

National Institute of Medical Herbalists, 56 Longbrook Street, Exeter, Devon EX4 6AH

Royal Horticultural Association, Wisley, Woking, Surrey GU23 6QB

Soil Association, 86–88 Colston Street, Bristol, Avon BS1 5BB

Sutton Seeds, Hele Road, Torquay, Devon TQ2 7QJ

Thompson & Morgan, London Road, Ispwich IP2 0BA

Unwins Seeds, Histon, Cambridge, Cambridgeshire CB4 4CE

BIBLIOGRAPHY

Biggs, M., *The Complete Book of Vegetables*, Kyle Cathie, 1997

Bruce, M., *Commonsense Compost Making*, Faber/Soil Association, 1967

Brown, L., *The Cook's Garden Century*, 1990

Buczacki, S., *Best Soft Fruit*, Hamlyn, 1994

Calborn, M., *The Good Old Fashioned Gardener*, Charles Letts & Co. Ltd., 1993

Carper, J., *The Food Pharmacy*, Simon & Schuster, 1989

Carper, J., *Food Your Miracle Medicine*, Simon & Schuster, 1994

Culpeper's Complete Herbal, Wordsworth Editions, 1995

Elliot, R. and de Paoli, C., *The Food Pharmacy*, Tiger Books,1994

Elphinstone, M. and Langley, J., *The Organic Gardener's Handbook*, Thorsons, 1990

Ewin J., *The Plants We Need to Eat*, Thorsons, 1997

Fernie, W., *Herbal Simples*, Wright & Sons, 1914

Flowerdew, B., *The Companion Garden*, Kyle Cathie, 1994

Gerard's Herbal, Senate, 1994

Gregg, R. and Philbrick, M., *Companion Plants*, Watkins, 1967

Grieve, M., *A Modern Herbal*, Penguin, 1976

Hamilton, G. (ed.), *Organic Gardening*, Dorling Kindersley, 1997

Hurley, J., *The Good Herb*, W. Morrow & Co, 1995

Hurst, K., *Herbs and the Kitchen Garden*, Sienna, 1996

Larkcom J., *Creative Vegetable Gardening*, Mitchell Beazley, 1997

McIntyre, A., *The Complete Floral Healer*, Gaia, 1997

McIntyre, A., *The Apothecary's Garden*, Piatkus, 1997

Macdonald, J., *The Ornamental Kitchen Garden*, David & Charles, 1994

Mason, C., *The Ornamental Herb Garden*, Conran Octopus, 1997

Mességué, M., *Health Secrets of Plants and Herbs*, Collins, 1979

Michael, P., *All Good Things Around Us*, Ernest Benn Ltd., 1980

Midgley, J., *The Goodness of Potatoes and Root Vegetables*, Pavilion, 1992

Moody, M., *The Pleasure of Gardening Vegetables, Herbs and Fruits*, Anaya, 1992

Pavord, A., *The New Kitchen Garden*, Dorling Kindersley, 1996

Phillips, R. and Rix, M., *Vegetables*, Macmillan, 1995

Reader's Digest Foods that Harm, Foods that Heal, Reader's Digest, 1997

Seddon, G., *Your Kitchen Garden*, Mitchell Beazley, 1975

Soothill, E. and Thomas, M., *Nature's Wild Harvest*, New Orchard Editions, 1983

Valnet J., *Heal Yourself with Vegetables, Roots and Grains*, Cornerstone, New York, 1976

INDEX

Hyphenated page numbers following ailments indicate that there is scattered (not continuous) reference to these within the given pages.

hot flushes 104, 117
huckleberry 94–5
Hungarian grazing rye 129
hyperacidity 82
hyperactivity 109

I

immune system 20, 26–8, 34, 48, 62,
66, 70, 88, 96, 100, 103–4, 119
impetigo 29, 46
indigestion *see* digestion
infections 18–20, 46, 60–2, 100, 103,
106, 110–11, 113, 115, 118
inflammation 36, 48
influenza *see* flu
infused oils, making 163
infusions 17, 45
making 158
insect bites and stings 16, 18, 29, 40,
54, 86, 108, 110, 112, 114
insomnia 28, 52, 72, 101, 108–10, 113
insulin 32
intestinal infections 46
irritability 38, 118
irritable bowel syndrome 46, 52,
78–82, 109, 119

J

jams 154
jaundice 56
jellies 154
joint pain 34, 111

K

kale 30
kidney stones 28, 34, 96, 118
kitchen gardens 121–47

L

lactation *see* nursing
mothers
laryngitis 29
lavender 108
laxatives *see* constipation
leaf mould 130

leek 18–19
lemon balm 110
lethargy *see* tiredness
lettuce 52–3
lima bean 58
liver 26–30, 38–40, 44–6, 58, 62–4,
76, 82–4, 88, 102, 104, 118
lumbago 29
lupins 128

M

manures, garden 128–30, 136–7
marigold 104
marjoram 52, 113
marrow 42
marshmallow 119
mastitis 109, 118
mazzard 74
measles 60, 103
medieval garden plan 124
menopause 34, 50, 104, 109, 117
menstruation *see* period pains
menthol 111
migraines 29, 36, 108–9, 111–12,
114–15
mineral deficiencies *see*
vitamin and mineral
deficiencies
mint 111
mooli (radish) 62
morello cherry 74
mouth ulcers 86, 90–4, 108, 111, 117,
119
mouthwashes *see* gargles
mulches, garden 125–6
mumps 110
muscular pain 34, 101, 107–13
mushroom garden compost 130–1
mustard (green manure) 128
myrtleberry 94–5

N

nails 40
nausea 36, 44, 50, 72, 92, 101,
107–11, 117
nerve tonics 28, 112
nettle rash *see* urticaria

neuralgia 29, 36, 109–10
New Zealand spinach 66
night vision *see* vision
nosebleeds 84
nursing mothers 28, 50, 103
see also babies
nutrients
in foods 13
in soil 124

O

obesity 34
oedema 84
onion 16–17
oregano 113
ornamental vegetable
planting 135
overheating 40, 42

P

palpitations 108
paprika 36
parsley 114
parsnip 56–7
patio garden 122, 146
pea 60–1
peach 78–9
pear 80–1
peat substitutes 131
peppermint 111
peppers 36–7, 154
peptic ulcers 28, 42, 52, 64, 82, 104,
106
period pains 36, 50, 90, 104, 107,
110–11, 113–14, 117
pests and diseases, garden 137–9
pharyngitis 16
phlebitis 29
pH testing (soil) 123–4
pickling garden produce 153–4
pineapple mint 111
plum 76–7
PMS 109–10
polio virus 70
potager, plan for a 125
potato 64–5, 124
pot plants 135–6

PRINTED IN BELGIUM BY

proost

INTERNATIONAL BOOK PRODUCTION